Los Angeles Rams

Great Teams' Great Years

Los Angeles Rams

by Steve Bisheff

A National Football League Book

Macmillan Publishing Co., Inc.

New York

Collier Macmillan Publishers

London

Other Books in This Series
Cleveland Browns
Detroit Lions
New York Giants

796
BISHEF

A National Football League Book
Prepared by Creative Services Division, National
Football League Properties, Inc.
Publisher: *David Boss.*
Editor: *John Wiebusch.*
Managing Editor: *Tom Bennett.*
Associate Editors: *Patricia Cross,*
              Doug Kelly.
Art Director: *Bill Von Torne.*
Production Manager: *Patrick McKee.*
Production Staff: *Amy Yutani, Rob Meneilly.*
Executive Director: *Jack Wrobbel.*

Produced by The Ridge Press, Inc./Rutledge Books Division.
Copyright © 1973 by National Football League Properties,
Inc. All rights reserved. No part of this book may be
reproduced or transmitted in any form or by any means,
electronic or mechanical, including photocopying, recording
or by any information storage and retrieval system, without
permission in writing from the Publisher.

Macmillan Publishing Co., Inc., 866 Third Avenue, New
York, N.Y. 10022. Collier-Macmillan Canada Ltd., Toronto,
Ontario

Library of Congress Catalog Card Number: 73-2759
First Printing 1973
Printed in the United States of America

Contents

Introduction

It was a vast wasteland. An enormous area with people spilling into the cities at an alarming rate. The climate was warmer and the air was cleaner—well, for awhile, anyway. Easterners were rushing to get away from the snow and slush and overcrowded conditions. They were searching for a new home and a new way of life.

Daniel F. Reeves was one of them. Before anyone else, he understood the potential that was there. He was in the football buisness, the professional football business, and he felt he had an entertaining product. But he knew he had to find the proper audience for it.

It was there waiting for him in Southern California.

When Reeves moved the Cleveland Rams to Los Angeles in 1946, it was only the beginning. It was as if the Gold Rush had started all over again. In a sense it had. Only this time they came in sleek airplanes instead of battered covered wagons. Franchises began popping up the way towns had a hundred years earlier.

It was, above all, the greatest contribution made by this man and this team. Systematically, he altered the entire scope of professional sports in America. He expanded more than just part of the map, though. This was an owner of vision, a man who believed that gambles were necessary to be successful in business.

So he signed the first black professional football player. He experimented with television as a medium that could aid, not hinder, the future of his sport. And he hired and trained a fleet of the most competent people he could find.

Reeves initiated the most intricate of all the early professional scouting systems. He developed it into a science, and always the results were evident on the football field. Through the early years, while many teams suffered the usual growing pains, the Rams glittered with talent.

They were—and in many ways still are—the glamour team of professional football. Perhaps it is their close proximity to Hollywood. Or merely the fact that they have adapted so well to their environment. Whatever, there has been almost a tinsel quality about them. Superficial? In some ways, perhaps. Disappointing? Yes, they've been that too. But rarely, if ever, have they failed to generate widespread interest.

For years, football had been a genuine part of American culture, a game of tradition, something you associated with a season, a time, a mood. College football prospered because its atmosphere was incomparable. It has always been, to put it in today's vernacular, a happening.

Professional football was something else. This was nothing more than a game. No pompons, no campus picnics, no homecomings. In a sense, a certain spirit was missing. It lacked, also, the rustic appeal of professional baseball. An afternoon in the sun at the ballpark. The slow, casual, distinctive syncopation of batter versus pitcher.

These were merely lumbering men crashing into each other. They wore different colored jerseys and assorted headgear, and yet there was a sameness to them. Some of them were clever and quick and could move through a crowd cradling a football. But a certain spontaniety was missing.

Then the Rams introduced the man they called "Crazylegs." Elroy Hirsch was the full name. His specialty was faking out a defender, racing into the open spaces and spearing a perfectly thrown pass. He was not just a receiver. He was an artist. And he brought spectators to their feet. Suddenly, a new dimension had been added. There was suspense now on every down. Hirsch's effectiveness was buttressed by the other weapons available in the Ram arsenal. Waterfield and Van Brocklin were among the most gifted passers of any generation. Tom Fears, the receiver who lined up opposite Hirsch, was almost the perfect complement.

For runners, the Rams had big burly men who could sprint in the open field and quick, little scatbacks who could circle out of the backfield to catch passes. Early, their strategy was simple. They would spread their people all over the field, challenging the defense to go one-on-one with any of them. Van Brocklin and Waterfield were so accurate, and their receivers so gifted, some of their scores defied belief. Opposing coaches soon caught on, however. The first strain of zone defenses was produced to stop the Ram pass offense. The bombs were falling too regularly. Something had to be done.

Something finally was. But even in its modified form, the Los Angeles offensive pattern of the early '50s dictated the trend of professional football. The passers and receivers opened the game up, providing a startling showcase for home television. Soon every team would line up with people split out to catch passes.

Perhaps it was a result of their startling success in those early years. Or maybe it was just the way it had to be in an entertainment-minded city like Los Angeles. But, whatever the reason, the Rams were to make certain of one thing. Win or lose, they always had their share of big names. The Star Syndrome, some called it. It was enough to make them trade 11 players for an All-American linebacker named Les Richter, and nine more athletes for a dangerously old superstar like Ollie Matson.

Some of the jealousy and controversy that evolved in ensuing years would have been worthy of a Hollywood sound stage. By nature, Los Angeles was a difficult town in which to coach. Encountering financial troubles early, Reeves took in a number of partners who were there to cash in on the good years. But they were also around to voice their opinions. The balance of power was often hard to locate. For a series of coaches and general managers, decision-making became precarious.

A long, almost insufferable slump ended with the arrival of George Allen, a coach whose talent was only exceeded by his single-mindedness. What should have been the resumption of a happy period for the Rams turned into one of their most turbulent. Reeves was back in complete control now but Allen was not a coach who wanted to regularly confer with an owner. Allen was fired once, rehired and then fired a second and final time.

Quietly now, the Rams have begun a new era. Reeves left behind a legacy that remains very much alive. It is not enough to say that this man was liked by the people who worked for him. He generated a type of devotion and loyalty that is rarely found in any business, let alone sports.

The irony is that the franchise finally was sold to one of his oldest and closest friends, Carroll Rosenbloom, a man not unlike Reeves in that he has a reputation for caring deeply about those who work in his organization.

Los Angeles has changed immensely since those early years when the Rams were struggling for acceptance. The city has been inundated by major league sports. The entertainment dollar has been sliced into fragments instead of pieces.

But the professional football team is still prospering. On bright Sunday afternoons, the Coliseum remains alive with the same sort of excitement. And yes, there are still arguments over this player and that coach. There has been just that one world championship, the one way back in 1951. And so far, Los Angeles has only hosted the Super Bowl. It has never had a team in the game.

But the city's place in professional football history is secure. The Rams were the pioneers, the leaders, the first to move West. All the others came later. Seemingly, they always will be there, winning, losing, feuding and entertaining.

Dan Reeves wouldn't have wanted it any other way.

The Great Years

To a teenage boy growing up in Los Angeles during the early '50s, it was as much a part of life as algebra and driving permits. It was as emotional as acne, as enjoyable as evenings spent sipping root beer at the local A & W stand.

It was more than entertainment and fantasy. It was escape. For three hours every Sunday, the overwhelming problems disappeared. The insecurities, the arguments with your parents, the fleeting relationship with that pony-tailed girl down the street.

Only the sounds booming out of a radio or the visions flickering across a television screen mattered at all.

Fifteen years later, you look back on it and you smile.

And let the memories flow gentle on your mind.

The rides in those open trucks and the free tickets from the local boys' club. Soft summer evenings at the Los Angeles Coliseum watching No. 7, Bob Waterfield, and nudging your friend and saying, "Betcha don't know who he's married to." Your friend doesn't know. "Jane Russell, the movie star, that's who."

Hot afternoons spent in the second-story apartment and Bob Kelley's husky voice describing the game. You lie on your bed and stare at the ceiling, a football clutched in your hands. "Van Brocklin comes out on third and eight . . . barks signals . . . and drops back to pass . . . He lofts it long and deep . . . Hirsch has it at the 30 . . . He's at the 20 . . . the 10 . . . the 5 . . . TOUCHDOWN RAMS!" You leap happily in the air, and the squeaky mattress springs absorb more punishment. Then you get up and carefully recreate the play, dropping back to pass, lofting the ball and racing across the room. You dive to make the catch in the end zone that masquerades as your bed.

Chilly mornings in your robe and pajamas, sprawled out in front of the television. The smell of bacon and eggs floats out from the kitchen.

Your father hides behind the Sunday paper. You've been up waiting for an hour and a half. Finally, it's time for kickoff. When breakfast is ready, you're too excited to eat. Your mother doesn't understand. Your father grins and tells her not to worry about it. The bad guys in the black uniforms have all the luck. And finally, they win. The rest of your day is spoiled. You have homework to do, but you can't concentrate. How could they lose that one? . . . Damn it, how could they lose?

A searing September day and the perspiration rolls down both sides of your crew cut. Your friend's father has three tickets on the 40 and you can't believe he asked you to come along. On the 40! Jeez, you've never been closer than the end zone. The Detroit Lions are in town and you know them by heart. "That's Bobby Layne out there at quarterback," you announce, proudly. "He's a good one." The game isn't very good, though. Not that you'd ever know. You're too busy watching your heroes up close.

A long afternoon cramped into one of the last seats in the peristyle end zone, a good 100 yards away from the nearest goal post. Some 100,000 people are there to see the villians known as the Chicago Bears and to boo George Halas. Jon Arnett . . . Jaguar Jon, they called him . . . sprints and swivels his way through that menacing defense all day long. You never really see any of the runs, just catch a glimpse of No. 26 from the back every now and then. But the next day, at school, you describe each move in detail. Your buddies are impressed.

The Rams really started it all in Southern California. Oh, there were USC and UCLA and a couple of Pacific Coast League baseball teams, the Los Angeles Angels and Hollywood Stars. You followed them. Each of them. But none meant anything once you discovered the Rams. This was the big time. Major league sports had arrived.

The late Daniel F. Reeves . . . handsome, urbane, Irish, and rich. In 1946, he moved his football team, the Rams, from Cleveland to Los Angeles, and set up his brokerage firm in Beverly Hills. With him in this 1947 photo is Bill John, business manager of the Rams. Reeves died of cancer at the age of 58 in 1971. He was elected to the Pro Football Hall of Fame in 1967. His career in the game widened not only the scope of football, but of all professional sports as well.

No one realized it then, but the man all of us in Los Angeles had to thank was a tough little pixie of an Irishman named Daniel Farrell Reeves. Once the Rams squeezed their way through, the flood began. The Brooklyn Dodgers moved West, the American League expanded to Los Angeles, the basketball Lakers arrived, followed soon after by the hockey Kings. And that was just in Los Angeles. The Bay Area welcomed the San Francisco 49ers and Giants, the Oakland Raiders and Athletics and the California Seals. Further south, San Diego shoved its way into the picture with the football Chargers, baseball Padres and the ill-fated basketball Rockets.

All because of Reeves.

"Dan broke the barrier," said Wellington Mara, president of the New York Giants. "I very well remember sitting in at the league meetings with my father and brother when Dan had to overcome the severest of opposition from all sides, particularly the Giants, in order to get permission to make the move." Mara agreed that someone, sometime would have had to take the gamble. "But, the fact is," he added, "it *was* Dan who took the 'first small step' that become 'the giant leap' for organized sports."

Reeves did not stop experimenting once he arrived in Los Angeles. In fact, it is doubtful if any sport has seen an innovator to match him. Some of his moves were gambles, others weren't. All contained fresh, new ideas. Ideas that were to help pro football off the launching pad.

Even before Branch Rickey brought the late Jackie Robinson to Brooklyn, Reeves signed a black man to a pro contract. The man was Kenny Washington, an aging UCLA hero who ironically played in the same collegiate backfield with Robinson. Washington signed with the Rams in 1946. Robinson didn't make it to Brooklyn until the next year.

It was Reeves who organized the first full-time scouting staff, an ingenious system of evaluating and drafting players that soon spread throughout the sport.

It was Reeves who was the first to establish "away game" television policies, perhaps the one single key to the amazing growth enjoyed by the National Football League.

It was Reeves who established the "Free Football for Kids" program, so that Los Angeles youngsters, like this one, could get in free to see the Rams play.

To appreciate what Reeves did, you have to realize what Los Angeles was like in the late '40s and early '50s. There were few freeways, only sprawling surface streets that led to all corners of a town just starting to grow. Only a few television antennas could be seen dotting the landscape, and a big night during the week was a walk to the neighbor's house on the corner to watch the Milton Berle Show on a tiny 12-inch screen.

The population was beginning to explode, though. It was moving out to the suburbs. The monster that would become Los Angeles was just starting to realize it had tenacles.

Reeves realized it as soon as anyone. Fortunately, he had the capital to do something about it. The son of the founder of the Daniel Reeves grocery chain in New York, Dan would be heir to an $11,000,000 fortune accumulated when some 600 of these stores were sold in 1940 to Safeway. As a youngster, Dan started in the chain's investment office. His seat on the New York Stock Exchange was assured by 1946, the year he moved the Rams to Los Angeles and set up his own brokerage in the prestigious environs of Beverly Hills.

Dan Reeves lived well, but he rarely flaunted his money. After driving Fords for years, one day he splurged and bought a Buick. Sheepishly, he explained, "I'm trying to improve my image with my bankers." Later, after the seemingly endless squabbles between Reeves and former

Ram co-owners closed, Dan bought control of the club in private auction in 1962. The price: $7.1 million. Reeves called his wife at home and said, "Mary, we've bought the Rams. Can we afford it?"

A native New Yorker born June 30, 1912, Reeves had been a football fan ever since captaining the Newman Prep School team of Lakewood, N.J., where he was both a quarterback and a man in motion. The story is told that one day, against a team from Staten Island, Dan went in motion on every play in the first half and caught the passes that kept the game close. He remained in motion the second half but fooled his opponents by sending his fullback successfully up the middle for critical yardage. Eventually, his team won the game and Reeves was to be awarded the Semple Cup as the Best Athlete at Newman.

Young Reeves had his first introduction into professional football at the age of 27 when he purchased the Jersey City Giants, a team in the defunct American League. He made early unsuccessful attempts to purchase the Pittsburgh Steelers and Philadelphia Eagles before finally settling on the Cleveland Rams in 1941.

When World War II intervened, Reeves served as a second lieutenant in the Air Force. He became Captain Reeves before returning to civilian life in the fall of 1945, just in time to see Bob Waterfield lead the Rams to the world championship in a playoff game with the Washington Redskins.

Upon his return, Reeves set about building his club into a colorful and consistent winner. His method may have changed the entire fabric of pro football. His common thread was a scouting system so well conceived it began to reap its harvest immediately. He did a large share of the work himself. His headquarters was an office where he kept a map divided into six sections. Each section was represented by a head scout

and dozens of "bird dogs," as they were called then.

"The secret of our success," said Dan Reeves, "is thoroughness."

The result? A steady flow of talent. Not just big name, All-America talent. But players discovered off the back roads and small towns, players unknown to the rest of professional football. Players like Tank Younger, Night Train Lane, Big Daddy Lipscomb and Vitamin T. Smith.

The scene was the Oliver Hotel in South Bend, Ind. Ram line coach George Trafton and chief scout Eddie Kotal had Jack Zilly and Gerry Cowhig, two fine Notre Dame players, in their room, trying to convince them to sign with the Rams. Cowhig's roommate at Notre Dame was the son of Mickey McBride, owner of the Browns, and Cowhig felt he owed it to his pal to sign with Cleveland. "I want to go out for a walk," Cowhig said, hoping to get out of the room. Trafton immediately pulled the bed away from the wall. "If you need a walk," he said, "walk around that bed." Cowhig and Zilly signed with the Rams.

"It is an indisputable fact that the Rams' scouting system, which Dan devised and implemented, was years ahead of its time and the forerunner to the present computerized systems," said Wellington Mara, the New York Giants' president.

Tex Schramm, the present Dallas president and general manager, was one of Reeves' early lieutenants in Los Angeles. "Dan's scouting system was so much more sophisticated than the other teams' at the time and it had a definite bearing on the draft. Whereas other teams were looking to get one or two players out of the first 25, the Rams were getting five, six, seven out of the first 18. By the early 1950s, every team was copying the Rams' scouting form. In fact, one team went so far as to make an exact copy of the questionnaire that the Rams sent out, including a bunch of squares. But the team had no idea what

the squares were or how to make use of them."

Those who have worked for Dan Reeves always mention one word in describing him: Loyalty. If an employee encountered trouble, any kind of trouble, Dan was there to help. Norm Van Brocklin, who is not generally known as the sentimental type, told this Reeves story not long ago. Van Brocklin had just been informed he had been traded by the Rams to Philadelphia. "Dan called and invited Gloria [Mrs. Van Brocklin] and me to his house for dinner. He said the reason was that I was his wife Mary's favorite player and she was mad at Dan for trading me. As we were leaving the house, he slipped me an envelope. When we got home and opened it we found three checks for $500 each, made out to our daughters, Karen, Lynne and Judy."

A young boy's grandfather in the late '40s would describe them as "picture boxes." He would stare at the picture from the wooden "box" and shake his head. He would ask questions. He would be unable to fully comprehend. Television was too new, too strange. Radio, to him, was still a miracle. Voices coming from all across the world. Music available by the flip of a switch. But this . . . this was too much. To the children growing up in the postwar era, television was more like a fascinating toy. It was "Time for Beany," "The Lone Ranger," "The Cisco Kid," and, of course, "Superman." Hours were spent sitting in front of the glowing screen, and bedtime became that much more difficult for frustrated parents.

The advent of this magical invention undoubtedly changed the lifestyles of millions of Americans. It also altered the texture of American sports.

To Dan Reeves, the possibilities seemed endless. He knew this was a new way to communicate, a new way to introduce professional football to people who never had been exposed before. It was simply a matter of how . . . and when.

Bill John, the Rams' present business manager and the only remaining executive who originally arrived in Los Angeles with Reeves from Cleveland, remembers when Dan first came to him in 1950 with the suggestion they televise home football games from the Coliseum. "I was shocked," said John. "I said, 'By God, man, don't you like money?' As it turned out, though, it was a great decision. One of Dan's best. Because things just took off and zoomed the following year."

The experiment with televised home games convinced Reeves that the answer was close. He knew if he continued the policy, however, attendance would never improve. People wouldn't pay to see what they could get for free. So Dan Reeves audiblized. He decided on a plan which would bring people televised games on the road. It offered Ram followers half the schedule and, at the same time, whetted their appetites for more.

Football fans in Los Angeles quickly turned into gluttons. They couldn't get enough. A Los Angeles Times Charity Game in 1951 against the Washington Redskins drew an astonishing crowd of 95,985. It remains the largest professional gathering ever for a preseason game. From 1950 through 1959 in Los Angeles, some 10 league games drew over 90,000 each. One meeting, between the Rams and their dreaded rivals from San Francisco, attracted 102,368, another record that is still in the books.

The fan interest was unparalleled. Two people who resided in Hillman, New Mexico, some 900 miles away, bought season tickets annually. Dues-paying members of the new Rams Booster Club included people from Honolulu, Kansas City, New York and London. A Los Angeles psychiatrist was said to have prescribed Ram tickets for a patient subject to mild attacks of melancholia.

A fan walked into the Rams' business office one day several months before the first game of the 1955 season. He was a veteran season ticket

holder. "I'm in love," he reported happily. "I'm going to get married this fall, and I'd like to buy a season ticket for my fiancee." The receptionist offered her congratulations and said she would arrange the ticket immediately. "Just one more thing," the man added. "My girl doesn't know much about football yet, and I've been following the Rams since I was 15 years old. I'd like to concentrate on the game. Could you put her in a seat about 17 rows away from me?"

By then, of course, the Rams had become one of professional sports' most lucrative franchises. That was only because Reeves had managed to avoid drowning in all that red ink when he first arrived in Los Angeles. In that not-so-wonderful year of 1947, Dan, in fact, blew some $200,000—a substantial sum in those days. He was desperate. He needed someone to share the losses until the red ink turned to black.

So for the startling price of $1 each, four major partners—Fred Levy, Edwin W. Pauley, Hal Seley and Bob Hope—were handed 66⅔ per cent of the club. With one provision. They would henceforth participate accordingly in the losses. Naturally, even Reeves could not know that three years later television would turn this into one of the country's new gold mines. As it turned out, in 1962, it cost Dan $4.8 million to buy back what he had given away for $4. But, more importantly, he had persevered. He had kept the franchise pulse beating when it appeared about to expire. It cost him. It cost him dearly. But those who knew him felt, if necessary, he would have done it the same way all over again.

When asked, in the middle of his team's attendance explosion, the reason for the Rams' success, Reeves would never fail to mention the power of the press. "The kind of treatment of the men in the various media has been a big factor," he said. "We have enjoyed wonderful support from virtually everyone in the press, radio and televison area."

But, like everything else, this was an area Reeves worked at himself. He cultivated friendships. He took pains to make certain he always had a competent man working as his publicity director. And he carefully arranged a deal with the influential *Los Angeles Times* upon his arrival in town. It resulted in the *Times Charity* Game, and besides the prestige resulting from the event, it provided the Rams instant coverage in the town's most important newspaper.

In the rush to claim press box seats at the Los Angeles Coliseum one year, a writer for a small weekly was informed that he would no longer be welcomed. Space had run out and Coliseum officials decided that only writers from daily papers would be alloted seats. The writer woke up a few days later to find a note from Dan Reeves in his mail box. "I just want you to know there always will be two seats for you in the press box—for all Ram games—as a personal friend of the President."

Radio and television were not forgotten, either. Reeves was careful to hire one of the best play-by-play announcers in sports in the late Bob Kelley, who was once also secretary of the club. When Dan came West from Cleveland, he brought Kelley with him. It was tantamount to the Dodgers introducing Vince Scully to a new segment of West Coast fans a few years later. Scully and Kelley created new fans all by themselves through their broadcasts.

Kelley could be controversial. He had his own radio sports show on KMPC in Los Angeles, and besides barbs and occasional potshots at other announcers in town, you were certain to get all the inside information on the Rams. On the day of the National Football League draft, for instance, no one covered the Rams' new selections like Kelley. If you were a sports fan, you made it a regular procedure to pause nightly from 6 to 6:15 to listen to Ol'Kell.

The transition from radio to television did not

Times were not always good for Reeves and his Rams, however. Heavy financial losses were incurred in the first few years after the move from Cleveland. To make ends meet, Reeves took in four partners—Fred Levy, Hal Seley and Ed Pauley (left to right) and comedian Bob Hope. Each paid $1 for his share of the team. In other years, it would prove to be a terrific investment for them, but for the time being. Reeves' benefactors were prepared to share the losses—which were substantial.

bother Kelley as much as many announcers of the time. His precise descriptions of the televised road games didn't hurt Ram interest, either.

"I like to describe the difference between radio and television this way," Kelley said. "Radio broadcasting requires a complete word picture. The announcer must tell the listener what is happening, where it is happening and supply all the details. Television commentary, on the other hand, just requires the announcer to supply the 'captions' for the picture. Television also permits the announcer to spend more time telling the viewers about the 'inside' story of what is going on. It enables the person at home to watch a red dog as the announcer explains what a red dog is."

No one did this better than Kelley. He threw phrases like "double wing," "full house backfield" and "red dog" around. But he always paused for the proper explanations. He knew the game, and besides announcing, he educated the Los Angeles public.

And so, the Rams began to take on their own special personality. Everything about them seemed to stir excitement. Even their uniforms were different, a bright gold with what was—and may still be—the most distinctive headgear in football.

Fred Gehrke is remembered best as an outstanding halfback on the Cleveland Rams team of 1945, the team that captured the world championship. In the decisive game of that season. Gehrke raced to two touchdowns, the first two times he touched the ball, against Green Bay. Still, it was another contribution, one made off the playing field, that had more impact. The first art major to play in the NFL, Gehrke one day decided to paint the helmets of his teammates. "Dan (Reeves) was always trying to improve our uniforms," said Gehrke, "and I guess that got me thinking about the helmet. Anyway, I made a pen-and-ink sketch of a ram's horns one

day in 1947 and showed it to our new coach, Bob Snyder. He said he couldn't visualize it on headgear and told me to go home and paint it on a helmet. So I took one of those gosh-awful brown leather helmets and painted it blue, then made a free rendering of a ram's horns in gold."

Eventually, Gehrke painted all the Ram helmets, free of charge. The Rams were only asked to supply the paint. That's how Los Angeles became the first pro team to have its own helmet insignia. Now every team but Cleveland has one. Gehrke's innovation did not go unnoticed. The present director of personnel and assistant general manager with the Denver Broncos was presented with the NFL's new Daniel F. Reeves Pioneer Award in a special 1972 ceremony at Professional Football's Hall of Fame in Canton, Ohio.

Gehrke was a typical Reeves' employee. Men of vision always seemed to be working for the Rams. Someone counted up the number recently and settled on close to 80 Ram-trained coaches and leaders presently active in sports—the majority of them in the National Football League. You can start with the commissioner, Pete Rozelle. "The big thing," says Rozelle, "is that Dan always took an intense pride in his people both in the Los Angeles club and as they moved along. Many executives fight to hold onto the men in whom they have a large investment. Dan's employees were his friends, and he took a friend's interest in them as they went to other organizations."

The irony is that for all the good people he trained in his organization, he never seemed able to hire a coach for a long term. Ram head coaches, on the average, have lasted two or three years on the job.

Reeves felt you needed great coaching and the best players. And to his everlasting credit, he was always striving to find the coach who could draw the best out of his players.

On a September night in 1948, the late Maxwell Stiles, who covered the Rams for years for the *Los Angeles Mirror,* boarded the chartered Ram airliner at Los Angeles International Airport and began inquiring for Bob Snyder, the head coach. Stiles could not find him. Finally, in the back of the aircraft, Stiles stumbled upon a nervous, graying 56-year-old man who asked, "Who are you looking for, Max?" Stiles replied: "I'm looking for the head man." "You're talking to him now," said Clark Shaughnessy.

Shaugnessy may have had the greatest football mind of them all. His experience included a distinguished career at the University of Chicago and a role as the leader of Stanford's renowned Rose Bowl team of 1940. At Stanford, he was credited with popularizing the T-formation and he advanced from there to the staff of George Halas' Bears in Chicago.

Shaughnessy's mission in Los Angeles was a difficult one. When he took over in 1948, the Los Angeles Dons of the now defunct All America Football Conference reigned as the most popular professional football team in town. They had struggled, themselves, but by 1948, they were averaging 41,096 spectators. The Rams were under 34,000. Still, Shaughnessy shook the Rams up and managed to win four of the last five games to finish at 6-5-1.

Clark Shaughnessy used to eat and sleep football. That was it. That was his life. Nothing else really mattered. Because of his preoccupation with the game, he would often find himself in trouble. Like with the law. No one in the club was cited for more traffic violations. Forced to spend too much time in a courthouse one day waiting to pay off his usual handful of tickets, Clark approached the sergeant with an idea. "Couldn't I just leave $500 here on deposit?" he said. Names were another problem. "I don't think he ever knew what my name was," swears Tank Younger. "I was simply 'Big Boy' to him." Unfortu- *nately, Younger was just one of several players known as "Big Boy" to the coach. Once Shaughnessy became disgusted at a practice and shouted to a hulking player: "Hey, Big Boy, you better get going or you won't be here Monday." The player was regular fullback Dick Hoerner.*

In 1949, with Reeves and Ram owners admittedly concerned, Shaughnessy produced the first divisional championship since the team moved out of Ohio. He did it with his usual ingenuity, and he did it with a myriad of offensive sets and assignments. His playbook was not the kind players cherished. "If he can sit down and write out 50 per cent of the plays he has given us this year," grumbled Bob Waterfield, who was never the grumbling type, "I'll learn this new stuff. Otherwise, nuts."

Waterfield learned it. So did the rest of the Rams. But the discontent lingered. Fortunately, a year later the National Football League absorbed the All America Football Conference, leaving the Rams as the lone pro team in Los Angeles. It was a victory of sorts for Shaughnessy. But he wasn't around to enjoy it. He was fired. The charge against him was vaguely described as "internal friction." It would not be the last time a Ram coach would be fired under unusual circumstances, never fully explained.

If in the next five years, there would be one distinguishing characteristic of the professional football team in Los Angeles, you would describe it as color. The Rams did everything colorfully, with a flair. Maybe it was because of the inspiration of Hollywood. Maybe because of the image the rest of the country had of a team that spent more time mingling with movie stars than practicing. But probably, it had more to do with a collection of marvelous football players, men who worked hard at their jobs and played hard when they weren't working. And men who knew how to enjoy themselves. The Rams lost their share of football games. But they never lost

The Rams' image, and the consuming passion felt for the team by Los Angeles fans, were nurtured by these two individuals. Fred Gehrke (left) was a backfield star, along with Bob Waterfield, on the 1945 championship team in Cleveland. An art major, Gehrke was as good with a brush in his hand as he was with a football, and in 1947 he painted Rams' horns on the team's helmets. It was the first, and in the opinion of many, still the most distinctive of all the helmet designs in pro football. The late Bob Kelley, who moved west with the Rams in 1946, was the team announcer. He was informed, at times caustic, and always interesting.

their sense of humor. At times, they needed it.

On their way to the conference championship in 1950, the Rams went into Philadelphia in the fourth game of the season with a 2-1 record, riding a two-game winning streak. It was a game in which they were unable to do anything right. The Eagles led at the half, 28-0. Owner Edwin Pauley was in attendance at the game with his good friend, General Mark Clark. Pauley thought the occasion called for an inspirational speech at halftime and, who better to deliver it than General Clark? He brought the General to the dressing room during intermission and the military leader delivered an impassioned speech about courage, fighting against odds, the cause is never lost, etc. Instilled with renewed spirit, the Rams sprinted back onto the field for the start of the second half. They kicked off to Russ Craft of the Eagles who caught the ball three yards deep in his end zone and ran 103 yards for the touchdown that made it 35-0. On the Ram bench, halfback Vitamin T. Smith leaned over to a teammate and drawled: "Wonder what the General would suggest now?"

Once asked for his formula to success with the Rams, Dan Reeves was quick to answer. "There are only two things necessary," he said. "First you get the best players. Then you get the coach who can get the best out of them."

In Los Angeles, Reeves and the Rams were somewhat more successful with players than they were with coaches.

Some believe the team borrowed the "Star Syndrome." from nearby studios like MGM and 20th Century Fox. Whatever prompted them to go after big names, the method turned out to be immensely enjoyable, both artistically and financially.

If pressed to come up with the six biggest names of The Great Years in Los Angeles, most Ram historians would probably choose, appropriately enough, two quarterbacks, two re-

ceivers and two defensive players. The quarterbacks were Bob Waterfield and Norm Van Brocklin. The receivers Elroy Hirsch and Tom Fears. The defensive players Don Paul and Les Richter.

Even today, among those in the Los Angeles organization, his name is spoken of in almost a revered tone. Only one other man is so honored, and his name is Dan Reeves. Perhaps it is fitting, then, that Bob Waterfield be coupled with the man who made it all possible.

Because without Waterfield, it is doubtful if Reeves could have brought it off.

Waterfield was there from the beginning when Reeves purchased the team in Cleveland. Well, almost from the beginning. Dan actually bought the club in 1941 and shortly afterward went into the service. It was when he returned that he first looked down on the field and saw a team quarterbacked by Bob Waterfield.

The year was 1945, and the rookie from UCLA took the Rams to the world championship. The quarterback turned out to be more than rookie of the year. He was also the league's most valuable player.

And he was the superstar Reeves needed to lure support in a new town. His descendants have been many ... Sandy Koufax ... Elgin Baylor ... Lew Alcindor ... Roman Gabriel ... Maury Wills ... O. J. Simpson ... Jerry West ... but Bob Waterfield was first. The first personality to bring people out, the first to generate interest, the first one kids began to imitate.

The year was 1948. The world champion Philadelphia Eagles were pouring it on the Rams, 28-0. Then, with 16 minutes to go, Bob Waterfield got hot. Four times he threw and four times Ram receivers raced under the football to catch touchdown passes. Final score: Eagles 28, Rams 28.

If Waterfield lacked anything, it was charisma, the flamboyant personality of a Joe Namath. Or even the color of a Van Brocklin. He

Bob Waterfield (left), one of the greatest quarterbacks of his era, was a superb passer, runner, punter and placekicker. And when he played there, he was a first-rate defensive safetyman, too. He had quarterbacked the Rams to the championship in their last season in Cleveland, 1945. Four years later, he and coach Clark Shaughnessey took the Rams to the title game again, only this time they were shut out in the rain by Steve Van Buren (right) and the Philadelphia Eagles 14-0.

has been described by some as sullen. But really he was simply a quiet man who often found it difficult to express himself. Especially in front of reporters.

In his own circle of friends, however, he was a dominant figure. And although to some the fire often seemed to be missing, it was always burning brightly on the playing field. He was a leader of unparalleled proportions. Players may have offered advice in other huddles. But no one spoke when Waterfield crouched down to call a play. He was the boss and he was capable of inspiring a team beyond its physical limits.

"Waterfield," wrote Bob Oates, then of the *Los Angeles Examiner*, "led the Rams with the surety of Churchill and the quiet dignity of Ed Murrow."

He led by example. He played under duress. He played with pain. But always, he played with great dignity.

The 1950 Rams-Bears playoff game is remembered for many things. But most players recall it by first mentioning Bob Waterfield's performance after a flu siege that left him so weak he practically couldn't run onto the field. They saw it. But many of them didn't believe it when Waterfield threw three touchdown passes to win the game, 24-14. "It was incredible," said Tom Fears, who caught all three scoring passes. "The more energy he expended, the stronger he seemed to get. It was so unbelievable that I feared a sudden and complete collapse. Until the end of the game I was never convinced Bob would be able to keep the show on the road." But he did. Bob Waterfield did more than that. He led the team to four divisional titles and two world championships, one in Cleveland, a second in Los Angeles. It has been 21 years since he retired, and the Rams have yet to win their third.

Norm Van Brocklin was and perhaps still is the most controversial of all Los Angeles Rams, past or present. His talent was unquestioned. He

was a passer of consummate artistry. And as a technician, there may have been none better. Anywhere. He read defenses and he knew how to take advantage of opposing players' mistakes.

But he was, always, an enigma. A man nobody really knew, nobody was really close to. He was a competitor, a tremendous competitor, but he was also a practical joker and a man whose emotions could often spill out in anger.

During the Van Brocklin Era, it was a rule quickly learned. Stay loose during practice. Better yet, pay attention. Van Brocklin always had a football in his hand—at practice, during chalk talks, even when there was time out on the field. Van Brocklin wanted everyone to concentrate. Anyone who didn't would pay the price. Van Brocklin would throw the ball at him—whether he was 10, 20 or 30 yards away. And the pass would almost always hit the poor, unsuspecting player in the head.

Van Brocklin always has been a man of strong convictions. He believed in many things. But, mostly, he believed in himself. It was a trait that often made it difficult for his head coach.

Once, in a 1953 game against the 49ers, the Rams were leading 20-0 and the quarterback known as "The Dutchman" was in punt formation on the 13-yard line. His *own* 13 yard line. Van Brocklin decided this would be a nice time to gamble. He uncorked a pass—a pass that was perfectly thrown—to Night Train Lane. But Night Train dropped it. San Francisco took over, scored immediately and proceeded to win one of the wildest games in the spectacular Ram-49ers series, 31-30.

Another powerful Van Brocklin theory is that there should be one quarterback. Just one. He should be The Man. And, most of all, he should call the plays.

"I don't mean that you can be without reserve strength," he said. "But your quarterback has to be your leader out there on the field and if the

players or coaches or the press or anybody starts choosing sides on which of your quarterbacks is better than the other, you can tear the guts right out of your ballclub."

Van's idea of how an offense should be run was simple. "You give the quarterback a 'ready' list and feed him information from upstairs in the spotting booth, but he's the only one who can get the feel on the field.

"Clark Shaughnessy, who was my first pro coach, had the right idea. He used to tell me that playing quarterback is like driving a team of 10 mules. You've got 10 reins to use, and you can pull and push or do anything you want with them. Well, you can't do that from the sidelines."

Van Brocklin never did completely get his way in Los Angeles. Never was he the only quarterback in town. When he arrived, he had to share the time with Bob Waterfield. Then, later, he was forced to alternate with Billy Wade.

Van Brocklin was very big on nicknames. Everyone on the Rams had to have one. Dutch saw to that. When a sleek rookie receiver named Bob Boyd showed up in 1950, Van Brocklin immediately dubbed him "Seabiscuit." In one game that year, the Rams took possession, unexpectedly, just before time ran out in the first half. Boyd was sent in along with Van Brocklin. In the huddle, Van called what, for him was a rather typical play. "Seabiscuit to the post and everybody block, on two." Seabiscuit outran the single safety, Van Brocklin threw a 60-yard spiral and the Rams had seven points.

Glenn Davis arrived from West Point as "Mr. Outside," a Heisman Trophy winner and one of the greatest collegiate running backs of all time. When he got to the Ram camp, however, he assumed a new name. He was "Buttercups," courtesy of Van Brocklin. Tom Fears, Van Brocklin's favorite target through the years, was sensitive about premature baldness. So naturally Fears became "Skinhead."

Maybe Van Brocklin's funniest nickname, though, belonged to an offensive lineman named Bob Cross. Van called him "Look Out." One day a rookie asked why. "Because whenever Cross watches a defender go by him, he always yells "Look out, Dutch."

There were times, of course, when a mere nickname wasn't enough. Tom McCormack, a talkative running back, was, naturally, "Motor Mouth." One day at a Ram practice, Van Brocklin couldn't stand McCormack's chatter any longer. When McCormack went on the field, Van nailed his cowboy boots to the ceiling and placed a paper full of . . . uh, a liquid of sorts into the toe of one boot. When McCormack came in he got a stool to get the boots down. Then he got the liquid right in his face.

When two dominant personalities get together on a football team, one of them usually has to go. In the case of Sid Gillman and Van Brocklin, it was Dutch who went. But not before the two endured their share of successful and stormy moments.

It was Van Brocklin who was the leader on Gillman's first team, the one that captured the Western Division championship for the rookie coach from Cincinnati. It was also Van who threw five interceptions as the Rams absorbed a decisive 38-14 beating at the hands of Cleveland in the title game.

After that loss to the Browns, Gillman began using Wade more and more. If it didn't divide the team, it certainly divided the fans. And it upset Van Brocklin more than anyone.

One year, when the club was suffering through a losing streak, it was staying in a Washington, D.C. hotel. An accordion player had been hired to serenade the players and staff during the team dinner on Thanksgiving Day. Van Brocklin called the accordionist over and requested a special song dedicated to Gillman and the coaching staff. The gentleman went to the cen-

ter of the room, made the dedication announcement, then began to play.... "*So Long, It's Been Good To Know You.*"

The song turned out to be prophetic. Soon after that, Van Brocklin went to the general manager, Pete Rozelle, and requested to be traded. He was dealt to Philadelphia, where he would eventually produce his second world championship. This time for the Eagles.

Tom Fears and Elroy Hirsch, the two Ram receivers, are difficult to separate simply because they were there together, complementing one another. They presented opposing defenses with still another problem when confronting Los Angeles.

On whom do you concentrate? Take the bomb away from Hirsch and Fears kills you with those first down catches. Double Tom and Elroy murders you deep.

"*You know,*" an assistant coach named Red Hickey said in 1951, "*there have been good ends in this league. Lots of 'em. I doubt if anyone could say for sure which of the great ones was the best. But I do know this. Collectively, Hirsch and Fears are the tops. The best pair of offensive ends I've ever seen.*"

The statement is over 20 years old now but it is one you still hear repeated by knowledgeable football men.

"We always considered Tom our 'bread and butter' guy—the first down getter," said Hickey. "He may not have had sprinter's speed, but he seemed to run just fast enough. He took that touchdown pass against the Browns right between two defenders and you know who got to the goal first." (Hickey was referring to the 73-yard pass from Van Brocklin that won the 1951 world championship.)

"Elroy, on the other hand, was our speed boy. Give him a short pass and he'd run away from defenders. He was a college halfback, you'll recall, and five or six of his 17 touchdown passes in

1951 were on little screens where he did most of his work after the catch. On the long ones, he'd simply get behind the deep man and if the ball was there, he'd get it. His technique of looking the ball all the way into his hands made him a great receiver. I can't recall Hirsch dropping a ball he could get his hands on."

Ram followers recall one drop. It was in 1957, a season in which Hirsch had been sidelined with injuries. His first appearance came in a game against Detroit. It was late in the fourth quarter and it appeared the Rams would lose another close one. In desperation, almost, Hirsch was sent in. Billy Wade faded back and Elroy raced into the secondary and beat the Lions' Jim David. It looked like a classic Hirsch catch. But the ball bounced off his hands and dribbled away. The Rams were on an extended road trip and spent the next week in Dearborn, Mich., practicing. "We were staying at a beautiful hotel, with lots of trees and open spaces," remembers Mickey Dukich, the Rams' film man. "Every time I looked out in the evening I saw Elroy walking by himself. He walked that way for hours. That dropped pass really disturbed him. He just kept walking for hours every night." A few months later, Elroy Hirsch announced his retirement from football.

No one turned the game of professional football into an entertainment spectacle quicker than Hirsch. The nickname "Crazylegs" was enough, by itself, to guarantee him plenty of publicity. But he would have earned it no matter what his name had been. Along with Waterfield and Van Brocklin, it was Elroy who really perfected "The Bomb." The play that provided football with an answer to baseball's home run. The long pass that could turn defeat into victory. The play that could explode at any moment. When Hirsch was in the game, the danger of such a game-breaking ·play was always imminent.

Much of the credit belonged to Elroy's uncanny ability to catch a pass while moving at full speed, without turning around. Remember Willie Mays' famous catch of Vic Wertz' drive in the 1954 World Series? Big deal. "Crazylegs" used to come up with one of those once a game.

"A lot of folks have asked me how I can see behind me on those over-the-head catches," said Hirsch. "Actually, it's a matter of footwork. I get a bead on the ball with my head turned toward it. Then I look back directly upside down and follow it in. The trick is rather simple. Anyone can learn it. You make sure you hold your head steady by not twisting the upper part of your body. You adjust direction with your feet."

The year 1951 may have been the most amazing ever compiled by a wide receiver. The Rams played a 12-game schedule. Hirsch caught 17 touchdowns in those 12 games. Each pass averaged—we said averaged—48 yards.

The statistic is so startling, it should not be admissable without evidence. So here it is, Elroy Hirsch's 1951 touchdown chart, catch-by-catch:

Opp.	Yards	Passer
1. Yankees	41	Van Brocklin
2. Yankees	47	Van Brocklin
3. Yankees	26	Van Brocklin
4. Yankees	1	Van Brocklin
5. Browns	37	Waterfield
6. Lions	70	Waterfield
7. Packers	81	Van Brocklin
8. 49ers	79	Van Brocklin
9. 49ers	76	Waterfield
10. Cardinals	51	Waterfield
11. Cardinals	53	Van Brocklin
12. Yankees	33	Van Brocklin
13. Redskins	3	Waterfield
14. Bears	91	Waterfield
15. Packers	72	Waterfield
16. Packers	37	Waterfield
17. Packers	19	Waterfield

Hirsch, of course, became so popular he eventually had a motion picture made about his life. "Crazylegs, All American," starred Elroy, himself, and launched the blond, good-looking Hirsch on a brief acting career. It also prompted his early retirement, something he eventually reconsidered when Dan Reeves called a year later and asked if he would please come back and play. The bright lights of Hollywood were nice. But they never appealed to Hirsch as much as the tense atmosphere of a crowded football stadium.

"It's tough when you're accustomed to having 50,000 people watch you every week and then all of a sudden—boom—there's no one to watch you any more," said Hirsch. "You hate to give it up. You hang on as long as you can. I guess it's the ham in me. It seems to be in my blood. I felt I had quit too soon. I first felt it the day I quit." What happened that day might have changed most men's minds.

It was the final game of the 1954 season. The Rams were playing Green Bay at home. Hirsch previously had announced it would be his final appearance in a Ram uniform. When the gun went off at the end of the game, thousands of youngsters raced out onto the field and surrounded him. They began tugging at his uniform. His jersey, bearing the familiar No. 40, was quickly torn to shreds. His pants were next to go, followed by his shoulder and hip pads. If the post-game show had been on television, it would have been rated X. Finally, reduced to only a skimpy athletic supporter, Elroy Hirsch trotted off the Coliseum field, tears streaming down his face.

There are coaches and players around the National Football League who will tell you that Tom Fears was the best receiver ever to play the game. The best all around. He could catch the deep pass—he did, after all, field the most important bomb in Ram history to win the world

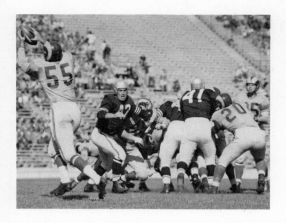

championship—and he could certainly catch the clutch, third down variety.

Because he was on the same team with Hirsch and because Elroy was so effective deep, Fears was noted as a man who specialized in the short stuff, the "hooks," as the players like to call them. Not many of them like to catch them. It's no fun. Fears, himself, once said catching hook passes was like "committing suicide a little at a time." You catch the ball and you wait to get cracked. If you're lucky, maybe you have a split second to make a fake or to dart to one side and hope the onrushing tackler has guessed wrong. But more often than not, the jolt arrives from behind just as the ball reaches you. Your hands and fingers must ignore the pain. And as you go down, your only thought has to be holding onto the football.

It takes concentration, and Fears concentrated as hard as any receiver who ever lived. Latter-day football fans would object, offering, perhaps, Raymond Berry as a strong candidate. But Berry played in a different era and worked with just one passer, John Unitas. Fears, playing without even a face mask for protection, had to adjust to the two distinct styles of Waterfield and Van Brocklin. How well did he make the adjustment? In 1950, playing a 12-game schedule, he caught 84 passes, a feat that stood as an NFL record until the Bears' Johnny Morris caught 93 in 1964.

Off the field, Fears was the quiet, intense type. Although good friends with Hirsch, there was something of a natural rivalry among the two. Noting Elroy's great success with his "Crazylegs" nickname, Fears was always looking for a catchy one of his own. Once he even asked friends to help. The best they could come up with was was "01 '55." Somehow, that just didn't make it. Especially after he was assigned No. 80 following a 1951 rules change that standardized jersey numbers.

As consistent as Fears was, his performance got even better in the money games. He was a tremendous clutch receiver. In the 1950 play-off game with Chicago, he caught three touchdown passes to highlight the 24-14 victory over the Bears. And, in the dressing room after the Rams' 24-17 victory over Cleveland for the 1951 world title, Paul Brown looked up at reporters and said, "Gentlemen, the difference out there today was Tom Fears. We just couldn't handle him." It was nothing to feel bad about. Through the years, the Browns were not alone.

When, in order, the Rams developed middle linebackers named Don Paul and Les Richter, frustrated opponents must have looked around, scratched their heads and wondered if Dan Reeves was working on some mysterious evolutionary process.

Paul and Richter were that much alike. Les even assumed Don's infamous title as "the dirtiest player in football." Part of it, of course, had to do with the fact that Paul was still around when Richter broke in, and later he was on the Ram coaching staff watching and helping Les to mature into an all-pro linebacker.

The Rams were playing the Philadelphia Eagles in a 1950 game when, suddenly, the referee blew his whistle and called time out. He walked over to Don Paul, took him by one arm and led him off the field. Paul couldn't figure it out. He was told later that blood was spotted flowing out of one ear. Paul, it turns out, was hit about the way a fighter gets hits when his jaw is broken. Don Paul's jaw bone was jolted out of its socket. But he never said anything. He would have continued playing if the referee hadn't seen it. A doctor later told him he was the first man he'd seen walk off the field after a blow like that. The doctor said it didn't make sense. He said most men would have been unconscious.

A second round draft choice out of UCLA in 1947, Paul joined the Rams in 1948, was captain

of the defensive platoon through a memorable eight-game winning streak in 1952, and eventually succeeded Waterfield as team captain in 1953. His name was a familiar one on Western Pro Bowl rosters.

Still, like Richter, Paul was most famous as a "bad guy." Admittedly, it was a role he cherished. "It isn't what you do," he said. "It's what they see you do."

They never saw all the things Paul did. He made sure of that. But opposing players made certain officials knew what was going on. They screamed and yelled throughout the game and Don enjoyed every minute of it. When, in 1954, Detroit's Leon Hart described Paul as "the dirtiest player in football," Don was tempted to send him a thank you card. It was not a rap. To Paul, it was a compliment.

As if to make sure the title was well-deserved, Paul went out the Sunday following Hart's statement and quickly "clotheslined" Green Bay's Max McGee. The Packers' wide receiver was racing out for a pass, when an arm was suddenly in the way and down he went. Paul and the Rams were socked for a 15-yard penalty for roughing the receiver. Don shrugged it off. "You have to show these guys who's boss," he said.

At National Football League gatherings, it was referred to for a long time as "The Trade." It was a deal that was beyond comprehension. In 1952, the Rams sent 11 football players to the Dallas Texans. In return, they received one. An All-America guard from the University of California named Les Richter.

The Texans got Dick Hoerner, once a member of the team's famous Bull Elephant backfield, along with Tom Keane, George Sims, Joe Reed, Dave Anderson, Billy Baggett, Rich McKissack, Jack Halliday, Richard Wilkins, Aubry Phillips and Vic Vasicek. Eleven for one. It seemed incredible. For awhile, it seemed a lot

worse than that to fans in Los Angeles. Two years of military duty interrupted Richter's professional career, and when he finally strapped on his first pair of shoulder pads for the Rams, his performance was . . . well, let's just say he didn't overwhelm anyone.

It was the second half of a game at San Francisco in Les Richter's first season, 1954. Richter was so tired he could hardly get up after each play. Don Paul, the man Les was being counted on to replace as the focal point of the defense, was still playing. Paul watched Richter until he finally had had enough. "Listen rookie," he roared, "either you are the first one up on every play and forming that huddle for me or one of us is going to leave this field in a horizontal position. And it sure as hell isn't going to be me."

They say that was the turning point for Richter. Les even said so himself. "I came out of that game with more than an aching rear," he recalled. "I learned that hustle and desire are 60 percent of defense and unless you have those two things, all your knowledge and ability aren't worth a thing."

Richter inherited more than an attitude from Paul. He inherited Don's old reputation. "Les Richter seems to like trouble," said Detroit quarterback Bobby Layne. "He goes out of his way looking for it. You can never class him with the great ones as long as he keeps up this dirty stuff." Norm Van Brocklin, who had just taken over as new coach in Minnesota, was, as usual, more descriptive. "Richter," said Van Brocklin, "is an overrated oaf. If he could just go as hard while the ball is in play as he does after the whistle, he'd be one helluva boy. But he doesn't and isn't."

Richter turned into one of the National Football League's premier villains in one celebrated moment during his rookie year. On a kickoff against Baltimore, Les decided to go after the Colts' monstrous Don Joyce. He not only flat-

26

Tom Fears (left) and Elroy Hirsch (right) were the most feared pair of receivers in football. Fears was a draft choice in 1948 after his All-America career at UCLA, and Hirsch joined the team a year later from the Chicago Rockets of the defunct All-America Football Conference. Fears had speed and great moves; Hirsch had even more speed.

tened Joyce, he upset the huge lineman by making one of his famous remarks. Joyce gave Richter a shove as he got up, and before anyone knew what had happened the two were engaged in a wrestling match. That's when Joyce jerked off Les' helmet and hit him over the head with it. The blow sent Richter to the hospital for the first time. Fourteen stitches were required over his right eye. And although he had taken the worst of it, he came out of that game as a marked man. "Dirty Les," they began calling him.

No one appreciated Richter's methods as much as Paul, who stayed on as an assistant coach after his playing days were over. "Les will lean over to a teammate," said Paul, "and whisper, 'See that big Bob St. Clair over there? Man, has he worked up a head of steam. Now watch. I'll lean over and call him a gutless pussycat, and we'll see what he'll do. Les also will probably give St. Clair's helmet a jerk. This'll make St. Clair sore, and he'll spend the whole day playing Les instead of the ballgame. That means we've got one less guy to worry about."

No one in the NFL infuriated opposing players more consistently than Richter. One afternoon in 1955, Philadelphia's all-pro Pete Pihos was racing out for a pass. Richter calmly hooked him with an elbow and wrestled him to the ground. Then Les rushed to the other side of the field to attempt to bring down the ballcarrier. Pihos got up, chased after Richter and as soon as he caught up with him, let Les have it. Pihos swung his foot mightily and connected. It was a bullseye. The kick landed with all its fury in the middle of Les Richter's ample rear. When films were shown of that game, players all around the league must have applauded.

Retaliation didn't stop Richter, though. His routine never altered. "Richter would get killed if he took that helmet off," said Bobby Walston, a Philadelphia wide receiver. "It's a life saver to him. That's why you never see him take

it off. He must have it riveted on. There's one guy who wouldn't walk down an alley by himself after a game, but he's going to get his pretty soon. He's been asking for it for a long time. He likes to take 'cheap shots' at you. Nobody dares turn their backs on him. He's always in there pitching after the whistle."

In one game against the Eagles, Richter started roughing up Van Brocklin, his former teammate. He started in the first quarter and kept up a running feud with the Dutchman throughout the game. Finally, when the game ended, Philadelphia linebacker Bob Pellegrini roared across the field, jumped Richter and started fighting. Pellegrini then took a strong hold on the Ram linebacker while several Eagle players got in some good licks. It could have developed into a brutal beating. But, finally, the police arrived and broke it up.

Sid Gillman, one of Richter's head coaches with the Rams, was quick to defend his all-star linebacker. "Criticism of Les as a dirty player is extremely unfair," said Gillman. "First of all, there are only two or three downright dirty players in the league. Les is the kind of boy who plays the game to the hilt. He's rough, but he's not dirty. He's a fine competitor. In 1956, against Baltimore, Les collided with the bench on a sideline tackle and had his leg ripped open. There was a two-and-a-half inch gash which took several stitches to close. Yet he came back to finish the game. Later, the wound became infected, but Les never missed a practice session nor was he out of any game action. In one Bears' game, he played himself literally into the ground. He was so completely exhausted that he went into convulsions in the locker room and it was two hours after the game before we could move him."

"Sure," Richter admitted, "I play rough. But that's what the Rams pay me for, and that's what the fans pay to see. We've got a few dirty players

in the league, let's be honest about it. But everyone knows who they are, and they don't get away with much. There's a big distinction between playing hard and playing dirty. It's natural that an offensive player is going to cry. Say he's a halfback. You know he doesn't like to get hit. He can't hit back, either. Frank Gifford of the Giants is one of my closest friends. He calls us linebackers a bunch of dirty so-and-sos. That's all right. I call him a crybaby, kiddingly. You could hit a man like Tobin Rote of the Lions with a sledge hammer and he'd get up without a word and run back to the huddle. Y.A. Tittle and Billy Wade get mad when they're hit unnecessarily but they run right back, too. Of course, we have some quarterbacks in the league who are real crybabies, too." Richter never did identify the crybabies.

"If you don't like to knock somebody down, you have no business in this game," Les Richter always said. "Either you knock somebody down, or you get knocked down yourself. If you're the aggressor, there's less chance of getting dropped. There's also less likelihood of sustaining an injury. It's as simple as that. Call it survival of the fittest or common sense, but it's more fun to knock than to be knocked."

Les Richter never missed a Rams game. He played with a fractured cheekbone, broken hand, busted ribs, trick knee, broken toe and an entire assortment of sickening bumps and bruises.

"Richter was 'up' for every game he ever played," wrote Bud Furillo in the *Los Angeles Herald-Examiner*. "Four different coaches never had to boot him in the backside to get his emotions in gear."

"Les didn't leave his heart in San Francisco, but he left part of an ear there," wrote Jim Murray in the *Los Angeles Times*. "He left a few teeth embedded in helmets here and there around the league. And there are parts of foreign soil that are forever Richter's because there are still strips of his flesh clinging to plankings and chalk lines in places like Wrigley Field, Chicago and Tiger Stadium, Detroit. He was a one-man walking wounded march. He limped off every field."

They finally got around to giving him a day at the Los Angeles Coliseum on Oct. 27, 1963. Les Richter, the noted villain, wept. He has received many tributes before and since, but teammate Eddie Meador, later an all-pro himself, probably put it best: "Les set a standard for me as a professional. No player I've ever known has given so much of himself."

It was an offense unlike any other, before or since. Two of the great quarterbacks in National Football League history took turns throwing bombs. The best pair of receivers ever to start for one team were there catching passes. The quick, little scatback runners were complemented by the burly, but amazingly fast fullbacks—the Bull Elephants as they were to become known—to drive opposing linebackers nuts.

This was before pro football ever thought about expansion. Before many teams had organized a scouting system as intricate as the one in Los Angeles. Dan Reeves and the Rams had cornered the market, and nowhere had their monopoly been so amply demonstrated than at the skilled positions.

Bob Waterfield, Norm Van Brocklin, Tom Fears, Elroy Hirsch, Bob Boyd, V.T. Smith, Glenn Davis, Tommy Kalmanir, Tank Younger, Dick Hoerner, Deacon Dan Towler . . . the list is awesome, and it doesn't end there.

There were enough talented passers, runners and catchers to stock a half dozen football teams. Together, they meshed into the best gate attraction in sports. The Rams were something else. First and 10 on their own five-yard line? Don't go away. Waterfield to Hirsch and presto! You could have a 95-yard touchdown play.

It happened all the time, from anywhere on the football field.

Clearly, this was not the era of defense in Los Angeles. The scores tell you that. In 1950, the Rams beat the New York Yankees, 45-28. Baltimore fell 70-27. Detroit got it, 65-24. Green Bay suffered twice, 45-14 and 51-14. Against the Lions, the Ram offense produced 41 points—in the third quarter.

The records? Well, they took a worse beating than the opposition.

That 1950 club scored 466 points in 12 games. It gained 3,709 yards passing, collected 278 first downs. It scored 64 touchdowns. Think about that . . . 64 touchdowns. That's an average of over five a game.

Van Brocklin and Waterfield completed 55.8 percent of their passes, and, together, they threw for 34 touchdowns.

The onslaught continued in 1951. Van Brocklin led the National Football League's passers in '50, Waterfield was No. 1 in '51. Fears caught 84 passes to set an NFL record and finish first among receivers in '50. Hirsch speared 66, including 17 for touchdowns, to top all the league's catchers in '51.

If the 1951 club wasn't as spectacular, it was more balanced. Glenn Davis was the top Ram rusher in '50 with 437 yards. Towler more than doubled that total the following year, cruising for 890 and averaging 6.2 a carry.

The '51 team amassed more total yards, some 5,506, than any club in Ram history.

Although most of the Ram reputation on offense was manufactured through the air, it was never because of a lack of running backs. For a long time, the halfbacks in Los Angeles were quick, shifty little people who could catch as well as run. Clark Shaughnessy got so carried away with players like Kalmanir, V.T. Smith and Jerry Williams, he conceived a rather unusual attack. One in which no one blocked. None of the backs, that is. Everyone was a receiver. The quarterback only had to find the open man, al-

though, admittedly, there were times when he had to find him rather quickly.

It was later, midway through the 1951 championship season under Joe Stydahar, that the Rams turned to a different approach. The analysts on the Los Angeles coaching staff suddenly decided they had a bull market. Why not take advantage of it? Really, what they had were three bulls. Their names were Dan Towler, Paul Younger and Dick Hoerner.

"We were in the middle of the season," recalled Elroy Hirsch. "The Bears were out in front with four teams tied for second. The 49ers had just clobbered us, 44-17, at Kezar Stadium, and by a quirk in the schedule we had to face them again the following Sunday at the Coliseum. The 49ers had made us look like rummies. Their offense had pounded away at our line which had been weakened by injuries and their defense had come up with a way to stop our record-setting passing game. Buck Shaw inserted two fleet halfbacks as his outside linebackers and they matched our halfbacks pound for pound and speed for speed. Coach Stydahar and his staff knew that every team in the league could come up with the same kind of answer and stop us. But at Gilmore Field's Tuesday practice, a countermove jelled. The Rams had not one, not two, but three of the biggest, strongest, fastest and most devastating fullbacks at a time. So Younger was playing defense and Towler was alternating at fullback with Hoerner. Then came the idea. Why not use them all at once?"

That's how the Bull Elephant backfield was born. The Rams felt by combining the talents of these three power backs, they would be giving up little speed. All three were unusually fast for their size. They would not be forsaking the passing game, either, because all three could catch the ball.

On the afternoon of the second 49er game, Stydahar had two separate backfields ready.

When San Francisco went with Jim Powers and Verl Lillywhite, their two smallest, quickest outside linebackers, Jumbo struck with his Bull Elephants. When the 49ers countered with bulky Norm Standlee and Don Burke backing up the line, Stydahar switched to a faster combination, going with either Hoerner or Towler at fullback and inserting Glenn Davis and V.T. Smith at halfback.

The strategy was too much for the 49ers, who were worn down by the Elephants and finally beaten on a 76-yard Waterfield to Hirsch touchdown pass. The final score was 23-16.

The Bull Elephants had given a new dimension to the Ram offense. But opposing defenses were wising up to it. When Los Angeles reached Chicago four weeks later for a pivotal game with the Bears, George Halas was ready.

Chicago moved out in front early, 14-0, and on the sideline, the Rams knew something had to be done to get back in the game quickly. Waterfield and Hirsch agreed "to try one" on the first play. In those days, they called it a "play number pass." Today, it is more commonly referred to as play action. With the Chicago defense keying on the three Bulls in the backfield, Waterfield faked beautifully from his own nine-yard line and lofted a bomb to Hirsch, who had slipped behind everyone in the secondary. It was a 91-yard pass play, a new all-time Ram record at that point, and it was also the play that turned the game around. Now forced to be more pass concious, the Bears were ripe to get run over by the Elephants. Towler, Younger and Hoerner combined for 205 yards rushing and caught 5 passes between them for 133 more. The Rams won easily, 42-17.

"There's never been a backfield like it," said Hirsch. "Imagine, three sprinters, weighing a total of 666 pounds, bulling their way downfield together. Two of them, shoulder to shoulder, blocking for a third, and all of them capable of matching speed with most of the league's top halfbacks. I'll never forget the picture we created with the Bulls' plays—like one we called '27-M-Sockem.' I took the defensive end outside, the tackle turned the defensive tackle in, and Hoerner and Younger, shoulder-to-shoulder, flew head-on at the linebacker with Towler, shifty as a scatback, carrying the ball behind them. It was an awesome sight and good for 15 yards almost anytime. As I said, there's never been a backfield like it."

If the players were dominant in Los Angeles, so were the coaches. Throughout Ram history, they have moved controversially through town, stirring anger, splitting factions and often leaving for mysterious reasons, few of which were their own.

Even in the years spanning 1949-55—the most successful years in club annals—there were four coaches in seven seasons. It gives you an idea of what must have gone on when the Rams were losing.

The job passed from Clark Shaughnessy to Joe Stydahar to Hampton Pool and, finally, to Sid Gillman. And each time bitterness was expressed, angry words were splashed across the city's sports pages and phones rang in loud protest at the Ram business office.

Clark Shaughnessy was still getting phone calls of congratulations for capturing the 1949 divisional championship when another call came. The one telling him he had been fired. When informed that Stydahar, his assistant, would be replacing him, Shaughnessy went into a rage, claiming Joe had stolen his job. "I hired Joe," he said, "but when he gets through coaching the Rams I'll be able to take any high school team in the country and beat him."

Stydahar lasted for 32 months, during which he found enough time to win two divisional championships and a world championship. He also managed to accomplish something all

other coaches of his era had tried and failed. He managed to beat Paul Brown in a money game.

Jumbo, they called him. He was a big, friendly hunk of an ex-tackle, a man out of West Virginia who earned all-pro honors on Chicago's famous Monsters of the Midway. The smile matched the 280-pound physique and he quickly became one of the most popular and colorful figures in Los Angeles.

He was the prototype football coach, the kind you used to see in the movies. He liked his beer and an occasional "beezer," his own name for a jigger of bourbon. He puffed on big, black cigars when his cheek wasn't bulging with chewing tobacco and his language was, according to the *Los Angeles Times'* Frank Finch ". . . liberally laced with some of the more pungent words in the Anglo-Saxon tongue."

Joe Stydahar was one of a family of five brothers and five sisters. Born March 3, 1912, in Kaylor, Pa., his father, a Croation immigrant, earned his living in the dungeon-like atmosphere of the Shinnston, West Virginia, coal mines.

Young Joe was always big, always well coordinated. Twice, he was all-state in football, once at tackle and once as a fullback. Although chubby, he was the best prep basketball center in West Virginia and the regular third baseman for the Shinnston varsity baseball team.

Jock Sutherland, who prowled the West Virginia hillside searching for prospects, quickly signed him up for the University of Pittsburgh, where Jumbo stayed one month before getting homesick. He returned to West Virginia, enrolling at the state university. As a senior, he achieved All-Eastern, Little All-America and All-America mention, playing in the Shrine East-West game and the College All-Star game. And in 1936, George Halas made him the Chicago Bears' No. 1 draft pick.

"That was the turning point of my life," Joe

Stydahar would often say. "Halas has been like a second father to me. I didn't know anything about football until I had a chance to play for him."

It was in Chicago that Stydahar became one of the great football players of his time. He was a regular on the All-NFL team from 1937 through 1940, and there is no way to judge how good he might have become if his career hadn't been interrupted by a tour of duty in the Navy. He was a lieutenant in charge of a gun crew aboard the carrier USS Monterey in the Pacific during the War.

With the Bears, Jumbo was on five Western Division championship teams and a member of three world's champions. Those were the original Monsters of the Midway, and it is where Stydahar developed his philosophy of the game of football.

The Rams had just been routed 49-14 in a 1950 game with Philadelphia. Stydahar stormed into the dressing room and started to roar at his players. "No wonder you guys got kicked around," he fumed. "Every guy on the team has still got all his teeth."

It was Jumbo's feeling that a player who didn't pay regular visits to his dentist wasn't putting out on the football field. "When you charge," he said, "you gotta keep your head up. You lose a lot of teeth that way, but you also make a lot of tackles."

Stydahar honestly believed that theory. It was the only way he knew how to play the game. Once, after blocking a punt against Detroit and coming close to blocking another, Stydahar ran into a Lion blocker who was getting desperate. The man missed his block, but made sure he didn't miss with his elbow. It crashed against Stydahar's mouth and knocked out four teeth. Jumbo played 35 more minutes that day and remained in severe pain during the Bears' long, eight-hour trip back to Chicago.

Dr. Bill Osmanski, the former Bear fullback, told this story about Stydahar: "One day we were playing Brooklyn, and Bruiser Kinard, the Dodgers' great tackle, was giving me a bad time. Once I was knocked out and when Joe picked me up he asked who did it. I told him I wasn't sure. That it was either No. 52 or 25. Well, a couple of plays later Stydahar and Kinard crashed together so hard that the force of the collison opened a deep gash in Kinard's arm and he had to go to the clubhouse to have it stitched up. The officials believed just a collision couldn't cause such damage. They thought Joe must have been carrying a knife. In fact, they made a thorough search of all of us for concealed weapons. They even looked in Stydahar's mouth to see if he could have bitten Kinard. That was a waste of time if I ever saw one. Joe couldn't bite anybody. Not without teeth!"

In the service, Stydahar refused to play football. "I just didn't have the heart to play against some of those kids," he said. "They were just too damned small."

On the other hand, Jumbo never was one to avoid a good fight. He remains just as much a legend in the Navy as he does in football.

Apparently, his most famous episode occurred in a Philippine port, where he came across three Marine flyers who had gained something of a reputation as "the bully boys of the Pacific." Jumbo found them one afternoon working over a sailor.

As the story goes, Stydahar pulled the battered sailor to his feet, while fending off the three attackers. One of the Marines took his best punch at Stydahar and the blow landed flush on Jumbo's jaw. "I never got hit harder in my life," Joe would say, later. But that only infuriated him more. When it was over, the three Marines were lying there unconscious and Joe and the sailor walked away. Word of the brawl didn't take long to get around and Stydahar was summoned to the Captain's quarters shortly afterward.

"Stydahar," he growled, "I understand that an officer of this ship was involved in a shore brawl recently. Do you know anything about it?" "No sir," said Joe. "Stydahar, you are a (bleep) liar. Dismissed." And then the Captain roared with laughter.

So it was two-fisted Joe Stydahar who took over the Ram coaching job and carefully blended all that talent into a championship team. Jumbo handled the delicate problem at quarterback as well as anyone. When two talents like Waterfield and Van Brocklin are on the same squad, someone is always going to be unhappy. But Stydahar picked his spots, alternating them, never playing one against the other. He made it work so well that the two even wound up rooting for one another.

Stydahar stirred emotions much like Vince Lombardi. He was a big, lovable bulldog. At the same time, he managed to win the respect of his players and that made him even more popular. Except, of course, when Jumbo got tough. And he could get tough. He developed a strong affection for his players early, but he was careful to make sure they weren't putting anything over on him. When punishment was to be doled out, Stydahar never flinched.

The Rams were playing a preseason game in September 1951, Little Rock, Ark. After the game, which ended at 11:30, Jumbo began to get suspicious when none of the players were seen in the vicinity of the hotel. By 2 a.m., he was fuming. He telephoned Tom Fears' room. There was no answer. He called several more rooms. Same result. Finally, on a hunch, he dialed a Little Rock night spot he had heard about. Jumbo asked for Jack Finlay, the veteran guard. Disguising his voice to resemble that of a certain Ram player, Stydahar inquired of Finlay, "Any Rams there, Jack?" The reply confirmed Stydahar's suspicions. "Yeah, we're all here. Come on down." Stydahar exploded. "Listen, playboy,"

A new dimension was added to the already powerful Rams offense midway through the '51 title season. With three big, fast fullbacks on his team, Stydahar put them all in the game at the same time. They became "The Bull Elephant Backfield." The "bulls" were (left to right) Dick Hoerner, Paul (Tank) Younger and Dan Towler. Their average size was 222 pounds.

he screamed, "this is Joe Stydahar and I'll give you guys 30 minutes to get back here. You're all fined a hundred dollars, and it'll cost you another hundred if you're not back in 30 minutes.

The crackdown was a headline story back in Los Angeles and the repercussions continued for days. Before he was finished, Stydahar wound up fining 28 Rams $7,900. "I can't afford the fine," complained one lineman. "I am in debt. I haven't made a nickel since the season started. Other players are hit even harder. Some of our fellows are married and have two and three children to take care of. They are living on money they haven't earned yet and running up bills."

Stydahar, backed by Reeves, insisted the fines would stick. "This type of thing happens to all teams somewhere along the line," he said. "The team must just realize that this is serious business and it takes training and discipline to have a winning team. If I didn't feel this team had such a great chance of going a long way, I might not have taken such severe action." In the Rams' next game, they were beaten by the Chicago Cardinals, 36-21. It was Los Angeles' first loss of the season. Not long after that, Stydahar's fines were rescinded.

It was Jumbo's nature. He was, in turn, suspicious and compassionate. After the explosion, he often liked to joke about his actions. He especially enjoyed the story of another room check he made one midnight in Salt Lake City, Utah, when the Little Rock incident was still fresh in his mind. Stydahar set out from his three-room corner suite and started down the hotel corridor. He knocked on the first door and, as in Little Rock, there was no answer. Jumbo blanched. "Damn those guys," he sputtered. "They're out again." Noting the number on the door was 825, he struck a match to read his copy of the room list. In his anger, his big fist shook so he could barely make out the words. Finally, he shoved the list at assistant coach Red Hickey,

who was making the tour with him. "Who is that so-and-so in 825?" he shouted. Hickey ran a finger down the list and then smiled. "825," he said, "is you, Joe."

At the age of 39, Joe Stydahar had swaggered into the National Football League, taken over the Rams and won the world championship. He had a lovely wife, Yolanda, a robust three-year-old son named David and another child on the way. He also had a new three-year contract, compliments of Reeves and the happy Ram management.

For a man whose original appointment had drawn such mixed reviews, it was quite an achievement. Jumbo was humble about it. He distributed the plaudits equally among members of his staff.

"I know this sounds corny," he said, "but my coaching staff couldn't possibly get the credit it deserves for the success of the Rams. Each has done wonders in his own department. Red Hickey has polished up our ends, Elroy Hirsch and Tom Fears, until they're the best in the game and you saw for yourself what our defensive men, Larry Brink and Andy Robustelli, did to Otto Graham in the championship game. When we started practicing last July, as you know, we didn't have any veteran tackles in camp. Yet Ray Richards rebuilt our offensive line from tackle to tackle and developed the rookie tackle of the year on defense, Jim Winkler."

Then Stydahar paused to pay tribute to the man who helped design his offense. As it turned out, it was to be one of the most ironic statements Jumbo would ever make.

"I hate to think of the long hours Hamp Pool spent in designing plays for Bob Waterfield and Norm Van Brocklin, and working out a pass defense which was the second best in the league," Stydahar said. "To my way of thinking, Pool is the best young coach in football."

A former teammate of Stydahar before the

war in Chicago and a close friend, Pool had been carefully chosen by Jumbo as his top assistant. "The deterioration of their relationship," wrote Bob Oates, then of the *Los Angeles Examiner,* "under the stresses of coaching a high-powered football team was at once the most influential and the most tragic thing that ever happened to either man or to the team they served. All things considered, the coaching job they did together in 1950-51 was the best the Rams had in the years from 1937 to 1954."

Stydahar coached the way most modern coaches do today. He was, basically, an organizer, a morale booster and a public relations man of sorts. Pool was the architect, a man with a fascinating mind and one of the few original thinkers in the game. Jumbo was the pal of the players. Pool was the enemy. When they had a gripe, they ran to Stydahar. More often than not, the gripe concerned Pool.

The problem really began when Stydahar relied so much on Pool, when he placed him in charge of both the offense and the defense. Jumbo thought it would work better that way, and it did. Except that egos and pride soon clouded the picture. Pool's name was dominating most newspaper stories. He was the topic of most conversatons among Ram friends and family. He was regarded as a young genius and perhaps Stydahar realized what he had done. And perhaps just a tinge of jealousy was involved. "He didn't understand," said Bob Oates, "that applause for Pool was applause for Stydahar."

So Jumbo moved to rectify the situation. He reclaimed the responsibility for the offense and the defense. His timing was not good. Two months later, the Rams were engulfed in a mild slump. Reeves tried vainly to get Jumbo to delegate the auhority the way it used to be. Stydahar remained stubborn. "Either I go or Pool goes," he said. Reeves was not one to be pushed like that. Of the two, he decided to stick with Pool.

So a few months after Joe Stydahar had praised Hamp Pool as the finest young football coach in America, he had another statement to make. It appeared in print in Sid Ziff's column in the Los Angeles Mirror. *Jumbo told Ziff: "I'll hate Hamp Pool until the day I die."*

It was some 15 years later, after he already had been inducted into the Pro Football Hall of Fame, that Stydahar was asked if he would have changed anything in his career. This is what he said:

"Well, there's one thing I would have changed. A man thinks he's grown up and he finds out sometimes he's acting like a little boy. That's the one time in my life I would change, the two years I was coach of the Los Angeles Rams. For the way I acted, I mean. I used my pride, instead of my mind. I thought I was so big I couldn't be replaced. Nobody's that big, not in football, not in anything. I know that now. I didn't then."

The transition from Joe Stydahar to Hampton Pool could not be an easy one. Not when two completely opposite personalities were involved. Unlike Jumbo, whose emotions were there for everyone to see and hear, Pool was more complex. He was described first as an intellectual, but one who did not believe pure intelligence was enough to win in the National Football League. So, according to some, he paraded as a tough guy, a man driven by a passion to succeed. The two roles made him doubly difficult to understand. Especially to players who were accustomed to a relatively simple man like Stydahar.

"That man is two men," said Tank Younger, *referring to Pool. "Maybe more. From January to July you couldn't meet a sweeter guy. But after football starts, I don't know what happens to him. He hardens up like this here ground."*

Emotion was the most important unknown in football to Pool. He spent hours trying to find a solution, a hint on how to break through the facade that hid a player's emotional makeup. He

was, in fact, ahead of his time. When he traveled to Stanford University and the Center for Advanced Study in the Behavioral Sciences, it was looked on as a rather strange move. When he came up with personality tests for the players, they were considered something of a waste of time. Twenty years later, however, successful organizations like the Dallas Cowboys are utilizing the same methods.

As a technician, few Ram coaches ever have matched Pool. His knowledge of offense, in particular, bordered on genius. His ingenuity was one of the primary reasons for the flashy, wide open style created by the pro football team in Los Angeles.

It was Pool who discovered that the Rams simply had too many fine receivers for opposing teams to cover. If spread properly across the field, at least one of them would be covered one-on-one. At the time, it was a revelation that changed the entire scope of football in the NFL. The Rams began blitzing people with that withering pass offense and opponents were driven to experiment with new defenses. Something had to be found to cut down the effectiveness of the Ram passing attack. Most teams tried some sort of combination involving zones. But, in the end, it was Pool, forced to combat other teams who had adopted the Rams' offensive style, who came up with the defense to stop it. In his first year, he won eight straight games to tie for the Western Division title in 1952. The key to his streak was an aggressive defense featuring Dick (Night Train) Lane. Night Train set a new National Football League record that season, intercepting 14 passes and returning them for 298 yards and two touchdowns.

Despite his success in a defense drawn up by Pool, Lane epitomized the discontent on the Rams. Later, he told how he felt toward Stydahar and then Pool. "He (Stydahar) was great with the players. He understood them. But the Rams had other problems. Anyway, Hamp Pool eventually replaced Stydahar as head coach, and, well, I didn't do so well for him. He was different than Stydahar. I don't think he cared for the players."

Pool cared. It's just that he was transfixed by X's and O's. He could sit for hours drawing up plays. And although many of them eventually helped the Rams win football games, they also took valuable time away from establishing a rapport with the men he coached. Because of his intense involvement in strategy, the thought of possible defeat magnified in his mind. He became almost frightened of it.

"Only those who are really scared they're going to lose will develop a genuine desire to win," he said. Pool had the desire.

The scene was on the long plane ride home after a 31-21 loss to Detroit in the 1952 playoffs. Hopes for a second straight world championship were gone, and Pool was seen sitting on the floor of the airplane. "What are you thinking about, Hamp?" a writer asked. The coach replied matter-of-factly: "Wouldn't it be wonderful if we ran into a mountain?"

Pool's apparent distant attitude toward players was a mystery to friends and reporters. "When out of sight of his players," wrote Bob Oates, "he was invariably courteous, a gracious, friendly, gay companion. Socially, he was the life of the party. An invitation to Hamp Pool, in fact, insured the success of any party."

Pool's football experience was as varied as his moods. He played at three different colleges, Stanford, California and West Point. And he learned six different positions, end, guard, center, halfback, fullback and quarterback. After playing for the Chicago Bears, he coached at five separate places in five years, including Fort Pierce Navy, San Jose, San Bernardino, Miami and Chicago. When he accepted the job as Los Angeles head coach at age 37, he became the first native Californian to lead the Rams.

But he, too, ran into problems. His work schedule was one of them. It began early and ended late. There were few days off. He never complained, but his assistants did. They didn't care for the long hours or the way Pool's time was distributed. They felt much of it was wasted.

Hamp came up with innovations like a "performance chart" that carefully accounted for each player on every play of each game. Perhaps more than anything else, this is what created a deep fissure on Pool's Ram teams. The assistant coaches objected to the chart, and, naturally, so did the players. In professional football today, of course, all teams grade their players similarly. In the early '50s, though, Hamp Pool's ideas were sadly, a bit too far advanced.

The mutiny started slowly, but began to grow as the months passed. The players, aware that some of the assistants were grumbling, increased their complaints.

Pool had difficulty handling it. Most men would have. This was an intellectual, however, and had he attempted to deal with it logically, he might have been better off. Instead, he got too tangled up emotionally.

The Rams gave one of the saddest offensive exhibitions in their history in a 1954 game against Detroit. Ultimately, they lost, 21-3, failing to score a touchdown for the first time in 67 consecutive games. Frustrated, Pool tried to shake his team up at halftime. He delivered an old-fashioned fight talk, built around the ancient request to "get out there and FIGHT!" As a final gesture of emphasis, Pool smashed a closed fist on a dressing room table. He was so caught up in his message, he neglected to look down at the table first. There, sitting innocently, was a pile of oranges prepared for halftime nourishment. Predictably, the results were catastrophic. The oranges were reduced to pulp and juice, most of which were sprayed over the head coach's neatly pressed gray flannels and blue sports jacket. It was a scene from a slapstick comedy, but in a troubled dressing room, the laughs were missing.

It was Pool's nature not to be concerned with certain details. Like signing a coaching contract, for instance. In his three years with the Rams, he never did sign one.

On the day he succeeded Stydahar after the first league game in 1952, time was short. There was a practice to conduct and considerable paperwork to do. Reeves and Pool had a brief five minute conference and as Hamp stepped out of the owner's office, Dan was reported to have called after him. "We'll get together one of these days and talk contract." But they never did. Even after his first season ended with the Rams tied for the divisional championship, he didn't ask for a raise. The University of Washington reportedly wanted him, offering in the vicinity of $27,500 a year. He turned it down to stay in Los Angeles and coach the Rams for a salary that was estimated to be $18,000.

But if he caused few ripples in the front office, he created many in the locker room. The "Stydahar men," in particular, seemed out to get him. In 1954, four of his five assistants resigned and the private debates became public. The newspapers ran interviews with several of the ex-coaches, all of whom had few nice things to say about Pool. One story strongly criticized Hamp for reading aloud to the squad from Norman Vincent Peale's book entitled, "The Power of Positive Thinking."

It finally got to be too much. One week after the end of the 1954 season, Hamp Pool quit. Although Reeves considered him an excellent coach, he did not hesitate in accepting the resignation. He confided that many of the wounds appeared too deep.

As always, Pool was unconventional, even upon leaving. He asked for no compensation. He was offered six months' salary as a settlement. He took it and departed.

Hamp Pool (far left), successor to Stydahar as head coach, was an intellectual, hard-driving leader who knew football strategy as well as anyone. He worked long hours and devised performance charts for grading his players. Pool resigned in 1954, and a widespread search for the new coach followed. The new boss of the Rams was Sid Gillman (near left) of the University of Cincinnati. He coached the Rams for the next five seasons. Jon Arnett (right) was the first player selected by Los Angeles in the 1957 draft. He became one of the most exciting stars of the Gillman era.

And so the Great Search began. It was more of a manhunt, really. The whole town got in on it. Everyone had an opinion on whom the next coach of the Los Angeles Rams should be.

All the biggest names in football were thrown into the fish bowl and plucked out one by one to be examined as possibilities. Writers and broadcasters rarely have had so much fun. They were making guesses about their guesses. One day it was going to be Bud Wilkinson of Oklahoma, and you could almost picture sincere-looking Bud strolling down the Coliseum sidelines. Twenty-four hours later, the newspapers reported Wilkinson was out and Eddie Erdelatz of Navy was in. It went on and on like that. Other names that cropped up included Jordan Olivar of Yale, Bobby Dodd of Georgia Tech and Wally Butts of Georgia. Those were just the college coaches.

There were plenty of pro candidates, too. Naturally, there was considerable backing for Paul Brown, although no one really knew what it would take to lure him away from Cleveland. Buck Shaw of San Francisco was another. Buddy Parker, they said, would be more than happy to leave Detroit if the right offer came along. And Ram assistant coach Red Hickey let the news leak out that he was interested. Days passed and no decision was reached. By now, newspapers had organized their own campaigns, championing their own personal candidates. Shaw, Hickey, Olivar and Brown were the most popular. A public opinion poll was conducted by sportswriters George T. Davis and John B. Old, and the reaction was amazing. Thousands of people wrote in, most of them suggesting Shaw, the 49er coach who had beaten the Rams more than they liked to remember.

Now weeks had gone by, and the situation turned into something of a folly. One writer launched a new drive to rehire Pool. Another wondered if Pool and Shaw might be able to switch jobs. Meanwhile, the rumors were doing wonders for some of the reported candidates. Erdelatz received an impressive new contract from the Naval Academy. The Air Force Academy signed Shaw. Bob Blackman, another who was mentioned, was hired by Dartmouth. San Francisco whisked Hickey away and Yale provided Olivar with a nice raise.

Finally, 39 days after the search began, it ended. The man chosen was perhaps the least known of all those mentioned. "Rams Hire Sid Gillman," screamed the headlines the next day. Most people had to read the story further to find out who Sid Gillman was. It turns out he was the head coach at the University of Cincinnati, and, as Ram fans would learn in the next few days, one of the most respected football men in the business, pro or college.

The Rams signed him in a Chicago hotel after meeting with co-owners Ed Pauley and Fred Levy. Wilkinson, it turned out, had recommended him for the job, and Army's Red Blaik was quoted as saying, "Gillman is the wisest choice." Red Sanders of UCLA agreed. "Gillman is absolutely the tops," he said.

Born in Minneapolis in 1911, Gillman grew up in the heart of Big 10 football country. He attended Ohio State, where he played end and received All Big 10 and All-America mention in 1931-33. He played with the collegians in the first College All-Star game in 1934 and also participated in the East-West game the same season. Following graduation, he played one year with the Cleveland Rams in 1935 before moving into coaching.

He served as an assistant coach at Denison University, Ohio State and Miami of Ohio. Then, in 1944, he accepted the job as head coach at Miami of Ohio, succeeding Stu Holcomb. His record was impressive. In four years at the Oxford, Ohio, school, he won 31 games, losing only six with one tie. In 1948, he became Blaik's line

coach on an Army team that was to go undefeated. And in 1949, he was offered the head coaching job at the University of Cincinnati, where he remained until the Rams beckoned.

Although Cincinnati is regarded as a small school in intercollegiate football, Gillman gained a wide reputation by lecturing at clinics. His theories were so well accepted, other coaches began to imitate him. When your teams are imitated, you know you've made it as a football coach.

In the early 1940s, Gillman was one of the first to begin alternating small units of specialists for offense and defense. As it turned out, this was the beginning of the two-platoon system. Gillman also used the "belly series." He used to call it the "ride-in series." The quarterback would plant the ball in a running back's stomach, forcing the defense to guess whether he'd leave it there or keep it himself. Blocking technique was another Gillman obsession. The old-line thinking forced blockers to concentrate on one specific defender, going after him no matter where he might wind up on the field. In Gillman's system, the blocker would go after the nearest opposing jersey.

Gillman's No. 1 tool was his trusty motion picture projector. "If they ever make movies illegal," he once said, "I'll quit football." Paul Brown kept him well-fortified with films for years and Gillman studied the Cleveland plays carefully. Many people will tell you that there is no better way to learn the game than to study a Paul Brown team in action.

Gillman had only one hobby. His work. There were no vacations, only occasional trips to wherever Sid was lecturing that week.

His wife, Esther, his high school sweetheart, was understanding about Gillman's work schedule. She had to be. There was no other choice. Fortunately, she had a fine sense of humor. "Sid must be a stupid football coach," she said, one day, assessing her husband, *"No*

other coach has to work that hard to get ahead."

Gillman was not walking into the best coaching situation in the country. Los Angeles had become infatuated with its pro football team, and everyone in town—the fans, the writers, the players, the owners, the broadcasters—had an opinion. It was impossible to please them all. To survive, a coach had to appease them, and, most of all, he had to win.

As a small college coach joining the pros, Gillman was faced with another major problem. The veterans, the hardened professionals who had proven their worth, were waiting to be shown. They were skeptical. They doubted a rookie coach could walk off a Cincinnati campus and take charge in the National Football League.

They were right. But Gillman foiled them, in part, by admitting that he needed help. He approached the seasoned veterans, like Van Brocklin, Fears and Paul, and told them, in effect, if you stick by me now, I'll stick by you later.

It worked. For one happy season, it worked.

But it wasn't easy. The Rams were struck down by injuries, especially on offense. It was their good fortune, however, to uncover a small, gifted runner from Maryland named Ron Waller. Waller, a second round choice, had been drafted primarily as a defensive back. That's what he played as a starter in the College All-Star game in Chicago.

When Waller reported to the Ram camp, however, Gillman took one look at him and announced he would be deployed at wide receiver. So Ron Waller, ex-defensive back, spent his first preseason in the National Football League running pass patterns.

Ron Waller remembers that first summer in Redlands, Calif. There was the oppressive heat and there was Gene (Big Daddy) Lipscomb. "Back then," said Waller, "there was no place in

Bill Wade (far left) was the Rams' first draft choice in 1952 but didn't join the team until 1954 because of Navy service. The quarterbacks before and after him were perhaps better known, but it is Wade who holds the club record for passing yardage in a season—2,875 in 1958. Two all-pro stars of the 1955 Western Conference championship team were guard Duane Putnam and running back Ron Waller (left). Three aspirants for the quarterbacking job in '58 were, left to right, rookies Bobby Cox of Minnesota, Frank Ryan of Rice and incumbent Wade.

town for a black guy to get his hair cut. So I used to drive Big Daddy to San Bernardino, where there was no problem getting a haircut. Funny, but I guess he was always grateful to me for that. Later, when he was traded to the Colts and we'd play Baltimore, he always tried to protect me. He was always looking out for me. When I'd get tackled, he'd try to prevent his teammates from piling on. And when I'd get hit hard, he'd always rush over and say, 'You okay, Ron?' He never forgot that small favor I used to do for him.''

Only two players in the league were smaller than Waller. They were Eddie LeBaron, the Washington quarterback, and Doak Walker, the Detroit immortal. The smallest Ram remained at wide receiver until late in the exhibition season when regular running back Skeet Quinlan went down with a knee injury.

Waller was moved to running back and told to learn the plays. Although he opened the regular season as a wide receiver, he was soon switched permanently to running back.

It turned out to be a lucky experiment, because the Rams were soon decimated by injuries at running back. The situation got so bad that their first draft choice that year, linebacker Larry Morris, had to move to fullback for the first time since his freshman year at Georgia Tech. A highly-regarded 220-pound All-America, Morris had won a starting job on defense. But he, like Waller an exceptional athlete, was able to handle other jobs. Although he never established himself as a powerful running threat, he handled the blocking assignments well, and that's all Gillman asked of him.

Waller did most of the running, although admittedly he had an advantage. He had a powerful ally in Duane Putnam, a second-year guard from the College of the Pacific. Putnam finished his rookie year weighing only 193 pounds, but a diligent off-season weight program matured him into a 230-pounder who had lost little of his exceptional speed. In 1955, Putnam may have enjoyed the greatest season of any offensive guard in Ram history. He was voted all-pro, and the sight of Duane pulling out of the line to lead a sweep always brought Ram fans to the edge of their seats.

The 1955 Rams remain one of the most interesting of Los Angeles teams, starting from the front office, through the coaching staff and finally the players. The general manager, for instance, was a rising, young executive named Pete Rozelle. The director of publicity was Bert Rose. Gillman's end coach was George Allen. And his quarterback was Norman Van Brocklin.

The man known as "Dutch" had been in complete command of the Ram offense since Waterfield's retirement in 1952. But this was the first time he directed the team to a divisional championship by himself.

The Rams were playing the Green Bay Packers that year and on a routine play, Ron Waller attempted to cross-body block a Packer defensive player. He missed and the man stepped over him, crunching his cleats into Waller's face. "I thought my nose was gone," remembers Waller. "The blood was coming from the bridge of my nose and forehead. I was bleeding like a stuck pig. Van Brocklin came over, looked at me and the blood was dripping down, and he calmly called my number on a pass play. I couldn't believe it. He threw the ball and somehow I caught it. But it must have been purely on instinct. I learned a lot about Van Brocklin that day."

All afternoons were not that bleak for Waller in 1955. The little man from Maryland ran for 716 yards, more than any rookie runner in Ram history. He worked some at wide receiver and wound up playing every minute of every offensive play, beside being part of the kickoff and punt return teams. He finished fourth in the league in rushing and was named to the all-pro team.

The Rams and Gillman didn't win the Western Division easily. Their friends from Chicago made sure of that. The Bears mauled them twice, 30-21 and 24-3, and were in close pursuit right on through December.

In fact, in the last game of the season, the Rams needed a victory over Green Bay or the championship would be lost. A modest crowd was expected at the Coliseum to see the Packers, who were not yet regarded as one of the NFL's bigger draws. But there was something at stake this day, and the town knew it. One of the biggest game day sales in Ram history produced a crowd of over 90,000. The Rams and Waller didn't disappoint them. Ron scored three touchdowns, one on a long run early in the first quarter, and the Rams won, 31-17. Los Angeles had captured its fourth conference title in seven years.

The ensuing world championship game with Cleveland provided the Rams with a foreboding look into the future. On a gloomy, rain-spattered day in Los Angeles, Van Brocklin—*the* Norm Van Brocklin—was intercepted five times.

Otto Graham sloshed through the wetness, passing crisply and running spectacularly. Paul Brown and his Cleveland Browns, beaten 24-17 by the Rams in the 1951 championship game, had been waiting four years for their revenge. Now their wait was over. The Rams were overwhelmed, 38-14.

With that game in mind, Gillman was to plot a shakeup of sorts in the off-season, making moves that would eventually stir controversy and cause problems. But then, why should he be any different?

No one ever found complete happiness coaching the Rams. Not even in The Great Years. The pressure was constant. It was applied from all sides. The fans would not just cheer or boo, depending upon how the game was going. They were there to coach, to offer advice, wanted or not. In field goal territory, for instance, the chant was always loud and clear. "Go For It . . . Go For It . . ." They never believed in field goals in Los Angeles. Not when they had seen touchdowns come so easily in years past. Nor would they tolerate a quarterback not of their choosing, and the chants of "We Want Van Brocklin!" or "We Want Wade!" or "We Want Ryan!" were to drive more than one coach up the walls.

It is little wonder, then, even after Gillman signed a four-year contract—the longest ever offered a Ram coach by Reeves—he received some wise advice from Melvin Durslag in an open-letter column that appeared in the *Los Angeles Examiner.*

"Don't fool with any real estate here," Durslag wrote. "Rent."

Yet, for all the incongruities, professional football in Los Angeles in the early '50s had an aura about it. There was the sense that something classical was taking shape. A sport that would capture the mood of a nation was starting to take its first strong grip. And these people were in on it. They were there from the beginning.

David Boss, the publisher of *PRO!,* the official magazine of the National Football League, expressed the feeling in a 1972 story describing the various stadia in the league. He talked about a Ram game in the '50s, and what it meant to be there:

" . . . I climbed a stairway of the Los Angeles Memorial Coliseum with my brother. It was 11:30 a.m. on a Sunday in November, but the stadium was crowded already. I will never forget the sensation of first entering the Coliseum. It was one of this country's first monumental stadia and, to this day, it still provides a special thrill to walk through its concrete tunnels. History resides there. It seems to permeate the place.

On this day, the Rams were meeting their archrivals from San Francisco and 102,368 people were gathering to watch the duel between Norm Van Brocklin and Y.A. Tittle. We sat in row 79,

the last row at the top of the stadium, far above the playing field. Squashed together into a mass of wall-to-wall people, we screamed ourselves hoarse as we watched an apocalyptical game. We were sharing something special, my brother and I, and like everyone else in the Coliseum that day we knew it. We were a part of the largest crowd in the history of pro football and it almost seemed as if we were shouting not only for the teams, but for ourselves, cheering the very glory of the monster our massed bodies had created."

The teenager who grew up following the Rams is an adult involved in other endeavors now. The early fascination of Los Angeles' first major league team left a large imprint, though. It is an imprint that affected a lot of other people's lives, too.

The teenager now an adult lives and works in another town, but the reaction is still the same. On a chartered airplane streaking through the darkness of a winter's night, the pilot announces that day's pro football scores.

". . . and in Los Angeles, the Vikings defeated the Rams 45-41 . . ." It shouldn't mean that much anymore. Another game in another season. The outcome wouldn't affect his life. But strangely it bothered him almost the way it had 20 years earlier. He wouldn't pout about it like he had then. He wouldn't refuse his evening meal.

But the score, that crazy score, bugged him. "Damn it," he thought, "there's no way they should lose when they score 41 points."

And then he sat back in his seat and smiled that same silly nostalgic smile.

It had been 25 years, and the occasion was the Rams' Silver Anniversary in Los Angeles.

Dan Reeves, who had made the decision to move West, was asked, in the spring of 1970, to select an all-time Los Angeles Ram team. He agreed, although he insisted that active players must be exempt from consideration for the team.

This is the team he selected:

QUARTERBACKS—Bob Waterfield and Norm Van Brocklin.

RUNNING BACKS—Paul (Tank) Younger, Deacon Dan Towler and Ron Waller.

WIDE RECEIVERS—Elroy Hirsch, Tom Fears and Jim Benton.

OFFENSIVE LINEMEN—Gil Bouley and Frank Varrichione, tackles; Duane Putnam and Milan Lazetich, guards; and Leon McLaughlin, center.

DEFENSIVE LINEMEN—Andy Robustelli and Larry Brink, ends; Dick Huffman and Frank Fuller, tackles.

LINEBACKERS—Don Paul, Fred Naumetz and Les Richter.

DEFENSIVE BACKS—Will Sherman, Jerry Williams, Woodley Lewis and Don Burroughs.

The Rams' owner did not comment on all the selections. But he did have a few things to say.

"Waterfield was a complete leader and quarterback," said Reeves, "and he was a winner. Van Brocklin, on his greatest days, was the greatest of passers.

"Hirsch was the most spectacular end in the history of football. Nobody else has ever done what he did so consistently. But Jack Snow has a lot of the Hirsch flair in him. I've enjoyed watching Snow. Hirsch and Fears were the two kinds of ends everybody still wants—the home run hitter and the .400 singles hitter."

On the team, in general, Reeves commented:

"They were not necessarily big men. But many of them were self-made, and they all had leadership and the desire to win, to do it regardless."

The Memories

Dan Reev

WORLD CHAMPIONSHIP PLAYOFF
NATIONAL FOOTBALL LEAGUE

13th Annual Game

CLEVELAND STADIUM
DEC. 16, 1945
25c

CLEVELAND RAMS
Western Champions

VS.

WASHINGTON REDSKINS
Eastern Champions

Championship game of 1945 saw the Cleveland Rams defeat the Washington Redskins 15-14 for the NFL title.

Kenny Washington, UCLA star who joined Bob Waterfield, Tom Harmon, in 1946 backfield.

The Rams' helmet, painted by halfback and artist Fred Gehrke.

Bob Waterfield, consummate leader and all-round quarterback. He could pass, run, punt and kick placements. He stood out in an era of great quarterbacks in pro football.

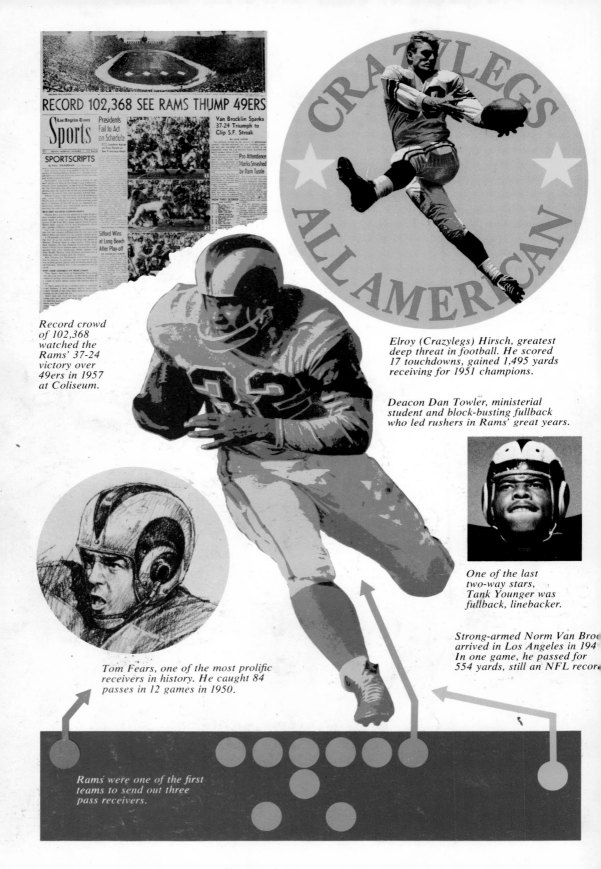

RECORD 102,368 SEE RAMS THUMP 49ERS

Los Angeles Times Sports

SPORTSCRIPTS

Record crowd of 102,368 watched the Rams' 37-24 victory over 49ers in 1957 at Coliseum.

CRAZYLEGS ALL AMERICAN

Elroy (Crazylegs) Hirsch, greatest deep threat in football. He scored 17 touchdowns, gained 1,495 yards receiving for 1951 champions.

Deacon Dan Towler, ministerial student and block-busting fullback who led rushers in Rams' great years.

One of the last two-way stars, Tank Younger was fullback, linebacker.

Strong-armed Norm Van Broc arrived in Los Angeles in 194 In one game, he passed for 554 yards, still an NFL recor

Tom Fears, one of the most prolific receivers in history. He caught 84 passes in 12 games in 1950.

Rams were one of the first teams to send out three pass receivers.

Tall and durable, Roman Gabriel (left) led
the George Allen-coached teams of 1966-70.

Defensive tackle Merlin Olsen (above) has been
selected for Pro Bowl every year of his career.

The second "Fearsome Foursome" (below): Lamar Lundy, Roger Brown, Merlin Olsen, Deacon Jones.

Carroll Rosenbloom became Rams' owner in 1972 after Robert Irsay purchased team from estate of late Dan Reeves, then sold it to Rosenbloom in exchange for control of Baltimore Colts.

Hopes for the future rest in young players like Isiah Robertson (left, stopping Vic Washington of the 49ers). The linebacker was first draft choice in 1971.

Willie Ellison (below) gained 247 yards against the New Orleans Saints Dec. 5, 1971, setting all-time NFL rushing record.

Bob Waterfield, QB, 1945-52. Inducted in 1965.

Elroy Hirsch, end, 1946-57. Inducted in 1968.

Norm Van Brocklin, QB, 1949-58. Inducted in 1971.

Tom Fears, end, 1948-56. Inducted in 1970.

Dan Reeves, owner, 1941-71. Inducted in 1967.

Ollie Matson, back, 1959-62. Inducted in 1972.

3

The Great Games

December 24, 1950

It was long before anything as clever as the Super Bowl had been devised. Seventeen years prior to that first Green Bay-Kansas City classic in Los Angeles, two teams from another era were playing for similar stakes.

It is an eerie trip through professional football's time machine.

The setting was Cleveland's Municipal Stadium, where, on a typical gray winter's day, the turf was frozen by winds howling off Lake Erie. The temperature at gametime was announced as 27 degrees. It seemed much lower.

The Browns, members of the All America Conference since it was first organized in 1946, had swept to four consecutive league championships and had proudly put in a claim as the best team in football.

The older, established NFL laughed it off. The All America Conference was one thing. The National Football League another. The skeptics wanted them to play the Bears, the Eagles, the Giants and the Rams first. Then talk about being No. 1.

In fact, when the AAFC was attempting to organize in '46, Elmer Layden, the Commissioner of the NFL, infamously advised the new league "to get a ball first."

Paul Brown went out and got one. He got a team, too. A pretty good one. And when it was finally allowed to play in the NFL, it proved its quality.

The Browns arrived in the establishment with their weapons intact. There was Otto Graham, the peerless quarterback, a brilliant place-kicker in Lou Groza and a hulking power runner named Marion Motley. There was also a fine defense and some flawless execution.

In their first season in the National Football League, the Browns outpointed the Bears 27-23 in an exhibition game; they defeated the Eagles twice; and they lost only to the Giants, who beat them twice but were unable to handle them when they met in the playoffs to resolve a tie.

In the game that counted most, Groza kicked New York out of the playoffs, 8-3.

But now there was Los Angeles to contend with. The Rams, professional football's mightiest offensive team. The franchise that had won a world championship in Cleveland and then had fled to the West Coast only five years earlier.

Bob Waterfield was a rookie fresh out of UCLA that season. He was also the first player ever to be selected as the league's most valuable in his initial season. That was five years ago. Now Waterfield was returning as one of pro football's most accomplished quarterbacks, the man some said was the most skilled all around player in the game.

Waterfield vs. Graham. The Rams vs. the Browns. The aristocracy vs. the outcasts.

The Hollywood Rams, they called them, and they lived up to their glamorous name. What they could do better than anyone else was find their way to the end zone. They scored 466 points during the season, 70 of them in one spectacular gulp against Baltimore.

They gained 5,420 yards, 3,709 of them passing. They manufactured 278 first downs and completed 253 passes, 31 for touchdowns.

And they had earned their spot in the championship round by defeating the physical Chicago Bears 24-14 in a bruising playoff game.

Paul Brown, the master tactician, knew that to beat Los Angeles he would have to cut down the effectiveness of the Ram passing game. And to do that, he would need a decent rush up front.

But he wasn't sure he could get it. Len Ford, his great defensive end, was the pivotal figure. The Browns worried about his condition. Big Len had his face mashed by Chicago's Pat Harder in a game Oct. 15. He suffered a fractured jaw, had been on a liquid diet and lost both weight and strength. He had not been active on the practice field and there were those who felt he was

Rams	14	0	14	0	28
Browns	7	6	7	10	30

in no condition to play again that year.

Ford was not among them. Len, noting the cracked ribs suffered by teammate George Young, asked to dress for the Rams and said he would be ready if needed. The other Cleveland injury was to Mac Speedie, the sleek wide receiver who had a badly pulled leg muscle.

The Rams' only serious injury was kept quiet. Norm Van Brocklin, the National Football League's leading passer during the regular season, suffered a broken rib on the third play of the playoff game with the Bears. He would get into this game with the Browns, but only for one play. The last one.

The mood of the game was set early. Twenty seconds after the opening kickoff, the Rams unveiled a play that had been planned for almost two weeks.

"We felt they would probably be keying on our fullback," Waterfield explained later. "So we thought we could take advantage of that right away."

The man who made the most of it was Glenn Davis, Mr. Outside from Army. Davis sprinted out of the backfield where a linebacker watched him fly by. Two defensive backs hurriedly tried to pick him up, but by then it was too late. Waterfield's picture pass found him gliding in the open. Touchdown. The play covered 82 yards and the stunned Brownies were down, 7-0.

Otto Graham was one of the few people in Municipal Stadium who seemed unperturbed. Automatic Otto calmly trotted out and got his own offense in working order. Running and passing, he moved Cleveland a brisk 72 yards, capping a typical Graham drive with a typical Graham pass, 32 yards to Dub Jones for the touchdown that tied it at 7.

While the defenses tried to adjust, both quarterbacks were taking full advantage. Now it was Waterfield and the Rams back at it. Tom Fears, who could get open in a crowded eleva-

tor, shook free twice to field passes that totaled 49 yards. Vitamin T. Smith and Dick Hoerner broke off some good runs and then Hoerner, a charter member of the Los Angeles "Bull Elephant" backfield, charged over from four yards out to make it 14-7, Rams.

The Cleveland defense began to get it together in the second period. Late in the quarter, Len Ford came in to replace Jim Martin at defensive end and the Brown linemen started to exert pressure on Waterfield.

Graham, meanwhile, continued to carve up the Ram secondary. The Rams had Elroy Hirsch and Tom Fears, two magnificent receivers.

But the Browns had a couple of fair targets themselves. One of them, lean Dante Lavelli, slanted between two Los Angeles defensive backs to catch a 35-yard pass for Cleveland's second touchdown midway in the period.

It should have been 14-14, except the snapback for Lou Groza's conversion attempt was fumbled by Tommy James, who scrambled, picked it up and threw the ball into the end zone where Tony Adamle dropped the ball.

James, the defensive back who practically grew up watching Paul Brown work his magic in Massillon, Ohio, was absolved of all blame afterward. Brown said the mistake was a result of a high center snap.

"But Tommy's a great competitor," said Brown. "His pass would have been a great play except that our boy muffed the ball in the end zone. I've known Tommy ever since he was a grade-school kid in Massillon. He's always been one of the finest football players I've ever known. He's just the tops. If he makes a mistake, we just write it off. We know no one else on our squad could have done it any better."

So the half ended with the Rams holding an insecure 14-13 advantage. The third quarter started much like the first. Before four minutes had elapsed Graham and Lavelli teamed up

The championship game of 1950 matched two offensive powerhouses, the Rams and the Browns, who were new to the NFL after winning the All-America Football Conference championship so often that the league went out of business. Los Angeles had Waterfield, Van Brocklin, Towler, Hirsch, Fears, et al. Cleveland ran up points with Otto Graham, Marion Motley, Mac Speedie and Dante Lavelli. With all that talent on the field, it was fitting that on the opening play, Glenn Davis (left) scored for the Rams on an 82-yard pass play from Waterfield. After the Browns tied it, Los Angeles went ahead again on a four-yard run by Dick Hoerner (right).

again. This time they covered 39 yards for the touchdown that put Cleveland in front, 20-14.

Graham-to-Lavelli. Waterfield-to-Fears. Both combinations were working. The man his teammates called "Buckets"—for Waterbuckets—completed passes to Fears and Vitamin T. and Los Angeles was planted on the Browns' 17 with a first down. The strategy from there was simple but direct. The ball was given to Hoerner. And given to him. And then given to him again. Seven straight times he snorted, put the horns of his Ram helmet down and bulled into the line. It wasn't too artistic. But it worked. Los Angeles recaptured the lead, 21-20.

What seemed like the turning point happened only a few seconds later. Motley, the Browns' fullback who had run so well in so many Cleveland games, was having a difficult afternoon. Some later theorized it was his own stubbornness that limited him. "Marion insisted on wearing cleats," Paul Brown explained afterward. "He told me he felt he could run all right in cleats, so there was nothing I could do. I think he'd have been much better off in basketball shoes."

It wasn't Motley's feet that created the problem, though. It was his hands. With a first and 10 on their own 20, the Browns gave the ball to their big fullback and watched him reach the line of scrimmage and then stop. Finding no opening, he attempted to reverse his field. He was chased back to the 7 where he not only was tackled but fumbled. Larry Brink, the giant defensive end, picked it up and ran it over for the touchdown that put the Rams ahead. 28-20. Los Angeles had scored twice in the space of 21 seconds, and in the City of Light, the flame was flickering.

With 15 minutes to play, Cleveland had to score twice and stop the most powerful offense professional football had ever seen. They went to work first on defense where the pass rush poured in on Waterfield. Under heavy pressure, the Ram quarterback threw a ball that was intercepted by

little Warren Lahr, defensive back of the Browns.

Then Graham took over. Carefully, ever so carefully, he initiated a drive that was to cover 65 yards. He threw the ball, mainly, but the passes were short, crisp passes, the type that are the hardest to stop. Nine times he found his receivers, including a series of five straight to Mr. Lavelli.

The ninth time, halfback Rex Bumgardner was the target. The play covered 19 yards and consummated in the end zone. Groza converted, and with 4:35 elapsed in the fourth period, only one point separated the two teams, 28-27.

Now the game took on an added aura of suspense. Each play, each move seemed magnified in importance. There was more at stake than just a football game. There was prestige involved. The reputation of two leagues would be determined in these closing minutes.

The momentum shifted back and forth. But with three minutes to play, Cleveland was only 24 yards away from the Los Angeles goal line when the impossible happened. Graham fumbled. Milan Lazetich recovered for the Rams and a groan of disbelief could be heard echoing through the windy corridors of Municipal Stadium.

"I wanted to die right there," said Graham. "It could have cost us the game. We were throwing the game away, anyway."

Almost. But not quite.

Three minutes, 180 seconds. That's all that stood between the Rams and the World Championship. They glanced at the clock and tried to take their time. A long huddle. A slow walk to the line of scrimmage. Anything to make that clock tick faster.

First down. Hoerner butted into the center of an aroused Browns' line. The loud collision gained only a few seconds. No yards. Second and 10. Again Hoerner. Again Cleveland met him at the line of scrimmage. Again no gain.

Third down. Davis, the sprinter, slithered through a sliver of daylight at right tackle and almost broke before he was cut down. Gain? Six yards. Fourth and four and Los Angeles would have to give up the football.

Waterfield—who did everything this day for the Rams—punted. A high, hanging punt that Cliff Lewis fielded and returned 13 yards, following his coach's orders by running out of bounds at the Cleveland 32.

The clock stopped and everyone glanced up again to look at it. The big hand was only one minute, 50 seconds away from completing its work for the day. The two minute warning had been given. The Browns were face to face with their last chance.

In the stands, spectators were on their feet, shaking out the chill and clapping their gloves. A chant rose and engulfed the huge arena . . . "GO . . . . . GO . . . . . GO . . . . ."

And Graham went. Fourteen yards on first down, scrambling out of tacklers' grasps after being unable to find Lavelli or anyone else open. First down on his own 46. Otto dropped back, looked and threw a strike to Bumgardner.

Another first down, this time on the Los Angeles 39. And the clock continued to move. Over on the sidelines, Lou Groza stirred around uncomfortably, warming up, taking practice kicks, swinging his right foot through the cold air.

Graham was far from finished. Again he dropped back, again he threw. Again it was caught, this time by Dub Jones for 16 more to the 23. Some couldn't bear to watch as the ticking grew louder and the time shorter But this was a great artist at work, and nothing was going to make him rush his strokes.

Otto was keeping his own time inside his helmet. He knew he had enough left for one more play, maybe two. The first one had to be a pass and it had to be perfect. It was. Bumgardner, oblivious to the pressure, clutched it tightly and

was wrestled to the ground at the Los Angeles 11.

Only one thing was wrong. The ball was not in good position for Groza. There was too much of an angle. But there were only 45 seconds on the clock. Graham thought that was enough. He was right.

He took the snap from center and groped at the Ram middle, diving to his right, placing the ball directly in front of the goal posts on a quarterback sneak that covered one meager but critical yard.

Now Tommy James kneeled down at the 16. He had to be thinking about the previous bad pass from center. He had to be hoping that this one would be true. It was. Center Hal Herring put it right in his hands. James placed it down cleanly and Groza took those three little steps and swung that deadly right foot.

In a classic photo of the moment, taken from behind the goal posts, the faces of the players on both teams are frozen, their movement suspended as the ball is seen hanging there between the uprights.

For Cleveland, it was a moment of joy. Then relief. For the Rams, anguish and despair.

Los Angeles had enough time for one more play after the Browns' kickoff. Van Brocklin, broken rib and all, was sent in to throw one long desperation pass. It was caught in the end zone. But by the Browns' Lahr. The interception ended the game and started the pandemonium.

It seemed as if all 29,751 people were pouring onto the field at one time. Stadium police vainly attempted to keep them in the stands. But they were overmatched. The players were mobbed. Groza was almost inundated. Hal Herring's jersey was ripped off.

Those who couldn't get near the players went after the goal posts and they tore them down in one gigantic surge.

After a considerable effort, the Browns managed to reach the safety of their dressing room.

The Rams were having good fortune in stopping Motley, Cleveland's big fullback. When he fumbled the ball deep in his own territory, all-pro end Larry Brink of Los Angeles picked up the ball and ran in for the touchdown which gave his team a 28-20 lead. Since Cleveland now had to score twice, and along the way stop the NFL's leading offense, it appeared that the Rams had wrapped up the championship. Otto Graham, however, was about to engineer one of the most incredible comebacks in NFL history.

Once there, they started their own celebration, shouting, screaming, laughing, hugging one another in exultation.

Paul Brown was wearing that familiar gray felt hat, but it had been squashed and battered from the hundreds who had offered congratulations as he made his way off the field. Normally composed and almost unemotional, Brown was visibly moved by his team's performance.

"This is the gamest bunch of guys in the world," he said, in barely more than a whisper. "Next to my wife and family, these guys are my life. What a Merry Christmas they've made it."

Someone wondered if he had been discouraged, or had given up, particularly when Graham fumbled late in the fourth period.

"I never gave up hope," said the coach. "I know this gang too well. I know they never quit. This is the greatest football team a coach ever had. Bless 'em all."

In a corner, the reporters swarmed around Groza, the huge tackle towering over them and smiling. "No, honest," he explained, "I wasn't nervous. I was just thinking of fundamentals, going over in my mind what to do. I didn't want to make any mistakes."

Then he turned and pointed to Joe Page. The New York Yankees' relief pitcher had come from his home near Pittsburgh to see the game and had managed to find his way to the Browns' dressing room to congratulate friends and fellow athletes. "Ask him," said Groza. "A guy doesn't get nervous in a tight spot like that."

"Like hell," Page boomed. "I get nervous plenty and so do you. Don't tell me you weren't worried about missing. I know what was going through your mind."

At a locker nearby, Graham was stripping off his soiled jersey. It was obvious he had taken a physical beating from the huge Ram linemen who repeatedly had knocked him to the frozen turf. His face was a mass of cuts and bruises and

he limped noticeably on a bruised knee.

"Somebody hit me in the back toward the end of the first half," said Otto. "I thought I was going to fold up right there. My knee buckled, but luckily it didn't stiffen up. It's just getting stiff now. It'll probably be plenty sore tomorrow."

Even in victory, there were some second guessers. Reporters wondered why the Browns didn't go for the touchdown before settling for the field goal.

"We had the ball with a first down on the Rams' 12," said Brown, "but the clock was running out. We have the greatest placekicker in the world in Lou Groza. So we sent in word to run one play to the right with Graham handling the ball to get it right in front of the goal posts. Otto did a good job of it and Lou booted the ball for the three points we needed. And that was the ballgame."

Graham, Groza and Godfrey weren't the only Cleveland heroes. There was Len Ford, who ignored that painful jaw injury to come in and play more than an entire half. Three times, big Len crashed in to spill a Ram ballcarrier for a large loss.

"I'll tell you how I feel," beamed Ford. "This is a wonderful group of fellows. Everybody pulls for the other fellow and you've just got to give it everything you've got. I felt good out there and I'm very happy I got to play. I wouldn't have wanted to miss this game for anything."

"Those who didn't go through this season with us can't possibly appreciate the struggle it has been," said Tony Adamle, the Cleveland team captain. "Sure, we lucked through a couple of games, but every team we played was like a bunch of wildcats after us. The great thing about our club was that we stayed with it. We hung on."

So did the Rams . . . until those last 16 seconds of the game.

Those who were there in Cleveland that day still consider the game one of the best in the history of professional football.

"There was never a game like this one," said Brown, repeatedly. Bert Bell, the National Football League Commissioner, agreed. "This was an instance in which a magnificently coached club which wouldn't give up overcame great opposition. The Browns overlook no detail in preparing for a game—they are ready for anything and they have that extra something of which champions are made.

"I would like to pay tribute to Joe Stydahar, the Los Angeles coach, who did a great job in his first year as head coach of the Rams. He did an outstanding job and we'll be hearing from him in the future. It was unfortunate that one of these two truly great teams had to lose."

Funny, but that's how the Rams felt.

"You've got to hand it to a ballclub like the Browns," said a disconsolate Stydahar. "They won simply because they refused to quit."

Bob Waterfield, who would never go on to become one of America's great orators, failed to say much. "It was just one of those things," he muttered. Later, Waterfield revealed that he felt personally responsible. He missed a 15-yard field goal in the second quarter, the only Ram field goal attempt of the afternoon. "All I could keep thinking," he said, "was that I owed every guy on our club $750." It was a typical Waterfield remark. The club, itself, never would have made it to the championship game without its gifted quarterback.

The post-game statistics only emphasized how close these two teams were in ability. The 44 first downs in the game were split evenly, 22 apiece. The Rams rushed for 106 yards, the Browns for 114. Cleveland passed for 298, Los Angeles for 312. The Rams wound up with a slight advantage in total yardage, 418 to 412. Even the turnovers almost evened out. The Rams were intercepted five times, but the Browns fumbled the ball away three times.

Individually, Los Angeles successfully stopped Motley, the 238-pound all-pro fullback, limiting him to just nine yards in six attempts. But, at the same time, the Rams' defense couldn't cope with Graham and his corps of receivers. Utilizing the so-called umbrella pass defense—a 5-3-3 with an uneven alignment of the three linebackers—Stydahar was hoping to cut off the Browns' favorite passes—the Z-outs to the sideline. But Graham not only still completed his outs, he hit on hooks and even a couple of bombs. All of this despite one of his best receivers, Mac Speedie, hurting with a pulled leg muscle.

With Speedie ineffective, Lavelli accepted the brunt of the responsibility and established a new championship game record, catching 11 passes, two for touchdowns. Dante's 11 receptions were good for 128 yards. Tom Fears of the Rams caught nine for 136.

Waterfield, although suffering five interceptions, completed 18 of 32 passes for 312 yards. Graham completed 22 of 33 for 278 yards and no interceptions.

It was a brilliant match of skills, one perhaps that could only be decided in the final seconds by a kicker like Groza. "The Toe," they called him, and in his memorable National Football League career, he kicked more than 250 field goals. But never would he kick another as significant or dramatic.

The upstart Browns, the renegades from the All America Conference, had proven their claim. They were professional football's best team. And the sport would not be shocked like this again for some 19 years, when another renegade team, the New York Jets, from another so-called "inferior" conference, would knock over the Baltimore Colts.

In 1950, a Los Angeles squad was witness to history. This time, pro football's most glamorous team came out second best.

But the Rams would be back.

Running and passing, Graham (right) drove the Browns 65 yards for a touchdown. His team now trailed 28-27. In the closing moments, the world would learn the worth of the Browns, as they faced their greatest test against the established NFL. The tension mounted when the Rams' Milan Lazetich recovered a Graham fumble. But the Browns held. Their leader maneuvered them into position for the winning field goal by Lou Groza from 16 yards out (below). Cleveland had won the championship. They would meet the Rams again, however, the next year, and that, too, would be a game to remember.

December 23, 1951

The perfect pass. That's what they called it. And under the circumstances, they may have been right. "That," said Tom Fears, "was the best thrown pass I ever caught in my life."

The forward pass under discussion traveled 73 precise yards. It found its way into Fears' hands by avoiding the straining reach of Cleveland defensive backs Tom James and Cliff Lewis. It occurred with 7:25 remaining in the fourth quarter of a game against the Browns at the Los Angeles Coliseum.

And it won the only world championship in the history of the Los Angeles franchise.

The story of the Rams' success in 1951 is not so much the fact that Norman Van Brocklin threw the football perfectly. But that he was there, on this team, on this day, in this particular situation. It was a credit to the genius of Dan Reeves and it was to set a precedent that the rest of the National Football League would follow for years to come.

When the pass was required, the Rams had the man to throw it. And they went out of their way to acquire him despite the fact they already owned a quarterback of distinction named Bob Waterfield.

It happened this way:

The date was December 1947. The Rams received a routine questionnaire filled out by Van Brocklin, then a sophomore at the University of Oregon. A single wing tailback his first year in college, Van Brocklin was pleased to find Oregon switching to the T-formation. Oregon was pleased, too, when the man known as "The Dutchman" quickly developed into an All-America. Anyway, the two key questions on the form were answered as follows:

Q—On a four-year basis, when does your class graduate?

A—1950.

Q—When will you graduate?

A—1949 ma.

Reeves and Eddie Kotal, the Rams' head scout, guessed at the interpretation of "ma." They figured Van Brocklin meant "maybe." And they were correct. In a postwar speed-up, intended to minimize the time spent on campus by war veterans with families, it was quite possible for a strongly dedicated student to graduate in three years.

Still, it didn't make sense that a busy football player would have either the time or the inclination to become that addicted to his books. Van Brocklin wasn't that enthused about studying. But his girl friend was. The young lady who was soon to become Mrs. Gloria Van Brocklin was an instructor at the University. And she was the driving force behind Van Brocklin's accelerated program.

In answering the Ram questionnaire, Van Brocklin checked his status. He had entered college in April, 1946. As of October, 1947, he had completed 101 of the 186 units required for graduation. Projecting his pace, he knew he had a chance to finish in 1949. When Norm became the best passer in college football his junior year, the Rams quickly accentuated their interest in what they called his ETG (estimated time of graduation). It appeared to be August of 1949.

On November 15, 1948, the National Football League held the first four rounds of its 1949 draft and the Rams unloaded their bombshell. They selected Bobby Thomason of VMI on the first round and then, three rounds later, afraid that their information might leak out, they picked Van Brocklin.

Immediately the selection was challenged by several other teams, whose scouting departments knew Van was a 1946 registrant. The general agreement was that he was not eligible. Reeves, aware that by gambling he could lose Van Brocklin forever, decided to take his chances. While they were upset, representatives of the other teams recognized the loophole on which Reeves

| Browns | 0 | 10 | 0 | 7 | 17 |
| Rams | 0 | 7 | 7 | 10 | 24 |

depended. The NFL by-laws state that no player shall be permitted to play on any (NFL) club until his original class in college has graduated, or until HE has graduated in a stepped-up course.

When the next semester began, Van Brocklin was in trouble. Three of the Physical Education courses he was planning to take during the six-week summer session would not be offered in 1949. Two of them were available in the regular spring semester, so Norm added those classes, leaving him shy on "Fundamentals of Body Movement and Conditioning." Eddie Kotal and his secretary got on the phone to colleges and universities across the country, hoping to find the course offered in the summer, or a similar one acceptable to the Oregon graduation judges.

Only one school could comply. Vassar.

While Norm, Gloria, the Rams and Vassar officials contemplated their problem, Oregon relented. If an acceptable tutor could be found, Van Brocklin could take the course in a six week period prior to June and would be given credit. A tutor was found. Van Brocklin coughed up the $75 fee and spent the rest of the semester studying, carrying 17 other hours, practicing teaching and also acting as a go-between as the future Mrs. Van Brocklin helped negotiate with the Rams.

The correspondence concerning money between Reeves and Van Brocklin was said to be classical. In one letter, Norm addressed the Ram owner as "Dangerous Danny McReeves." Finally, perhaps feeling outnumbered in the two-against-one negotiations, Reeves paid Van Brocklin what the quarterback thought he was worth.

And, somewhat exhausted, Van Brocklin was graduated on June 19, 1949.

Two years later, he was available when the Rams needed the bomb to beat the best team in football in what must still rank as the most important game they've ever played.

It was the philosophy of Reeves and his or-

ganization always to draft the best athlete available, regardless of position.

"Quarterbacks," explained Hampton Pool, an assistant coach in 1951, "came first, though. In other words, if we had owned five quarterbacks at the time, we'd have drafted a sixth if one as outstanding as Van Brocklin had been available. They just weren't that easy to come by. If you had a chance to get a great one, you grabbed him, no matter who you currently had playing the position."

"What Van Brocklin had going for him," said Pool, "was, first of all, an exceptionally strong arm. He could throw the ball as far as you needed to throw it. Then, he had big hands. They enabled him to throw any kind of pass. He could hang it up in the air, he could drill it or he could give you that nice soft touch on the screens. Probably even greater than his pure physical equipment, though, was his ability to come off the field after one series of plays, practically, and tell you exactly what the opponent's defense amounted to. He had this uncanny knack of getting a mental picture of almost everyone in that secondary. That's the thing that made him so successful. He could tell you when a middle linebacker was overrunning, not getting over to a certain spot, and then he'd keep that information in mind until just the right time—until you really needed it. Then he'd exploit it. He could do that better than anyone I've ever seen."

It was this particular ability that probably won the Rams the world championship. It seems Blanton Collier, then a Cleveland assistant, had spotted something wrong in his secondary early in that Dec. 23 game at the Los Angeles Coliseum. Sitting in the press box, he called down to the bench and alerted the Browns' secondary.

"One of the defensive backs, I forget exactly which, either James or Lewis, was playing too far on the outside," said Pool. "I remember seeing Collier after the game and he told me he had

warned the kid about it. He said that he told him he was leaving himself wide open for the bomb. He said he had told him early and that he was worried about it the rest of the afternoon.

"It was typical Van Brocklin to wait until the fourth quarter to unload like that. The pass was perfect, just perfect. I can't remember ever seeing a better one under that kind of pressure. It was as clutch a situation as you'll ever see, and the ball was right there."

The one play won the game, but there was more drama to this rematch than just one fleeting moment of perfection. Cleveland, the "outlaw" from the old All-America Conference, had established its superiority over all of professional football the previous season, coming from behind to nudge the Rams, 30-28, on Lou Groza's memorable field goal. And the Browns had beaten Los Angeles again in a regular season game in October.

Now there was talk of a Browns' dynasty. This was a team that had it all, and coming to the West Coast this bright, sunny afternoon, Cleveland had been established a six-point favorite to make it back-to-back National Football League championships and six straight championships overall.

The Browns were at their peak, having captured 11 straight Eastern Division games to coast into the title game. Los Angeles, on the other hand, had backed into the playoff. Only a startling San Francisco victory over Detroit, 21-17, on the final day of the regular season gave the Rams the Western Division championship. Los Angeles finished 8-4 to edge San Francisco and Detroit, both 7-4-1. Chicago was fourth, a mere game back at 7-5.

The Rams received the news of the 49ers' upset minutes after they had finished polishing off Green Bay, 42-14. "I ought to send Frankie Albert a Christmas present," smiled Bob Waterfield in the Los Angeles dressing room. "We ought to

hop a plane to San Francisco and treat those wonderful 49ers to a great, big dinner," said Reeves. "Just tell the Rams I'll appreciate four tickets for next Sunday's championship game," said Albert, the San Francisco quarterback.

The fact that their team had only split its last four games and had acquired assistance from San Francisco didn't dampen the enthusiasm of Rams fans or owners. "I don't care if the Rams got in through the service entrance," cracked Bob Hope, one of the stockholders. "As long as they got there."

And so the buildup began. If America's sportswriters were correct, Cleveland deserved its favoritism. The Browns had eight players selected on the all-pro team, the Rams two. Quarterback Otto Graham, halfback Dub Jones, end Dante Lavelli, tackle Lou Groza and center Frank Gatski were chosen on offense. End Len Ford, guard Bill Willis and defensive backs Tony Adamle and Warren Lahr were picked on defense. The only Rams to make the first team were Elroy Hirsch and fullback Deacon Dan Towler.

Graham had just completed what may have been his best season and, in December of this year, he was regarded as the No. 1 player in the sport.

"Otto is a pure passer," explained Paul Brown. "By that I mean he naturally throws the ball straight. A T-quarterback is something like a bank clerk. You can teach them to add and subtract, but not all of them will be honest. We coaches can teach a T-quarterback ball handling, but not to pass it straight like Graham does. Otto is at his best when we're in trouble and he has got us out of many a hole by the skin of our teeth. That's another mark of a fine athlete.

"He doesn't tighten up. He treats football as a game, which I firmly believe he enjoys. As such, the tougher the game, the more he seems to relax." Graham must have spent a very relaxing day in Los Angeles.

With their victory over the Rams in the title game the year before, the Browns had become the most feared team in football. Now they would again meet the Rams for the championship. No fewer than eight Browns made the all-pro team of 1951. The Rams, meanwhile, were represented by only two players—fullback Deacon Dan Towler and end Elroy Hirsch (left, Towler gets set to cut back behind Hirsch's block on Warren Lahr). It had been an especially good year for Towler. The most feared member of "The Bull Elephant Backfield" that season, he had averaged a sensational 6.7 yards a carry for the Rams.

As superb as Otto was throughout the season, he was never as spectacular as Hirsch, the pass receiver they called "Crazylegs." Elroy was the focal point of the Rams' offense, the one threat that forced defenses to change and opposing coaches to worry. He was always there, ready to bust one deep. And if you cheated by pulling a man off his side of the field, he would beat you every time. It's possible that no receiver ever has had a season like Hirsch enjoyed in 1951.

The statistics included 66 receptions for 1,495 yards, 284 more yards than the previous record—a record set by a gentleman named Don Hutson in 1942. Included in those 66 catches were 17—count 'em—17 for touchdowns. And, remember, this was in the days of the 12-game season. The 17 averaged over 50 yards per shot. He caught four against the New York Yankees one day, had a 91-yard bomb vs. the Bears, an 81-yarder against Green Bay and 79 and 76-yard trips at the expense of his old friends in San Francisco.

Bob Oates, who covered the Rams from the beginning in L.A., wrote in the *Los Angeles Examiner:* "No end ever did the things Elroy perpetrated this season. Another such year for Hirsch, or any end, would seem to be beyond attainment."

Of course, Graham and Hirsch were hardly the only threats on the field. For the Rams, both Waterfield and Van Brocklin were regarded as great passers. In fact, Bob edged Van, 8.8977 to 8.8917 for the league passing championship. On the season, this is the way the three quarterbacks matched up:

	Attmpts.	Comp.	Yards	TD
Graham	265	147	2205	17
Waterfield	176	88	1566	13
Van Brocklin	194	100	1725	13

The quarterbacks were not the only weapons these two teams could wheel out. Cleveland's backfield also featured Dub Jones, probably the most versatile halfback in football, and Ken Carpenter, the Oregon Statesman who was among the most underrated players in the league. Jones, a 6-4, 205-pound runner-receiver, scored six touchdowns in the Browns' 42-21 adventure over the Bears. And it was a screen pass to Carpenter that broke open the 38-28 win over the Rams in October.

Los Angeles, of course, still had its stable of bullish running backs, including Dick Hoerner, Tank Younger and Dan Towler, not to mention the quick, little scatback types like Vitamin T. Smith and The Cricket, Tommy Kalmanir.

And yet, this was a young Ram team with 13 rookies, six of them offensive tackles. When the team first reported in September, Joe Stydahar was worried about offensive tackle. Very worried. But from 11 candidates, he picked six. All six turned out to be quality players. Charley Toogood of Nebraska, Tom Dahms of San Diego State, Jack Halliday and Bobby Collier of SMU, Jim Winkler of Texas A&M and Don Simensen of St. Thomas (Minn.).

Defensively, both clubs were solid. Yet both knew that the key to this game could be the pass rush. None of the three quarterbacks could be given time to throw. Pressure had to be applied, or any one of them could blow his opponent out of the Coliseum.

And so, on a clear, sunny 71-degree afternoon —the kind of day to which Los Angeles had become accustomed before smog—a surprisingly disappointing crowd of 59,475 sat back to find out which of these two glamorous teams was the best in football.

Cleveland won the coin toss and elected to receive, starting its first drive from its own 23-yard line. Graham wasted little time in getting his team moving. Passes to Speedie and Lavelli gained 27 yards and just like that the Browns were in Ram territory.

Otto threw again to Lavelli for 16 yards to the Los Angeles 19, where the Rams' defense dug in. Three plays gained only three yards and that

71

At a time when the elements of victory were needed more than ever, they were there for the Rams. The great 1951 season was driving to a climax on the floor of the Coliseum. The combination of Van Brocklin's arm, as strong as any in football, and the reliable Tom Fears put together the play that brought Los Angeles its first world's championship. Van Brocklin retreated (left) and threw to Fears. The play covered 73 yards for a touchdown and gave the Rams the title, 24-17.

familiar hulking figure trotted onto the field. Only this time, from the 23-yard line, Lou Groza's kick sailed wide.

At the end of the tense first period, neither team had scored. Waterfield attempted to do something about the Coliseum's inactive scoreboard early in the second quarter. A pass to the Vitamin man, Smith, swallowed up 18 valuable yards and another to Hoerner got 13. First and 10 at the Browns' 25. Smith, on two carries, gained 11. Hoerner powered for four, then, three plays later, carried tacklers across with him from one yard out. Waterfield converted and the Rams were in front, 7-0.

The lead did not survive the end of the half. Groza, who a few minutes earlier had shanked a chip shot, stunned the partisan crowd when his 52-yard attempt floated powerfully through the uprights. The kick broke an NFL playoff record by a full 10 yards. It was 7-3 Rams, but Cleveland, its defense providing good field position, was back on the attack a few minutes later.

From his own 46, Graham proceeded to throw three passes. Each to a different receiver. Each on target. Each one caught. The final one, from 17 yards away, was fielded in the end zone by Jones, 10-7. Cleveland gave the Rams something to think about in the silence of their dressing room at halftime.

Los Angeles seemed like a team that needed a break. Early in the third quarter, Larry Brink provided them with one. He leveled Graham on the 30-yard line, forcing a fumble. Andy Robustelli, crashing in from the opposite end, picked up the ball and lumbered to the Cleveland 2-yard line before Motley caught up with him. The Browns' defense didn't surrender the yards easily. But three straight shots up the gut by Towler finally got the Rams their lead back, 14-10.

From his own 9, Graham, the superb competitor, cranked up again. Brink and Robustelli had worked him over much of the afternoon. But

Otto was not one to be intimidated. He passed to Jones for 14 yards, to Speedie for 10 and, with a first down on the Ram 48, he found the appropriately-named Speedie again for the go-ahead touchdown. Except that an official also had found a Browns' blocker holding. The points were wiped away and Cleveland's momentum was shattered.

It was at this point, shortly before the start of the final period, that Norm Van Brocklin was sent into the game. The Van Brocklin fan club greeted his appearance with an appropriate cheer. A year ago, in the championship game in Cleveland, Van Brocklin's sore ribs kept him out of all but one play, one final play. And Van had thrown a desperation bomb that was intercepted.

He could afford to be more careful this time. But The Dutchman was never one to be careful. After an incomplete pass to Hirsch, Norman faded back and looked for Fears. When he found him, he unloaded. The 48-yard strike gave the Rams a first down at the Cleveland one. It also gave the Browns a chance to show their character. Their defense rarely conceded anything, as Towler and Hoerner soon found out. Deacon Dan lost one, lost two more and then Hoerner was slammed down for no gain. With fourth and goal from the four, the Rams lined up in field goal formation. Glenn Davis, the holder, took the snap and sprinted around left end. It was a good idea, but too many Browns were there waiting. When they finally tackled him, the ball was on the 18 and Los Angeles had wasted a precious opportunity.

But this was a day the Rams would be afforded more than one chance. Marv Johnson, a rookie defensive back from San Jose State, intercepted a Graham pass and returned it 35 yards. Again the Rams were on the one yard line with first and goal. But again, they couldn't score a touchdown. This time it was penalties. One for backfield in motion, another for too much time. So on fourth

down from the 11, Waterfield kicked a 17-yard field goal that made it 17-10.

Stydahar made only one real change in the Rams defense. He poured halfbacks into the game, utilizing even Hirsch in the secondary, along with Jerry Williams, Bob Boyd, Woodley Lewis, Herb Rich and Norb Hecker. At one point, Los Angeles deployed four linemen and 7 backs. The object was to cut down the bomb. So Graham, one of the original scramblers, did the next best thing. He ran. His big gain covered 34 yards and maintained a classic 70-yard, 10-play drive. Carpenter capped it, running over from five yards with 7:50 to play.

So that's how it stood midway in the fourth quarter. 17-17. The world championship pennant was still there, hanging over the Coliseum, waiting for someone to grab it.

Groza kicked off. The Rams ran a play, Cleveland jumped offsides and Los Angeles stood second and three on its own 27.

It was at this point that the Rams needed a big play. They needed someone who could throw the long pass accurately. They needed someone who would not be affected by the pressure. And what they needed, Reeves, Kotal and the rest of the front office had provided. The hours of paper work, the phone calls, the frustrating negotiations all suddenly seemed worth it as the football spiraled beautifully through the air like a missile with a preordained target. Fears was there, as he had been so many times before, and the Rams were 24-17 winners. This had not been Tom's best season. A year earlier, there had been comparisons with Don Hutson. But now it was Hirsch they were comparing. Fears, his knee badly twisted, had run his 1951 patterns almost unnoticed, while the spotlight focused on another part of the field.

But at this moment, on this day, the Rams wouldn't have wanted anyone else going for the football.

Later, after the Los Angeles defense had fought off Graham and the Browns for the last time, the celebration started. The happy people rushed onto the field. Some of his more courageous players tried to lift the 300-pound coach known as Jumbo Joe onto their shoulders. They gave up after a few valiant yards. Inside the Ram dressing room, amid the whoops and the hollers, the praise flowed along with the champagne.

"It was just like last year, only this year we were lucky," said Don Paul, whose speech was interrupted by the arrival of a man in a foreign uniform, a uniform smudged by the soil and dirt of a hard afternoon's labor. Otto Graham had come to pay his respects.

"Great passing in there," said Paul. "I sure threw a nice one to you," smiled Graham, referring to Paul's interception, one of two the Rams were able to steal that day. "I'm too slow," said the Los Angeles linebacker. "I should have scored on that play."

Across the hall, Paul Brown spotted one of his players walking by dejectedly. "Hey, you, don't look so glum," he shouted. Then, in a moment's retrospect, he wondered aloud. "What do you think might have happened if Mac Speedie's touchdown hadn't been called back by a penalty? Would it have been a different ballgame? Football always hinges on such dinky little things.

"Maybe the Rams had it coming after the game last year in Cleveland. Call it poetic justice. I still say one team should never be favored over another in a playoff game. But I'm not disappointed about anything."

Graham, back in the solemn confines of his own dressing room, blamed himself as much as anyone. "I guess they were due to catch up with us. But I didn't help matters a bit. I threw away 10 points. It really wasn't the Rams that scared me. It was the law of averages. We were due to lose today."

Before his players scattered, Paul Brown called them together for one final message. "All good things must come to an end," he said. "It's too bad, but that's part of living. We can't kick after all the nice things that have happened to us. Keep your nose up." Graham went up to his coach privately. "I let you down, Paul," he said, quietly. "I'll try to make it up to you later." Paul looked at him and replied, "That's all right, Otto."

Long after the Browns had departed, the Rams were still there, dressing slowly as if they didn't want the afternoon to end. This was a special moment, and they were sharing it the same way they had shared the despair of that December day in Cleveland 12 months earlier.

In his cubicle, Norman Van Brocklin, two years removed from the University of Oregon campus, wore the grin that identifies a winner. "Boy," he said, "I'm going to have a party tonight. Our guys were really playing football. And those Browns. They are not only good, but they're tough. They never could stop Fears, though."

They could never stop Van Brocklin, either. In the brief time he appeared, Van threw six passes. Four were complete, one other was dropped by Hirsch, of all people. The four completions covered 128 yards. On that day, Fears caught four balls for 146 yards.

The final statistics once again pointed out how close these two teams were in ability. The Browns actually outgained the Rams in total yardage, 372 to 334. They outpassed them 280 to 253.

But the difference turned out to be one play. One pass. One quarterback. And one vigorous owner who capitalized on a loophole to draft a man who would rank among the greatest throwers in the history of football.

To the Rams, it was the perfect end to the story.

October 12, 1952

Trying to pick the best game Bob Waterfield ever played is like trying to decide what Bob Waterfield did best on a football field. No matter what you choose, you're going to get an argument.

A superb passer, a fine runner, an excellent punter and placekicker. In the often clichéd parlance of football, they would say he could do it all. Only this time, they were right. Maybe the best thing Bob Waterfield could do, though, was lead. He could take a team and move it and inspire it and push it beyond its limits.

"He was the toughest guy ever to walk into a huddle," said Elroy Hirsch. "I remember the time one of our backs was reluctant to carry the ball and Bob hauled off and slugged him right there in the huddle. And I remember once when I asked him to call a certain play because I felt I could beat the defensive man with that pattern. The pass was intercepted and when we got to the sidelines, Bob walked up beside me. 'Elroy,' he said, 'if you don't know what you're talking about, keep your damned mouth shut!' "

The year was 1952. The date Oct. 12. The site Marquette Stadium in Milwaukee, Wisconsin. But really, the foundation for this game was laid seven years earlier.

Bob Waterfield, UCLA All-American, left school in 1943 to enter the Army. He earned a commission as a second lieutenant at Fort Benning, Georgia, in September of 1943, and later received a medical discharge. In the National Football League draft that year, Waterfield was chosen on the third round by Bob Kelley, who would be the Rams' broadcaster and eventually one of Bob's best friends. Waterfield, however, decided to return to UCLA for the 1944 season. He enjoyed another distinguished year and was chosen to play in the East-West Shrine game, the showcase for the nation's top graduating seniors.

The game, appropriately held on Jan. 1, 1945, would signal the start of one of the most incredible seasons ever credited to any athlete in any sport.

That New Year's Day afternoon, at Kezar Stadium in San Francisco, Waterfield averaged 6.7 yards as a ballcarrier. He ran 13 yards for the winning touchdown in the West's 13-6 victory. He completed 11 passes, including the 45-yard bomb that set up his team's other touchdown. And, on five punts, one of which he intentionally angled for the coffin corner, he averaged 59.4 yards.

Ohio State's Heisman Trophy winner Les Horvath, who later was to join Waterfield on some great Ram teams, was the East safetyman that day. He had stood there helplessly and watched a pair of spectacular punts sail over his head. "It was inspiring, really inspiring," Horvath told reporters with a tone of reverence in his voice.

Waterfield's performance that day increased his market value—market values being what they were in those days. Now one of the more sought-after properties in sports, he negotiated with Rams' vice-president Chile Walsh and, on June 15, it was announced that Cleveland had signed itself a quarterback. "We ain't giving out the terms of the contract," said Walsh, "but he's married to Jane Russell, the movie star, and that didn't make signing him any easier." Guesses ranged from $6,500 to $8,000. Waterfield would later admit that the figure was $7,500. It was, of course, to be one of the biggest bargains in pro football history. But Walsh didn't realize it at the time. Neither did the late Franklin Lewis, columnist for the *Cleveland Press*. Lewis chastized Walsh and owner Dan Reeves for "throwing their money around."

"When you think," Lewis wrote, "that Parker Hall and Johnny Darke, two of the best backs ever to play in the National League, got top money around here with contracts that were under $7,000, it is a trifle shocking to discover that raw college recruits, weighted down with clippings, are being signed for that much money!"

In August 1945, the young Cleveland Rams went into training camp under new coach Adam Walsh, Chile's brother. They had drafted several

Rams	0	6	0	24	30
Packers	7	7	14	0	28

highly-regarded backs, but if others were impressed, the newspapermen covering the team weren't. They already had predicted the Rams would not break their record of failing to enjoy a winning season since their inception in 1937.

It did not take long for Waterfield to establish his identity. He threw two touchdown passes in his first camp game and it soon became clear that veteran Albie Reisz was no longer the regular quarterback. Bob provided an indication of things to come when he led the team to a 3-1 exhibition record, a record that included a victory over Sammy Baugh and the Washington Redskins, the first time the Rams ever had achieved such a feat.

It was in the Redskin game that Waterfield first displayed the "bootleg," the play that was to become his trademark. This is the way Bob Yonkers of the *Cleveland Press* described it:

"With the ball on Washington's 20, Waterfield sent Gehrke off tackle for six yards on first down and then pulled a neat trick out of the bag which caught the entire Washington team flat-footed. Instead of giving the ball to Gehrke, Bob kept it, and while Fred was faking beautifully roaring off tackle again, Waterfield was strolling around the opposite end for a touchdown. Not a hand was laid on him. Then, while the thousands cheered, he calmly kicked the extra point."

Captain Dan Reeves, after serving three years in the Air Force, was released and placed on inactive status the Thursday before the Rams' league opener with the Chicago Cardinals. That was the first time he saw Waterfield and the 1945 team play. Bob scored on the bootleg the very first time he tried it in a league game and Cleveland was off and winning, 21-0. The wins did not stop. When the Rams beat Detroit on Nov. 22, it was their eighth victory in nine games and it clinched the Western Division championship. Waterfield completed 10 passes to Jim Benton that day against the Lions. They were good for 303 yards, helping Benton break Don Hutson's single-game

record of 239 yards. Cleveland had a new hero.

A Cleveland newspaper headlined it this way: "Waterfield Best Cleveland Pitcher Since Bob Feller."

The story, however, focused more on the courage of the Ram quarterback. "Immediately after the battle the Rams trooped into their dressing quarters and one by one their eyes caught the sober, ashenfaced Waterfield. They remembered the painfully torn rib muscles and the fact he could not raise his arm above his head at midweek. They noted the thick band of white tape around his body and from Adam Walsh down, they spoke respectfully and admiringly.

"'It was the greatest exhibition of guts I've ever seen,' marveled assistant coach Bob Snyder.

"When he ran, when he passed, there was severe pain. It was worse when the Lions hit him, which they tried to do on every pass. Once Stan Batinski, the big guard, hit Waterfield so hard he knocked himself out. Waterfield took it. And if one man can win a football game, Waterfield won over the Lions yesterday."

The championship game against Washington—the rematch with Slingin' Sammy Baugh—was scheduled for Dec. 15. And on Dec. 14, the field at Cleveland Stadium appeared more suitable for a snow fight than a football game. An 18-inch layer of the white stuff lay on the tarpaulin, which was on top of 5,000 bales of hay. The hay was on top of the paper covering the turf. And the weatherman was predicting more snow on the day of the game.

The temperature? It never got above six degrees. But a rookie named Waterfield didn't seem to notice. He completed 14 of 27 passes, throwing one touchdown to Benton and another to Jim Gillette. The Rams won, 15-14, and the margin of victory turned out to be a Waterfield extra point that was partially blocked, slid along the crossbar and dropped across. In his first year in professional football, Bob Waterfield had taken his team

to world championship. The accolades flowed in.

Adam Walsh called him "the greatest T formation quarterback in the country." Dan Reeves had a different description for him. "He is the highest paid football player in the world," said Dan. The day before the title game, Reeves had signed Waterfield to a new three-year contract at a salary of $20,000 a year.

The voting was easy for sportswriters that year. Waterfield was the all-pro quarterback. He was also the Most Valuable Player. By unanimous vote. And that's the first and probably the last time a rookie quarterback will be so honored.

It is interesting to speculate whether Reeves would have made his dramatic post-season franchise switch to the West Coast without a natural gate attraction like Waterfield. It was a move that would change the entire character of professional sports, and certainly the man his teammates called "Buckets" played a prominent role in it.

From 1945 to 1952, Bob Waterfield was a superstar, the first ever in Los Angeles. How effective was he? Well, the Rams have been in the National Football League for 35 seasons, but except for the Waterfield years, they have won only one Western Division championship and, since the reorganization and merger, have yet to make it to an NFC Championship game. During Waterfield's eight seasons, however, they won two world titles, four Western Division crowns and lost another division championship in a playoff.

Naturally, everyone has his own favorite Waterfield story. Tom Fears still likes to talk about the 1950 playoff game with the Chicago Bears for the Western Division championship.

"We went into that Bear game with just one quarterback," said Fears. "Bob had come down with intestinal flu on Wednesday, was delirious with fever on Friday, hadn't eaten a solid meal since Tuesday, and was too weak to drive his own car to the Coliseum for the game. That left the entire load on Norm Van Brocklin's shoulders. Van

Brocklin didn't have it from the start. He couldn't hit a lick with his first eight passes. In the huddle I noticed that he was wincing—we found out later that he had cracked a rib on the second play of the game.

"In spite of Van Brocklin's passing troubles, most of the first quarter was a stalemate. Then, when Curly Morrison quick-kicked dead on our 37, Waterfield grabbed his helmet and went into the game. Apparently, Van Brocklin thought [Joe] Stydahar had sent Bob in, and by the time Van and Joe realized that Bob had entered the game on his own, it was too late. The first play Bob called was a handoff to Glenn Davis, who went 63 yards for a touchdown—only they called it back.

"From that moment on, Buckets seemed to gain strength. It was incredible. The more energy he expended, the stronger he seemed to get. It was so unbelievable that I feared a sudden and complete collapse. Until the end of the game, I was never convinced that Bob would be able to keep the show on the road. But pretty soon he was kicking a 43-yard field goal. And before the afternoon was over, we had connected for three touchdown passes, Bob and me, and we beat the Bears 24-14 for the Western title.

"I can explain some facets of that victory, but the story of Waterfield's physical endurance after the flu siege is another matter. I knew the facts. I saw the strength incredibly surge back. I was, to put it mildly, astounded. To explain it—I beg off. That must be somebody else's department."

Waterfield, after those eight glorious seasons, was given a day by fans in Los Angeles late in that final year of 1952. But as Bob's close friend and current Ram executive Jack Teele wrote, "It came only after Waterfield had given the fans their 'day' earlier in the year—on October 12, to be exact."

Typically, the performance came at a time when the Rams were badly in need of a boost, a shove, something to turn around a season that looked like it might evolve into a disaster. Rookie head

The game that was one of the most exciting ever played by Bob Waterfield was preceded by some hard times for the Rams. They were the world champions, yet by the third game of the 1952 season they found themselves riding a five-game losing streak. Three preseason losses had been followed by an opening day 37-7 shelling at the hands of the Browns (left, Ken Carpenter about to be stopped by Andy Robustelli). Then the Rams lost to Detroit 17-14. The troubles mounted as Stydahar's team fell behind the lightly regarded Packers.

coach Hampton Pool had seen his team lose its last five games in a row. The final three exhibitions were won by San Francisco (17-7), Philadelphia (35-14) and New York (30-17). In the first two league games, the streak continued. The Rams were beaten by Cleveland (37-7) and Detroit (17-14).

Nothing that happened in the first half that day in Milwaukee made anyone think the trend would be altered. The Rams, once again, were in trouble. With Waterfield on the bench, except for a couple of brief field goal attempts, Green Bay quickly assumed command of the football game.

The first Packer drive consumed 17 plays and covered 68 yards. It was littered with penalties and losses and it was hardly artistic. But when Bobby Floyd raced 14 yards on an end run, Green Bay had taken the lead. Fred Cone kicked the extra point and it was 7-0.

Woodley Lewis, one of the best kick runners in Ram history, shook things up momentarily, streaking 49 yards on a punt return as the quarter ended. But Woodley threw such a splendid fake on a Packer defender that he fell himself, 13 yards from the goal line. And he hadn't even been touched. That's the way things were going for the Rams. Los Angeles could not mount much offense so Waterfield was called upon to come in and kick it through from 16 yards out.

Green Bay gave the Rams another opportunity a few minutes later, but the visitors again failed to take full advantage. When a Babe Parilli punt sputtered only 14 yards before going out of bounds, all the Rams could get out of it was another Waterfield field goal, this time a 32-yarder.

Then the Packers struck again. Tobin Rote-to-Billy Howton was a passing combination that would cause Los Angeles grief for many seasons to come. This time, Rote and the rookie wide receiver from Rice were working from their own 31. Tobin threw a quick 11-yard slant to Howton, who sidestepped Larry Brink, cut diagonally

across the field, picked up some blockers and raced 69 yards for the touchdown that made it 14-6. The half ended that way.

Things got worse for the Rams in the third quarter. Green Bay owned the football for all but eight plays. Rote and Parilli each threw touchdown passes to Bob Mann, the former Michigan Rose Bowl hero, and as the fourth period opened, Los Angeles seemed hopelessly behind, 28-6.

A few minutes passed, and then, suddenly, it began to happen. Slowly, at first. But after a while you could begin to feel the momentum steadily surging. The Rams and their captain were about to put together one of the most amazing comebacks in professional football history.

Rather than try to explain it, we will let the architect of the rally, the man who put it all together, explain how he did it. This is Bob Waterfield's own description of the final 12 minutes of that memorable afternoon.

"A rally like that could never happen, of course, without the cooperation of the other team. The biggest single reason for what happened was that Green Bay crawled into its shell and tried to protect its lead with safe football.

"More than one pro team, including some Ram teams of other years, had gone down the drain for the same reason. I remember Paul Brown saying one time that he would rather be behind than ahead by a few points, in the fourth quarter.

"But we were behind 22 points in that fourth quarter in Milwaukee, and I don't think even Paul Brown would approve of that.

"What was the turning point? It wasn't any one thing, but I do remember that Tank Younger was the ballcarrier on the first play we did right all day.

"I had just checked the clock, confirming my suspicions that the fourth quarter was well under way, when I gave Tank the ball on a statue-of-liberty.

"It was second and nine, just the spot for the

Tanker and the statue in those days, and he gave the ball quite a ride.

"He went for 38 yards, and a minute later Deacon Dan Towler bucked over from the one-yard line. It was the Rams' first touchdown of the afternoon—we had made a couple of field goals for our six points in the first half and it cut Green Bay down from 28-6 to 28-13.

"This left us 15 points back. And with the clock moving right along we knew that we'd have to score two touchdowns and a field goal to win.

"It didn't matter to us in what particular order we did those things; and so, after Green Bay punted and we worked the ball down to the Packer 20-yard line, we went for the field goal next, on fourth and one.

"I heard afterward that one of the experts up in the press box almost blew the roof off screaming when he saw us go into field goal formation—eight minutes before the end of a game we were 'losing' by 28 to 13.

"To some of the Packers it also seemed like a weird thing to do, but we were playing to win, and we knew that if we didn't salvage three points this trip we were done. A field goal in this spot, we felt, would be as good as a touchdown. And it proved to be.

"Having narrowed Green Bay's lead by three more points, to 28-16, we next got a little luck. The Packers, who were starting to panic, fumbled the ball over to us.

"And then when Younger promptly fumbled for the Rams, Bob Carey picked up the ball without missing a stride and ran it in for an easy touchdown, about fifteen yards. Our conversion left us only five points behind, 28-23.

"I have often wondered if we would have won that game if Carey hadn't been out there blocking and in position to pick up an open-field fumble. The way we were going, we probably would have scored eventually, but it might have taken so much time that for us to score another touchdown

would have been completely out of the question.

"So Carey's touchdown put us in reach of the Packers with five minutes to play.

"We kicked off and our great defensive team stopped Green Bay again, but then Babe Parilli really put us in a hole. His high punt rolled dead on our eight-yard line.

"That left us 92 yards away from the winning touchdown, and only two-and-one half minutes to go for it.

"As I was heading out to the field, Andy Robustelli stopped me for a second. He had started the game at offensive guard, the only time he ever played it, but had come out injured, and now he looked at me and said, 'Take your time, Buckets.'

"It was pretty good advice. A passing team can go 92 yards in two minutes, all right, if it doesn't get reckless.

"You see, there's all kinds of pressure on both teams in such a situation. And with so much pressure on, there's a tendency to do things too fast—to try to push the clock.

"But the fact is that the best time in football to be deliberate and thorough is the last two minutes of a close game. Almost never, in pro football, can you pull a game out of the fire with a long reckless play.

"The team that fights the urge to try to win it all with one play is the team that has the best opportunity in the last couple of minutes.

"Robustelli, with unusual insight for a young player in the league, was just reminding us to 'proceed with deliberate speed.'

"Well, that's about the end of my story. It took us seven plays. Towler went six yards, Vitamin T. Smith four yards and Bob Carey 20 yards on a pass. On the next two passes, V.T. Smith moved us 30 yards to the Green Bay 32-yard line, and Tom Fears moved us 26 yards to the 6-yard line. V.T. got to the 3-yard line, and Towler got over.

"I think the big play was Fears' catch and run to the 6-yard line. It was a slant behind the line of

The feats of Bob Waterfield on an October afternoon, bringing his team from 22 points behind in the fourth quarter to win the game, amazed the new coach of the team, Hamp Pool (top, below). Joe Stydahar (bottom) had resigned after the team's dismal showing in the preseason. Pool and the Rams won the last eight games of the 1952 season and captured the division championship. The incredible game he had given the Rams in Milwaukee that day would always be remembered as the best of many great ones from No. 7. After a "day" in his honor, Waterfield retired at the end of the 1952 season.

scrimmage and I didn't have to throw the ball very far.

"The play was mostly a Fears run, and it must have been a great run. I didn't see it myself. I was giving Tom so much body English that I stumbled and grounded out.

"The next day, I had a pretty good excuse to stumble around some more, verbally, when people started asking me, 'What happened?' I hadn't seen much of the key plays—the Fears run and the field goals. The kicker, you see, if he's kicking properly with his head down, never does see his own field goals.

"Nevertheless, on October 12, 1952, I was there."

So were a handful of others. A lucky handful of 21,693.

Pool, stunned and at the same time greatly relieved after his first victory, never was one to praise players in the dressing room. But when the name Waterfield came up, he couldn't help himself.

"Bob's the greatest player I've ever seen when this club is behind. I still don't know how he brought us back this afternoon."

It wasn't the only time it happened. Four years earlier, against Philadelphia, the Eagles were leading 28-0 with sixteen minutes to play. The final score of the game: 28-28.

But, for all his honors and all his accomplishments, the game that day in Milwaukee—that 30-28 victory—may rank as his greatest achievement. Vincent X. Flaherty wrote it this way in the *Los Angeles Examiner*.

"As the black hands of the clock made their jerky circuit on tortoise legs, the Packers must have felt like wading into the icy waters of Lake Michigan until their hats floated. Games such as the Rams and the Rifle [Waterfield] played Sunday are the kind that set pro football apart, give it that extra touch of quality which makes it the finest game in the land."

November 2, 1958

It was, perhaps, the most distinguished first round in the history of the National Football League draft. The names on the list jump out at you. Paul Hornung . . . John Brodie . . . Ron Kramer . . . Jon Arnett . . . Len Dawson . . . Jim Brown . . . Jim Parker . . . Del Shofner . . .

It was also a time of difficult decision. The lights burned through the night in the offices of the Los Angeles Rams in January of 1957. The Rams would get the fourth player selected, unless they were lucky enough to inherit the bonus pick. The choice was a critical one. After recording an 8-3-1 record and winning the division championship in his first season, coach Sid Gillman's team was 4-8 in 1956. Gillman knew he needed help and he knew he needed it fast.

So the debate continued. Who should it be? One segment of Ram scouts recommended Brodie, although it was known San Francisco, choosing two spots ahead of the Rams, would possibly take him. Another group pushed for Brown, a runner, they said, with unmatched potential. Then there was Arnett, the local boy from Manual Arts High School in Los Angeles, the All-America from USC, the gifted breakaway threat who could bust a game open at any time.

A unanimous opinion had still not been reached on the day of the draft. In New York, early that January morning, came the first announcement. Green Bay had won the bonus. The Packers quickly picked Paul Hornung, the All-America from Notre Dame. San Francisco was next and one Ram decision was avoided. The 49ers went for Brodie.

Next it was Green Bay's turn again, with its regular first round pick. The Pack needed a tight end. They got one of the best ever in Michigan's Ron Kramer.

Now it was up to the Rams. The field had been narrowed down with the elimination of Brodie. Would it be Arnett or Brown? The flashy USC home run threat or the power man from Syracuse?

The Rams selected Arnett. Some say they let their box office dictate the pick. Others claim it was typical of this team. That this was one of their colossal errors, the kind from which you cannot recover.

But that was all hindsight. What people tend to forget is that Pittsburgh and then Cleveland followed and both were known to covet the same man. It was not Brown. It was Len Dawson. Pittsburgh picked first and got him. Poor Paul Brown had to settle for the greatest runner football ever produced.

The Rams were never sorry they chose Arnett. Okay, so they bypassed Brown, and everyone knew he was good. But no one had any idea he would be that good.

Los Angeles got exactly what it wanted in the rookie known as Jaguar Jon.

This was a runner of rare style. Not that big—about 5-11, 195. Not overpowering. And the speed was hardly extraordinary. What he had were the pure traits found in only a few. Balance, body control, and, most of all, instinct. Hugh McElhenny had it. Gale Sayers had it. But you are hard pressed to find many more. It is not something that can be taught.

"I really believe," Jon Arnett said once, "for the most part it's a case of you have it or you don't. You know what I mean? You see a bunch of kids playing tag. One kid seems to have a great knack for dodging, twisting away or outrunning the others. Chances are this kid, given the right environment and with the right physical breaks, would make a good halfback someday."

He created excitement anytime he touched the ball. He was an artist with his own unique strokes. The plays designed on blackboards were useless to him. He had no blueprint, no design. He moved where he sensed there was daylight. He cut where he felt there was room.

But there was more to it than that. "You watch Arnett some time," said the late Red Sanders,

Bears 7 7 7 14 35
Rams 17 14 10 0 41

when he was coaching at UCLA. "He even walks different than everyone else." Some claimed you could throw him off the top of a building and he'd land on his feet. It was balance developed as a high school gymnast.

"How did the sport of gymnastics actually help you?" he was asked. "Well," he answered, "it's hard to explain, but I can give you an example. Say you learn to do a back flip with a twist . . . a tumbler's stunt. After you master this maneuver, you become aware of the position of your feet and legs when you are upside-down in the air. You have gained better control of your body and you land in perfect balance. Now supposing you are upended by a tackler and your feet fly out from under you. There's no panic and the awareness of how to land in balance is there."

Arnett enjoyed many great days and broke off an endless string of memorable runs for the Rams. But the day he will always remember was a November afternoon in 1958. The day he personally destroyed the Chicago Bears.

The Rams and Bears groveled in the dirt twice every year. Once at menacing Wrigley Field and then again in the Coliseum at Los Angeles. Tickets were never easy to come by. Even if the records weren't too impressive, when the Rams played the Bears, something always happened.

Halas, of course was the great intimidator in those days. He'd roam the sidelines in his suit and hat, rushing down to argue with an official or shouting and pointing a finger at an opposing player. He was the most animated coach in professional football. They loved his act in Chicago. They despised it in L.A.

The first meeting in 1958 was typical. It was filled with controversy, questionable officiating and near fights. And, of course, the Bears won. The bad guys in the black uniforms were almost invincible against Los Angeles in the '50s. That victory in October of '58 was the eighth consecutive for Chicago over L.A.

Despite the domination, the Bears against the Rams was always great theater. Even the 31-10 win at Wrigley Field that year was entertaining. From the time the Rams opened it up with a 92-yard touchdown pass from Bill Wade to Del Shofner to the postgame accusation that the Ram phones had been bugged, the pace never slackened.

In the first period, a tackle on the Chicago sideline prompted a shoving match between the Bears' Abe Gibron, the Rams' Don Burroughs and the ever-present Halas. It ended with Richter jostling the Bears' coach and telling him "to get the hell away."

The Chicago defense, meanwhile, clamped tightly around Arnett, allowing him only 12 net yards in nine carries. Although Wade finished with 200 yards passing, he was intercepted four times. And as for the officiating . . . well, the Rams couldn't believe it. Eight times L.A. was penalized in the first half for an even 100 yards. The Bears were caught only twice. For the game, the Rams accrued 12 penalties for 145 yards and when the yardage lost on gains was added to that total, it was discovered the men with whistles had taken 233 yards away from them.

Afterwards, as if Gillman's team wasn't mad enough, assistant coach Bill Swiacki hinted that someone had been listening in as the Rams discussed offensive strategy over the phone at Wrigley Field.

"Before the game I tried to contact Lou Rymkus down on the field," said Swiacki. "Lou was busy, but instead I heard foreign voices on the line. And they weren't Ram voices." The offensive phone system was installed by the Bears for the benefit of visiting teams. Swiacki said there were two telephones in front of the Chicago bench. One was in ready use, the other only when the Rams had possession of the ball. The Los Angeles assistant said the tipoff came on a fourth down punting situation in the last quarter.

Adversaries for an afternoon in the Coliseum . . . the Rams and their Western Conference rivals, the Chicago Bears. George Halas (right) was the Bears' leader, scowling and plotting intrigue, or so claimed the Rams' fans. You could always count on a battle when Halas brought his Bears to the Coliseum. Bill George and Doug Atkins led the Chicago defense, and fullback Rick Casares (left) was the star of the offense.

Swiacki explained he had phoned down suggesting Shofner should fake a kick and pass. While Gillman thought over the idea, a Chicago sub raced onto the field and shouted something to his teammates. Swiacki did not go into it any further, other than pointing out the Rams ends were both held up at the line of scrimmage and Shofner wound up punting the ball.

Later, Halas, aware the Rams were contemplating a formal complaint about the officiating, lodged one of his own. He said it had been brought to his attention that a Los Angeles assistant in the press box had yelled down over the intercom to "Get that Galimore," referring to Willie Galimore, the Bears' elusive halfback. Halas made it sound like the order was suggesting bodily harm. The Rams, already angry, hotly denied the charge.

The bad blood that flowed between the two teams would only have to wait two more weeks to reach a new boiling point. On Nov. 2, the lines at the Coliseum ticket windows began forming early. By noon, it was clear the crowd for the rematch would be in excess of 100,000.

Chicago (4-1) was favored at odds that fluctuated from 3 to 6 points during the week. Los Angeles (2-3) was coming off a 41-24 loss to Detroit, but there had been strong suggestions that the Rams were thinking more about the Bears that day than they were the Lions.

What Chicago should have been thinking about was Arnett, although there was no way they could have prepared for the Rams' marvelous runner on this particular afternoon.

In 60 memorable minutes, this is what he accomplished:

1. A 72-yard run with a screen pass from Wade, taking the ball to the Chicago 3 to set up a touchdown.

2. A 36-yard punt return to the Bear 34 to set up a touchdown.

3. A 24-yard punt return to the Chicugo 36.

4. A 58-yard punt return to the Bear 38 to give the Rams field position for another touchdown.

5. A 52-yard run from scrimmage that took him to the 4-yard line and allowed the Rams still another opportunity to score.

6. A 38-yard run from scrimmage in the fourth period when a Chicago rally threatened to wipe out the Ram lead. This one gave Paige Cothren a shot at a field goal he eventually missed but it also put the Bears back in a hole from which they could not recover.

To the delight of a roaring mob of 100,470, Arnett finished the afternoon with a total of 298 yards, although somehow in his weaving journeys across the floor of the Coliseum, he never did score.

Afterwards, across the street in Julie's, the favorite postgame hangout of USC and Rams fans, the arguments raged over which of Arnett's runs was the best. Most seemed to favor the very first one, the short pass converted into a spectacular gain.

With huge Doug Atkins bearing down on him, Wade flipped a short screen to Arnett, who caught it and headed for the northern sideline. After faking out Fred Williams, he gave it one of his jaguar cuts and veered back toward the center of the field, where six Chicago defenders, including Atkins, Bill George and Joe Fortunato, surrounded him. Somehow, some way, he eluded them all and shook off a desperate diving tackle by Bill Bishop. It was a foot race after that, and because he had covered well over 100 yards, it was fatigue as much as Erich Barnes that finally caught him from behind.

The game was broken open in the second period when two of Arnett's flitting punt returns turned things around. With his 58-yard spectacular providing the impetus, the Rams lead at halftime grew to 31-14. When Chicago closed to within 31-21 in the third quarter, Jon busted his 52-yard run to set up the touchdown that made it a 16-point

87

Turning the corner, evading tacklers, almost falling, then recovering . . . Jon Arnett had exquisite grace, balance and agility. The Bears found him unstoppable this day. He rolled up yardage carrying the ball, catching passes and returning punts. It became a dizzying afternoon for the Bears.

cushion for Los Angeles. A lesser team might have quit, but the Bears refused to give up. Halas had put together perhaps the most volatile offense of his tenure in Chicago. The quarterbacks were Zeke Bratkowski and Ed Brown, neither of whom stood out in an era of Unitas, Layne, Tittle and Conerly. But both were experienced and could throw, and in the Windy City, they had a lot of powerful weapons at their disposal. In the backfield, there was Rick Casares, the prototype professional fullback. Large and strong, Casares was famous for putting his helmet down and rumbling between the tackles. More important, he was durable. He could carry the ball all day.

At halfback, there was Galimore, who, for a fascinating season or two, would prove to be as quick and elusive as Gale Sayers would later be over a longer period of time. Eventually killed in an automobile accident a few years later, Galimore was especially effective against the Rams. There were days against Los Angeles when Willie looked like the best running back in the league.

At wide receiver, Chicago had Harlon Hill, a rangy, country boy who might have been, at that time, the closest thing the NFL had seen to matching Elroy (Crazylegs) Hirsch. Hill was a superior deep threat, the player who most concerned opposing defenses. The Bears also had young Johnny Morris, the little man from the little school at UC Santa Barbara who would develop into one of the club's most exciting players.

Overall, the Ram defense did an excellent job containing Chicago on this bright November afternoon. Casares gouged out 113 yards in 23 carries but Galimore could only get 35 in seven tries. Bratkowski and Brown threw for 193 yards and three touchdowns, but they were intercepted twice, both times by Jack Morris.

Still, the Bears kept coming. That comfortable 31-14 halftime advantage slowly narrowed. Galimore caught a 12-yard touchdown pass from Bratkowski to narrow it to 31-21.

Arnett, of course, never did stop swiveling his way through the Chicago secondary. But even after his montage of surrealistic runs had helped make it 41-21, Halas' team didn't quit. Casares culminated one drive with a five-yard charge into the end zone, and then Bill McColl, the good doctor from Stanford, caught a 23-yard pass for another touchdown. Both times the PATs were converted by another gentleman of whom you may have heard. His name was George Blanda.

Now it was 41-35 and there were still six minutes and 31 seconds remaining. Shade began to creep along the closed end of the Coliseum and the fans were starting to fidget nervously. There was that jinx to worry about . . . the jinx of eight straight Los Angeles frustrations against the Bears.

Moments later, it appeared as if No. 9 might happen. Chicago had the ball and Hill was streaking into the sunlight at the peristyle end. He was open and the ball was there. Only this time, he dropped it at the Los Angeles 27.

Morris intercepted Bratkowski's next pass and the Rams ran out the clock.

In the Chicago dressing room, the writers waited for Hill. "No," he explained, sadly, "no one deflected the ball. I had it in my hands and dropped it. I caught the ball low but I didn't bring it up. It was a sure touchdown."

Halas, who had been the subject of boos and catcalls throughout the long, hot afternoon, said the fans didn't bother him. "I don't pay any attention to that stuff. People come because of pro football, not any phony publicity."

"The Rams are a fine football team and they played a great game," said the Bears' coach, "but after everything is said the game comes down to that dropped pass."

The Rams' dressing room was quiet, almost somber. The weary players seemed to smile in relief.

"Yes, the team had the desire today," said Sid

Gillman, still chewing vigorously on a stick of gum. "Arnett? Oh, my, I never saw so many punt returns. Jon was great, sure he was great."

It was Arnett's finest moment in a Rams career cluttered by frustration. No one was hurt more by the decline in ensuing years than the sleek running back from USC.

Forced to maneuver behind a makeshift offensive line, his statistics, as well as his reputation, suffered. He was an accomplished receiver and, when the blocking failures up front reached their peak, he was even shifted outside for awhile to catch passes. Still, around the league they sympathized with him and they speculated what he would have been like running behind Vince Lombardi's precison line in Green Bay.

Eventually, Arnett became one of the more outspoken veterans on the club. The consistent losing bugged him as much as the lack of qualified blockers. And when the team continued to bring in highly publicized, well-paid and untested rookies, Arnett grew even more unhappy. When word escaped that young Merlin Olsen would be presented $25,000, Arnett practically started a one-man revolution. Nor did it particularly please him that the Rams seemed infatuated with running backs. Why, he would sometimes wonder aloud, would they want an Ollie Matson or a Tom Wilson or a Dick Bass when they already had a Jon Arnett? Fans would often wonder the same thing.

Finally, slowed some by injuries and advancing age, Arnett fell out of favor in Los Angeles.

And the Rams, in their never-ending search for irony, managed to do it again. They traded him to the Bears.

December 9, 1967

"In sports the only measure of success is victory. We must sacrifice everything to this end. The man who can accept defeat and take his salary without feeling guilty is a thief. The average player in pro football makes around $25,000. I cannot think of a thing this money can buy that a loser could enjoy. Fancy cars and clothes and parties and pretty women are only window dressing. Winning is the only true goal. Only the winner is alive. The loser is dead, whether he knows it or not."—George Allen.

It was more than a winning era. It was a mystique. George Allen could cast a spell over players. He would pat them on their wallets, clap his hands and come up with one of those corny sayings of his and they'd believe. The players would get this funny, sort of glazed look in their eyes and they'd rush out to do or die for dear, old George.

In between the wins, the cheers and the clichés, the George Allen era was perhaps the stormiest in Ram history. From the beginning, when the Chicago Bears filed suit for a permanent injunction to try to restrain Allen from taking the job in Los Angeles, to four years later when George was fired for the second and final time by Dan Reeves. It was never smooth. It was always rocky.

The high point for Allen—what has to rank as his most memorable and emotional victory with the Rams—came on Dec. 9, 1967 against the Green Bay Packers at the Los Angeles Coliseum.

But to fully understand what transpired that day one has to examine more closely the Allen philosophy and how it affected the players he coached.

In 1966, his first full year with the Rams, George led the club to its best record in eight years, finishing 8-6. Now, prior to the 1967 season, he listed six objectives for making Los Angeles a champion.

"First, I wanted to bring in some players who knew how to win. The Rams had been losers for a long time, so I had to trade for players with a winning attitude. We got some and they helped. Second, we had to get over the idea we were building for the future. The Rams were always building. I said this is the year we win, not build. I kept veterans who could help immediately, not rookies who would be a help in the years to come. Third, the Rams were not a tough club mentally and I wanted to instill a feeling of toughness in them. Fourth, the Rams were losers on the road and I wanted to change that, too. When we beat Baltimore in Baltimore last year, I think we turned a corner. After that the club began to believe it could win away from home."

Allen made a serious effort to destroy the Rams' old Hollywood image. One Ram coach of the past had said that the trouble with the club was too many cars with the top down and too many girls. A rigid curfew and strict discipline got rid of both, thus accomplishing Allen's fifth objective. "As for the sixth," said George, "I wanted to put in a basic, simple offense to tie in with an improved defense. We didn't want any errors on offense. If you can bring the defense up and make no mistakes on offense, you can win."

And thus, the George Allen legend was born, buttressed always by an amazing list of quotes that were. . . well, pure George. Quotes like these:

"The harder I work, the luckier I get."

"I have told my teams that God, family and football are the three most important things in their lives. During the season, football comes first."

"We all need sleep. We all should have some leisure. Leisure time is the five or six hours you sleep at night."

"Sometimes I'll dig out rocks and throw them in the ocean. If I find one that is heavier and buried deeper in the sand than I believed, I'll stay with it until I've got it out. I won't let that rock defeat me. Life is a series of such challenges."

Packers	7	3	7	7	24
Rams	0	7	10	10	27

"Each of us has been put on earth with the ability to do something well. We cheat ourselves, we cheat those who are dependent on us, we cheat God if we do not use that ability as best we can. I know many have resented the demands I have made on them, but I believe they should thank me for driving them to make the most of themselves."

"Most persons give only 50 per cent, whether they realize it or not. Let them be objective and look at themselves and how they spend each day, and they will know I am right. They are wasting much of their days, their lives and themselves. I ask them to give 110 per cent in hopes of getting 100 per cent. I do not believe that is asking too much."

And finally . . "This is the profession they have chosen, so it is the one to which they must give everything they have. It does not matter whether you are working for the Ford Motor Company, the Los Angeles Rams football team or the corner grocery store; if you have pride in yourself, you must prod yourself to accomplish all that can be accomplished. We were not put on earth to have a good time, but to contribute all that is in us."

If you were to pick out one segment of a George Allen team that sets it apart from all others, you would have to choose the special teams. No other coach has been able to impart such pride in reserves whose afternoon's work entails only a few brief minutes in kicking situations. Allen set out to glorify them, to make them feel important and he has accomplished his task. Moreover, it has paid off handsomely for him. Allen teams have won more games with blocked kicks than any other two or three clubs combined.

Allen is proud of the fact his special teams spend so many hours on the practice field. "It takes time to cover every special team phase," he has said, "You can only do it if you have open-end practices. Some clubs practice an hour and a quarter, or an hour and 30 minutes, and that's it. And I'm not saying they're wrong. A player's attention

span is not much longer than that. But on our team we feel one thing is more important—not overlooking any details—regardless of how tired the players are. So we keep practicing each day until we've covered everything. And another thing, we like to put our best players on special teams. If a regular is better than a youngster as a special-team blocker, we use the regular."

The special teams were never to mean more to Allen than they did this day, when they brought his club back from the dead to one of his greatest triumphs.

The Rams began the 1967 season winning their first three regular season games easily. But in game four, at home, they were edged by the San Francisco 49ers, 27-24.

A 24-24 thriller at Baltimore's Memorial Stadium was followed by still another tie—this time 28-28—against Washington. But then George put together six straight victories, and going into the 13th week, the Los Angeles record was an impressive 9-1-2.

Still, Baltimore was keeping pace in the Coastal Division and the Rams not only required a win over the Packers, but a victory the following Sunday vs. the Colts to get into the playoffs.

Vince Lombardi's proud Pack had no such problems. They had clinched the Central Division and were merely playing out the string. About all a win would have meant was a clarification of whom they'd be meeting in the playoffs. If they beat the Rams, they could begin studying Baltimore films a week early. If they were to lose, they'd have to wait until the ensuing Rams-Colts game to find out who their opponents would be.

This was an unusual late-season Saturday game at the Coliseum, but 76,637 didn't let that bother them. They weren't about to be fooled by the calendar. It had been a long time since a pro football season had been climaxed this way in Los Angeles. The weather was typical for December, warm, with just a touch of crispness to the air.

Vince Lombardi (far left) and George Allen were about to send their teams into one of the most emotion-packed games that either man would ever coach. The Packers had to deal with a Rams' team made into a winner by Allen. Los Angeles led in the second half when Allen made a rare mistake, kicking off to Travis Williams. The Speedster returned 104 yards for a touchdown. It tied the score 17-17.

The Ram cadre of captains, Ed Meador, Joe Scibelli, Lamar Lundy and Les Josephson, strolled out to midfield, shook hands with the Packers' Willie Davis and Bob Skoronski and watched the coin flip into the air. Green Bay won the toss and elected to receive.

George Allen had one strict rule on kickoffs. Never kick the ball to a runner like Gale Sayers or Travis Williams. "The Roadrunner" was what they called Williams, and although he never developed into a consistent threat from scrimmage, he had become one of the most feared kick runners in football. Bruce Gossett followed orders and squibbed the ball downfield where Tommy Joe Crutcher, a linebacker, picked it up on the 18 and returned it seven yards.

From there, the familiar figures in the green and gold uniforms broke their first huddle and went to work. Bart Starr opened with what looked like it was supposed to be a sweep. Donny Anderson never made it to the line of scrimmage, though. Deacon Jones nailed him for a yard loss and the Coliseum had its first of many explosions. The Deacon was in his prime, an all-pro defensive end who, along with tackle Merlin Olsen, formed the foundation for Allen's great defenses. Earlier, three spectators had carefully unraveled a sign that read: "Deacon Jones For Secretary of Defense." The nickname was to stick.

Starr didn't wait long to loosen up the Ram defensive sets. With second and 11, he found Boyd Dowler on the right side for 29 yards and a first down on the Los Angeles 47. Anderson came inside on the next play, bursting briefly into the secondary for 13 yards to the Ram 34. Then the Secretary and his defense got tough. The drive stalled and Don Chandler attempted a 41-yard field goal. It sailed wide to the left.

Neither team could move the ball consistently through the rest of the first quarter, until Gossett's 46-yard field goal attempt was blocked by Lee Roy Caffey and recovered by Green Bay's defensive back Herb Adderley on the Los Angeles 43.

No one ever pounced on opponents' errors like the Pack. This time it took Starr four plays before he stepped back coolly and lofted a 30-yard pass to Carroll Dale for a touchdown. "Looks like the same old story," muttered a disgusted Ram official in the press box. "They wait until we make a mistake—and wham."

The jolt may have helped the Rams regain their senses. Now Los Angeles had the ball again and Roman Gabriel, developing into one of the best quarterbacks in the league, began a drive on his own 27. Dick Bass wriggled for five yards. Les Josephson swept for seven more.

With a first down on his 39, Gabriel faded to pass and Willie Davis and the Packer linemen went after him. Under heavy pressure, Gabriel managed to locate Bernie Casey with a mini-bomb for 40 yards. With a first on the Green Bay 21, Josephson rammed into a wall for no gain as the first quarter ended with Green Bay in front, 7-0. On second down, Gabe went back to the air, hitting Josephson for 11 and another first. On the nine now, the Rams' Tom Mack was detected holding. Gabriel had a difficult first and goal situation from the 24. A Bass draw got only one. Gabriel scrambled for seven more, setting up third and 16. Jack Snow, Gabe's most reliable receiver down through the years, faked once, cut to his left and beat Bob Jeter in the corner of the end zone. The pass was perfect. Rams 7, Packers 7.

While the Los Angeles defense continued to play well, Gabriel went to a slightly different game plan. He started throwing long. And the Packers started taking advantage of it. Adderley intercepted one ball and Willie Wood grabbed another, the latter steal giving Green Bay the ball on its own 47 with 2:30 left in the half. A Starr to Dowler 20-yard pass moved it close enough for Chandler to get a shot from 32 yards away. This time he didn't miss and the Pack left the field ahead, 10-7, at intermission.

Only that final interception kept it from being a complete draw for the first 30 minutes. Rarely have two teams finished so close statistically. Eighteen first downs were split evenly. Green Bay gained 163 total yards, the Rams 161.

Burned once, Gabriel switched back to his original strategy at the start of the second half, concentrating on quick look-in passes and relatively safe out patterns along the sidelines.

After Willie Ellison's splendid 43-yard return of the second half kickoff, the Rams went right to the attack. The underrated Josephson galloped up the gut for 9 and then sliced off right tackle for five. Gabriel, on a keeper, managed two and then passed to Casey for 15 and tight end Billy Truax for seven. Josie got three more inside and Bass squirmed for four and a first down at the 12. Josephson's one yard run was followed by another Gabriel-to-Snow connection. This time Jack beat Wood, the all-pro safety, for 11 yards and the touchdown that put his team in command for the first time, 14-10.

Green Bay couldn't move and Gabriel got the ball back moments later. From his 37, he generated another smart drive, one that covered 10 plays. A screen pass to Josephson got 19 yards and another completion to Casey was good for 17. At the 15, the Packers held and Gossett put the ball through for a 23-yard field goal and a seven point lead, 17-10.

At this point Allen, perhaps feeling a little more secure, made a ghastly mistake. He decided to kick the ball to Williams, the 6-1, 210-pound sprinter who had run a 9.3 100-yard dash at Arizona State. Travis caught the ball four yards deep in the end zone. He ran straight upfield where he crashed at full speed into Bob Nichols, a large Ram reserve tackle. The impact would have felled most men. All it did to Nichols was knock him out of one shoe. As for Williams, he bounced three yards sideways and landed balanced and running. When he hit the sideline, it was all over. Once he

got a step, no one ever caught him. It was a 104-yard touchdown run, Travis' fourth scoring return, a new record in the NFL, and it tied the score at 17.

"The deflating effect that this had on the Rams was colossal," wrote Melvin Durslag, the *Los Angeles Herald-Examiner's* columnist. "It hit with suffocating shock, and a game that might have taken a big turn for Los Angeles suddenly was tied, and Ram players were wondering about the next few minutes as if they had been separated from their mother."

The two teams traded mistakes early in the fourth period. A Starr pass was intercepted by Clancy Williams and returned to the Green Bay 25, from where the Rams could not make it to the end zone. They got as far as the eight and Gossett kicked a field goal from the 16. The Rams assumed the lead again, 20-17.

Five plays later, after thwarting Green Bay's offense, the Rams took over on their own 47, in remarkably good field position with a three-point lead and eight minutes remaining in the game. It took only one play to create panic in the Coliseum. Bass coughed up the ball and Jim Weatherwax recovered for the Packers. With 43 yards to navigate, Starr, the pilot you want to have in pressure situations, took his team to the Ram four in eight plays. From there, Chuck Mercein, a Yale man, of all things, scooted through left guard and fell over the goal line. Pack 24, Rams 20, and moments later, when a Ram drive stalled on the Green Bay 44, the fans started filtering toward the exits.

The Packers owned the football with 1:20 remaining. But the Ram defense hadn't conceded. They cut off Williams for a six-yard loss, allowed Mercein only three—and then knocked Anderson down for no gain. That made it fourth and 13.

This set up what may have been the Rams' most dramatic single play since the 1951 touchdown pass that won the world championship.

Allen had had his team working on a blocked punt play for weeks. Now, under duress, his special team would try to bring it off, just the way it had been planned. With only 54 seconds left on the big Coliseum clock, eight men were stationed on the line in gaps between the blockers. Tony Guillory, a substitute linebacker, was to play head-to-head on the center and go whichever way he felt was open.

"This time I went to my right," explained Guillory afterward. "The center's got his head down for the snap, so you get a good jump on him and I got off right with the ball. My assignment on the play is really to draw a block from the fullback, so one of the outside guys can come in free. This time nobody touched me and I came right up the middle."

Guillory hit the ball with the side of his left wrist and it wobbled into the hands of Claude Crabb, a substitute defensive back. The full rush had deposited a band of Rams in the Packer backfield and Crabb had an escort of seven excited teammates as he set out for the Green Bay goal line. Like a happy drunk, Guillory almost knocked Crabb down trying to get in front to block. "I can't see at all without my glasses," said Tony. "I didn't know Claude had the ball, and I couldn't read the numbers anyway."

Anderson circled around to the front of the milling group of Rams and finally tackled Crabb on the Packer five-yard line.

Now there were just 44 ticks remaining. But a quiet calm had pervaded the Rams, even if the crowd had long since become hysterical.

"I wasn't worried about scoring a touchdown," said defensive tackle Roger Brown, later. "When we blocked the punt, I knew we would get the score. If we had to pick up a man and throw him into the end zone with the ball, we're going to get the score. The touchdown was the frosting on the cake. The blocked punt was the winner, man."

Still, the touchdown was notable for its ex-quisite execution. The play was called Pass 46Z Corner and Gabriel called it on second and five after a previous pass had fallen incomplete, stopping the clock with 34 seconds left. Lined up in a tight formation, with both ends in close to the tackles, Gabe began barking signals. Casey was flanked a yard outside the Ram left end. Opposite him was Bob Jeter, with the Green Bay safeties a bit deeper in the end zone. At the snap, Gabriel faked a handoff to Tommy Mason, who drove straight ahead, carrying out the deception beautifully. The play action froze Jeter. "My responsibility depends on what the end does," explained the Packer defensive back later. "I have to read run if he blocks, and he did block."

In the Green Bay dressing room, Anderson was explaining how the play looked to him. "We were naturally expecting them to put on a big rush," said Donny. "It looked to me like they were set a little tighter in the middle than usual. I was already in the process of kicking the ball when I saw this guy [Guillory] coming in at me. There was nothing I could do then. I rushed the kick as much as I could, but it was too late.

"I never saw the ball after that."

"A lot of people were coming through there on us," said Crutcher. "I was supposed to pick out the most dangerous one and block him. I picked out a guy on the left end of the line. I thought he'd be the one. Donny is a left-footed kicker so you've got to protect him more on the left side. I didn't see the kick blocked. I just heard it."

Lombardi said Josephson, who ran for 73 yards, "was a key player for the Rams today."

"And their pass rush was just tremendous."

Starr agreed with the latter evaluation. "It was not by my choosing that I was running around way I was," said Bart. "I was just forced out of my pocket."

"That was a different Starr today," observed defensive end Lamar Lundy. "Usually when he is about to be hit he curls up in a ball and goes down.

The Rams regained the lead. This was a poised Packer team riding the crest, however, and Bart Starr took advantage of a fumble and moved Green Bay ahead again. Emotions wound tighter and tighter, and showed in the faces of the Rams: guard Tom Mack (left), linebacker Maxie Baughan (right) and Allen and his quarterback Roman Gabriel (below).

You also know where to find him—in the pocket. But, he was stepping out of it today."

The Deacon, celebrating his 29th birthday on this happy afternoon, agreed. "Starr put a fake on me the likes of which [Fran] Tarkenton never did. Whew, I feel I had 20 birthdays today. Look at those gray hairs."

When the Rams passed out their game balls, Guillory got his first. Then Charlie Cowan, the offensive tackle, was awarded one for the job he did on Green Bay's all-pro defensive end, Willie Davis. "The picture that most certainly remains this morning," wrote Bob Oates the next day in the *Los Angeles Herald-Examiner*, "is Charlie Cowan blocking Willie Davis, the all-pro Packer lineman. Snow ran perfect routes to score twice and Gabriel laid the ball in there when it counted, and all the time, when Davis danced, Cowan danced with him and shut him out."

Guillory's smile was the brightest in the Ram dressing room. The little-known linebacker from Lamar Tech had been nicknamed "Beowulf" in college because of his unusual feats of strength.

The strength of the Los Angeles performance on this bright Saturday was balance. Offensively and defensively, the Rams were solid in all departments, breaking down only once when Williams returned that kick for six quick points. "I was hit somewhere between our 10 and 15," explained Travis. "There was impact, but I slipped off and skinned out. Nobody touched me after that."

How good was the Ram defense? Well, Williams was also the Pack's best runner from scrimmage. But his figures weren't nearly as impressive. He finished with 26 yards on 12 carries.

The Rams outfirst downed the Pack, 20-12, outpassed them 222 to 120 and outrushed them 102-98. Overall, the final yardage totals read 324 for Los Angeles, 218 for Green Bay.

"This is a story only for those of you who believe in the Easter Bunny, leave cookies out for Santa Claus or think the story of Cinderella was a

On a team that put experience before all else, young linebacker Tony Guillory (left) had little chance to excel. He was relegated to the special teams, and played only parts of three seasons in Los Angeles. This day against the Packers, however, he made one of the greatest plays in Rams' history. With 54 seconds left in the game and his team behind, Guillory charged through to block a punt by Donny Anderson (below). Claude Crabb recovered and two plays later, Gabriel won it with a pass to Bernie Casey. The Los Angeles bench erupted as Allen exulted and Gabriel was lifted to the shoulders of a teammate.

documentary," wrote *Los Angeles Times* columnist Jim Murray.

"You will have to turn elsewhere for the score of Saturday's Rams-Packers game. You see, I saw only 59½ minutes of that game. And there are some wise guys around here who are trying to get me to believe the Rams won."

Allen believed it. Even after someone paused in the middle of the post-game celebration to inquire about the team's next assignment. "Baltimore?" said George. "I don't know about Baltimore. I'm going to drink a glass of milk and then I'm going to get dressed and have a slow glass of blackberry brandy and then I'll start to think about Baltimore."

It was George Allen's day, the afternoon all his mottos came to life. The Rams were to go on and beat Baltimore the next Sunday with a flawless display of football, 34-10. But the following week, in the Western Conference playoff in the Midwest, Green Bay and Lombardi came back to beat them soundly, 28-7.

Guillory's blocked punt and that scintillating victory would prove to be the highlight, the zenith, if you will, of George Allen's very successful and yet very controversial career in Los Angeles.

"We had been laughing stocks and he restored our pride," said Roman Gabriel. "He asked more of us than we wanted to give, but he proved it could be worthwhile."

Even George couldn't have written himself a better tribute than that.

Casey hesitated a moment as Jeter came up to meet the simulated run, then Bernie sprinted hard to his left into the clear, open spaces of the end zone. He caught—in fact, he almost caressed—the soft pass and Los Angeles won the game, 27-24.

Oh, Green Bay got the ball back and Starr had enough time to throw three desperate passes. But linebacker Maxie Baughan intercepted the last one as the gun sounded and Allen and his players, tears streaming from many of their eyes, hugged and danced as the fans swarmed down on them.

Green Bay had lost but Vince Lombardi and the Packers were able to walk off the field with their heads high. In a game they didn't need to win, they had gone all out. The integrity of the National Football League had been preserved.

"I'm proud of the performance of my football team," said Lombardi. "They're a credit to football, having the title won and playing as hard as they did today."

"They did their very best to beat us and almost did," said Allen. "It is the way the game should be played and knowing Lombardi, we didn't expect he would play it any other way. He could have been saving something for the game Dec. 23, but not Lombardi."

"We've worked on that blocked punt play since last July," continued George, "and spent a little time each week sharpening it up, but we don't use it much because you always run the risk of getting a 15-yard penalty for running into the kicker. This time it was a desperation move. The penalty wouldn't have meant anything, but blocking the kick did. What we do is put everybody in the gaps in their line and come in with more men than they've got blockers. It was no time to give up. As long as there was time on the clock we figured we had a chance. This was the opportunity of a lifetime and we could not pass it up."

"I could see all that money going down the drain," said Crabb. "I was on the right side, coming in. For some reason Tommy Joe Crutcher picked me up instead of Tony. I don't know why. I couldn't see it but when I heard the thud I knew the punt was blocked so I started looking around for the ball. We're trained to do that. The ball was bounding around and there was nobody near so I just picked it up and ran with it. Maybe I could have scored but I wasn't going to take a chance of losing the ball because we still had time to get the touchdown. I wasn't going to fumble."

The Players

Tom Fears

Position: Wide receiver
Years played: 1948-56
Height: 6 feet, 2 inches
Weight: 215
College: UCLA

The Los Angeles Rams of the early '50s might have had the greatest passing offense in the history of professional football. Why? The answers are easy. They had two marvelous passers and a pair of Hall of Fame ends. Bob Waterfield and Norm Van Brocklin throwing and Elroy Hirsch and Tom Fears catching. Hirsch and Fears. It's doubtful if there's ever been a better reciving tandem. They complemented each other beautifully. Elroy was the great deep threat, Tom the clutch third down man. Fears could do more than catch short passes, though. A 73-yard bomb he fielded from Van Brocklin is probably the greatest play in Rams' history. It won the team's only world championship. In 1950, Fears caught 84 passes that stood in a 12-game season. It was a record for a long time.

Perhaps more than anyone else, you were the first receiver who made an art out of catching the ball. Tell us some of your theories.

"Well, I've always felt the essential thing is concentration. You have to think about what you're trying to do. Then you map out a series of steps you will take. You look over the entire field and try to guess who will be picking you up. You have to have a preconceived plan. Then, as events occur, you have to come up with a solution and that has to happen by instinct."

What about your moves?

"You have to think about them ahead of time. I tried to save the best part of my fake for the next to last move. That's the one that has to be convincing. You almost have to convince yourself that that's a real move. Then, just like that, you have to cut it off and go for the ball."

Then what do you think about?

"That's where the real concentration starts coming in. You try to judge the way the ball is spinning. You have to give with it slightly. And you have to keep your eyes open. You can't blink. Then you have to make sure you have good hand position and you must remain oblivious to anything around you, such as the corner back."

That takes a certain amount of courage, doesn't it?

"Yes, I suppose so. The rest is simply a matter of training yourself. I try to tell my receivers the same thing today. You're gonna get hit, anyway. Right? Ninety-five percent of the time, you will. So why not catch the damn ball while you're at it."

What about after you catch it?

"Then you have to be aware of the depletion of the defense. You have to have an idea of where you go from there. A lot of receivers today use a little trick of snapping back after catching the ball."

Do as many receivers today think about pass catching the way you did?

"I don't think so."

But there have been some in recent years. Guys like Raymond Berry, for instance?

"Oh yes, he was certainly one. He had it all worked out scientifically. But for the most part today, with zone defenses, guys have more speed and natural talent. Basically, they try to run into areas that have been cleared out. I don't think they concentrate as much on refining the art of catching the ball."

What was the easiest pattern for you to run?

"The sideline pattern. You knew half the time you wouldn't even get hit."

What was the most difficult?

"Anything inside. When you caught a pass in the middle—whether it be a buttonhook, a quick look, or anything—there was lots of traffic from both sides. And you knew it. They were all tough."

How would you characterize yourself, physically, as a receiver?

"I was very quick. That was probably my biggest asset. But I only had average speed."

How average is average?

"I don't know. We never were really timed

much. Elroy Hirsch was faster than I was. But then, Bob Boyd was faster than I was."

How big were you then?

"About 6-2 and 215 or 218. I was good sized. As a matter of fact, in those days, I was one of the bigger ends around. But I'd be a little guy today."

It seems like a lot of the patterns you ran then would be run by tight ends today. Is that an accurate statement?

"That's exactly right."

For someone as technical as you were, wasn't it a disadvantage to have to adjust to two quarterbacks?

"No, not really. I think Waterfield and Van Brocklin were the two best quarterbacks that have ever been on one team. That's my own opinion, of course. But when one couldn't do it—and even they had an occasional bad day—the other would step right in and get the job done."

But didn't each one throw the ball differently?

"Not that much. Van Brocklin drilled it more and could throw with a little bit more variety. But both of them could lay it out there beautifully. I think if one had been lefthanded it would have been much more difficult. I caught Frankie Albert in a couple of All-Star games and that was a tough adjustment. The ball was spinning in the opposite direction of what I was used to."

The catch you made in the 1951 championship game has to be your most famous. What do you remember about it?

"Well, it wasn't any special play, I remember that. Van called it—I think it was late in the third quarter. He hit me perfectly, right in the seam between the two Cleveland defenders. I scooted in between them and they ran into each other trying to get me. That cut down their pursuit and I was able to go all the way."

Can you think of a bigger play you've ever made?

"No. That one did win our only championship. That has to be the most important."

How much help was it to you to have a receiver like Hirsch on the same team?

"It was helpful, no question about it. Not only that, we had a lot of backs who were all very mobile and fast. And all of them were good receivers, too. Guys like Vitamin T. Smith, Glenn Davis, Tommy Kalmanir. Basically, Hirsch was the deep threat and I was the short yardage specialist. But that can be exaggerated a bit. You know there's only four yards difference in our career averages. His is 18 something and mine was 14 something."

Are you pointing out you caught some bombs, too?

"What I'm saying is that it wasn't that simple. Elroy didn't just go long and I didn't just go short."

What kind of defenses were you seeing in those days?

"Mostly man-to-man, although several teams started specializing. What I mean by specializing is coming up with guys who exclusively played defensive halfback. Before that, a lot of players were going both ways. I can remember the Cards coming in with some very fast defensive backs. That, of course, made it tougher for those of us on offense."

Was the game rougher then?

"No, it wasn't rougher. But I honestly believe the players were more durable.

Did you get injured much?

"I was fortunate. I didn't have many injuries. I did hurt my knee in the latter part of my career and that about finished me up."

There were more famous "henchmen" back then. At least it seems that way. Do you agree?

"Yes, I think so. Guys like Ed Sprinkle with the Bears and Don Paul with the Rams were famous for that. The Bears always had their share of them, it seems. But I'll tell you the worst guy of them all. His name was Hardy Brown and he

Fears' great asset as a receiver was his quickness. Yet he ran pass patterns which today are assigned mostly to bigger, slower tight ends: the quick look-ins over the middle, where at any moment you might be belted by one of the linebackers. In Fears' day, the league had plenty of linebackers who liked nothing better than to do just that. Fortunately for him, one such man played on his own team—Don Paul (far left). Another great hitter in the early '50s was San Francisco's Hardy Brown (No. 33, left, pursuing Fears' receiving mate Elroy Hirsch).

played for the 49ers. He used to kill people. Really lay them out. There was nothing dirty about him. It was all perfectly legal. But he used to get guys all the time. He had this sort of explosive shoulder. When he cocked it and went out to get somebody, something usually happened. He put Otto Graham out one year, I remember. He used to knock somebody out of just about every game he played."

Were there any gimmicks that you used as a receiver?

"I used to put glue—or stickum—on my hands. Almost all backs and ends did. I think they still do. It was a case of just wanting a moist feeling on your hands. When you got tired, you ran out of spit. They put the stuff on their socks now, then touch down and feel it. I had a special pocket sewn on my pants around the middle of my thigh. I'd stick the stuff in there and went through a little ritual· so as never to give it away."

What was it like playing on the road then?

"I don't think you'd believe it. When we'd go on the road in those days it would be a three-week trip. Take Green Bay, for instance. Back then it was a kind of Siberia of football. Until Lombardi came along, of course, and after the glory years they had a long time ago. The threat would always be to watch out. You might get traded to Green Bay. When we played back there, they always nested you out somewhere away from everything. I remember Stevens Point in Wisconsin. It was some isolated place and you'd really get cabin fever. All there was to do was play cards. I tell you, fights would break out and everything else. Then there was Chicago. We used to stay at a hotel there that Abe Lincoln must have slept in. It had one of those elevators with one of those pull down things."

What about Kezar Stadium?

"We had some great games there. It was always sold out and there were always people scalping tickets in the hotels. The worst thing about Kezar was the dressing quarters. They weren't football dressing rooms. They were small, there was no place to hang your clothes and no air conditioning. Kezar, Franklin Field in Philly and Wrigley Field in Chicago. They were the three worst places to dress in, in that order. Today, the players have great conditions. Spacious dressing rooms, wall-to-wall carpets, ice water, excellent trainer's facilities. What a difference!"

Are you sorry you didn't play in this era?

"No. You can't ever look back. I enjoyed the game when we played it. I loved it, in fact."

Were you paid enough?

"Our salaries were fair because a lot of teams weren't making any money. Do you know that an established star back then was lucky to be drawing five figures. I don't think there was anyone in the league making $20,000 unless it was Otto Graham or someone like that. Today, there are guys on the taxi squad making that much. Besides, the benefits these players get today are fantastic. And they get paid for every damn thing beside. Everywhere they go, everything they do."

It sounds like it makes you mad. Does it?

"Only because I think today's players are selfish. The players who started all this and made all this possible, they don't get anything. I'm not talking about myself. I've always been able to get along. But I know some people who played in my time who are destitute today. They don't even have enough money to pay for operations they need. I met a former player not long ago in Las Vegas driving a cab. He had holes in his pants and looked like he hadn't eaten in days. That's a terrible thing. It all goes back to selfishness. These guys today want all of it for themselves. They don't care anything about the players who paved the way, who made all of this possible. I think it's a terrible thing."

Getting back to you and the Rams, which of your coaches made the biggest impression on you?

"I guess I've got to say Clark Shaughnessy. I think a lot of that had to do with the fact I'd just come up and was quite impressionable. Clark was a fine coach and a fine man. He was dedicated and he worked long, hard hours. If he had a fault, it was a tendency to work his players too long. He'd have these long meetings and long practices and a lot of the guys would lose interest. Clark had a very fertile mind. His teams had introduced many innovations. The man in motion . . . the three-receiver offense . . . advanced formations and variations. All of these things had to have a new language. He's come up with names like 'East Gee' or 'West Haw'— which came from a mule, or something. He had so many different names, he used to give prizes to anyone who could think of a good, relative name for one of his new ideas. He'd offer five bucks, or something like that. But really, he was the father of all these things. And I'm talking about defense as well as offense. A lot of the teams that use all those formations picked it up from Clark. The Bears still use it. George Allen picked it all up from him. So did Jim Dooley."

What did you think of Joe Stydahar and Hamp Pool?

"Joe was a real lovable guy. You wanted to do anything in the world to help him. He inspired you that way. Technically, his assistants did most of the coaching, which was a real good set-up and one that was ahead of its time. That's the way most teams handle it today. It was starting even then. A head coach suddenly had to wear so many different hats—priest, psychiatrist, doctor. You have to meet with the owners and talk over problems with the kids. More and more responsibilities have been delegated to the assistants."

Pool was a heady coach.

"He was a fine technician, a designer and architect of excellent plays. He prepared us for our games very well. If a team didn't change some things against us, we'd hit 'em in their weak spot and run up a big score."

Everyone agrees the Rams had tremendous talent in the early '50s. Why weren't they able to win more than one world title?

"I can't tell you. I think we should have won others."

Was it frustrating?

"Very. I remember one year, I think it was 1952, we had a playoff with Detroit. We're winning and it looks like we're going to make it a runaway when V.T. Smith hits me with a touchdown pass right before the half. But one of our linemen was penalized for holding. Then Bobby Layne hits Cloyce Box with a long touchdown pass. Now that's a 14 point difference in a matter of a minute and a half. That gave them the impetus. And we lost our lead and finally we got beat. Detroit went on to smash Cleveland in the world championship game that year. We had somewhat of a lull in '53 and '54. In 1955 we played for the championship again. But we didn't have the same kind of team then."

During this period, were you aware of the way pro football was growing in popularity?

"I'll say. I guess I was always very promotion minded. I can remember taking a projector, a screen and films with me to give talks around the Los Angeles area. You know how much we got paid for one of those nights? $10. Today, kids won't even consider going anywhere for less than $100. Anyway, I used to bug the Ram management and try to tell them that pro football was missing the boat. We weren't glamourizing the sport enough. For instance, we had movie stars in the stands, we had big, handsome guys playing the game. We weren't taking proper advantage of it. I used to see baseball films and although the sport was much less conducive to action, they handled it much better. Today, NFL

Fears pursued an active career as an NFL coach after his retirement from the playing field in 1956. After two years as a Rams' assistant to his former teammate, Bob Waterfield, he moved to the Green Bay staff of Vince Lombardi (left). Later, he spent three years as the first head coach of the New Orleans Saints.

Films does a tremendous job. But I could see the possibilities back even then."

Do you regret not being able to play today?

"I was very happy with my era, overall. It certainly was better than the one right before that when guys got paid 75 or 100 bucks a game. Even some of my contemporaries didn't have it as good as I did. A lot of them were playing for shaky organizations and they never knew from one week to the next if they were going to get their checks. I was fortunate to be with a good organization."

Who were some of the great characters you remember with the Rams?

"Where do I start? One that comes to mind immediately is Milan Lazetich, a guard from Michigan. He was not a man who went for any kind of training. He misused and mistreated his body terribly. He was always kind of tired and everyone always knew why. I remember Shaughnessy would give him the awful job of counting all the plays. And there were a lot of them under Clark. Laz would always be cheating on the calls. It used to break everyone up."

Who else stands out in your mind?

"Dick Huffman. Everyone called him Huff. He'd have been a great guard by today's standards. He weighed in excess of 260 pounds and he had great quickness. He was just a big, mean guy. He was one of the last of the great two-way players. He'd come in late on defense and shout across the line of scrimmage: "Come on in, girls." I remember one particular day in Pittsburgh. It was a muddy, muddy game and Huff had been wrestling in it all day. Then, afterward, they told him one of his sons had died. I can still picture that scene. Huff sitting in a corner and all you could see was the white of his eyes. The rest of him was all mud. And he just sat there with his head down, the picture of dejection. It was the kind of thing you just don't forget."

Who else?

"Well, the present general manager of the Rams is Don Klosterman, and he and I were roommates when he came to the club. Someone stuck the nickname 'Chicken Little' on him, and Klosty hated it. Just hated it. After all, he was the 'Duke of Del Rey' in his college days at Loyola in L.A. Anyway, the guys used to leave eggs in his dressing room stall and start cackling whenever he came in. It was really starting to drive Don nuts. One night, I was up almost the whole time convincing him that nicknames can really help a football player. Take Bulldog Turner, for instance. Or Crazylegs Hirsch. Anyway I thought I finally made him see it differently. Then we went to sleep. The first thing he said when he got up in the morning was, 'I still don't like Chicken Little.' I think I laughed for two days."

What about parties? You must have had some wild parties in L.A. then?

"No wilder than any others. Parties are parties. They're the same everywhere. I do remember one particular party we had at Dan Reeves' home, though. Everybody got to feeling pretty good and one of Dan's cooks had baked this giant cake the size of a football field. I mean, it was big! It had markers and stripes and in the middle there was this huge chocolate football. Someone asked Lazetich how far he thought he could kick the ball. Well, you know what happened next. He took the ball off and kicked it and the next morning, besides having football players asleep in the bathtubs and closets and everywhere else, there was chocolate in every corner of that damn house. Funny thing, but that was the last party we ever had at Dan Reeves' home."

Elroy Hirsch

Position: Wide receiver
Years played: 1949-57
Height: 6 feet, 2 inches
Weight: 190
College: Wisconsin

They called him "Crazylegs" because he had this funny, little waddle when he ran downfield. But there was nothing funny about the result.

Elroy Hirsch is regarded as one of the best pass receivers in the history of professional football. On the NFL's all-time, all-pro team, it was Hirsch and Don Hutson who were picked as the wide receivers. Elroy, perhaps more than any other player, was responsible for "The Bomb," the long pass that turned pro football into the exciting sport it is today. In 1951, Hirsch caught 17 touchdown passes in 12 games. The average length of each touchdown was 50 yards. He had an uncanny knack for catching a ball thrown over his head. The timing and the hands were unmatched. The speed was 4.4 seconds for 40 yards. Combine his talents with two of football's greatest passers—Bob Waterfield and Norm Van Brocklin—and you get an idea of what the opposition was up against back in the '50s. Hirsch retired after the 1957 season and is presently the athletic director at the University of Wisconsin.

Looking back now, what do you remember most about your years with the Rams?

"I think that basically they were my happiest years in football by far. We had a great gang of guys who thoroughly enjoyed playing football. I know it sounds corny, but these guys weren't as interested in money as much as the players are today. I'm sure if we played today, though, we'd all be just as interested in salaries and such."

You sound like you're a little jealous. Are you?

"I'm envious. But not jealous."

How much has the game changed since those days?

"Well, first there's the size of the players. They're much bigger and quicker now. The defenses are also lot more complex. But I don't really think the offenses have changed that much."

What kind of defenses did you see in the '50s?

"Oh, mainly 6-1, 5-2 or 5-3 sets. There were no complicated zones, bump and run or any of those things. When I first got to the Rams, it was a daring move to rush a linebacker. If you did it, everyone made a big thing of it. Today, defensive linemen are so much bigger and stronger, you can take a man off the line and not be hurt as much. Four people up front is a lot different than five or six."

Through the years, the Rams always had a "Hollywood" image. They were called playboys by various people around the league. The impression was they enjoyed themselves so much off the field they could never realize their potential on it. Was any of it true?

"As far as I knew, none of it was justified. I think much of it started when Waterfield married Jane Russell, the glamorous movie star. That was rather unusual, and the press made a big thing of it. But really it was our style that got people mad, I think. We were able to score so easily, while others had to slug it out. We had a tremendous passing offense—with Waterfield and Van Brocklin—and we were fortified with outstanding runners. The two meshed together so well that no one could defense us."

Who were the dominant figures on those great Ram teams?

"I guess you'd have to say Waterfield and Van Brocklin. You couldn't find two better throwers or two better minds for the game. They kind of complemented each other. Bob usually started and he'd come in and sort of probe the defense and set things up. He'd get the winning flow started. Many times, he'd set it up so well that Norm would come in and within three plays throw the bomb.

Still, they were two great football players competing for the same position. Was there any animosity between them?

"Well, there was great competition, I'll say

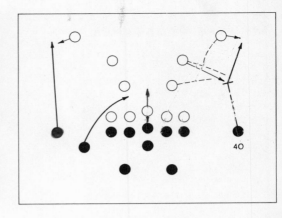

that. But I think most of the ill feeling was generated more by the press than anything else. I won't say they were great social buddies or anything. But no animosity ever came up in front of the team. I know both were unhappy when not playing, but that's only natural. Really, it was a great situation for the Rams. Waterfield was extremely quiet, kept to himself most of the time. He had very few really close friends. But if you needed something, he was always there, always willing to talk things out and help you if you needed help. He was the real level head on the club. I remember once we were dividing up playoff money and there was a move to cut out the trainers and equipment men. Well, Bob stood up and talked in that quiet way of his and put an end to that stuff right away. Van Brocklin was a more sensational type. He wanted to score right now. When he got in a game, he didn't want to fool around. Off the field, he was more of a fun lover, he socialized with more people, hung around with the guys more. When he became No. 1 after Waterfield retired in '52, Norm changed a lot, I think. He wasn't as carefree. He became more serious. He wasn't the Gary Good Guy he was in the previous four years. But he was still a fun lover and still worked as hard as anyone in practice. Together, they were really quite a pair. I feel fortunate to have come along at the same time."

Who's the greatest football player you've ever seen?

"You don't ask any easy questions, do you? Well, you have to break it down a little. For instance, the best runner was probably Hugh McElhenny of the 49ers. The best passer, I'd have to say Sonny Jurgensen, although Van Brocklin actually had a stronger arm. Sonny was the most accurate. But if you're talking about all-around football player, I have to say Waterfield. Do you realize he used to cover Don Hutson man-for-man? He also kicked off

into the end zone, did our placekicking, was a good runner and a fine short and long passer. He played hurt and although he wasn't blessed with great speed, he had a good running instinct. He just did it all."

Which coach did you respect most with the Rams?

"I'd have to say two. Clark Shaughnessy and Hamp Pool. They were two completely different types. Shaughnessy was more like a father. He'd always put an arm around you and talk gently. But I think he tried to teach too many plays and formations. It was difficult to absorb them all. Pool liked to play wide open like Shaughnessy, but Hamp had more of a game plan. More of a ready list, you might say, on offense. He was a very tough man, from the old school. I can honestly say I didn't realize how good a coach Pool was until I got out of football. He stressed conditioning. He was a tremendous conditioner. He wasn't trying to be popular. That's just the way he chose to coach."

Was Los Angeles a particularly tough town to coach in?

"I think so. It was so competitive. First of all, USC and UCLA make it tough. Then there was the press. We had a lot of newspapers in those days. Those guys were always trying to dig up some new, sensational story. Then, of course, it is tougher to keep track of players in a town like Los Angeles. It's not Green Bay. There are a lot more distractions."

You were a running back in college. How and when did you convert to a wide receiver?

"Well, in 1949 I was still a running back with the Rams when Shaughnessy put in these new spread formations. Many times I was flanked out and was thrown to quite a bit. Still, in 1950 I spent all preseason at halfback. Then someone got hurt—I think it was Jack Zilly—and in the season opener against the Bears in L.A., they put me in at right end. I got about a five-year

With Elroy Hirsch and Norm Van Brocklin, the term "bomb" entered the language of football. Elroy had the ability to catch a ball over his shoulder at full speed without breaking a stride (far left). To stop it, opponents tried many measures (left). Sometimes they worked, sometimes they didn't. Hirsch caught 53 touchdown passes, 17 in one amazing season—1951. He was at his best going all-out, so it was a little disconcerting to Elroy when Sid Gillman drew up precise patterns for him to run.

education in 60 minutes. I was held by the linebacker, tripped by the tackle, clipped by the cornerback, knocked off my feet almost constantly. Even though I think I caught a touchdown pass later on, I played an awful game and we lost. But I learned a lot. After that, the position seemed to be easy for me."

How about the nickname? Where and when did you get it?

"There are two stories. One segment claims it was a sports writer named Francis Powers in Chicago who wrote it first. Another that it was Stoney McGlynn in Milwaukee. I really think it was Powers. Whatever, I certainly didn't mind it. In fact, I think it helped.

Did the progress come quickly at wide receiver? Or was it a tough adjustment?

"I could always catch the ball. That part was easy. The toughest thing for me was getting free at the line of scrimmage. That and my blocking. I will not go down in football history for my blocking."

No one else utilized the deep pattern—or "The Bomb," as it's become known—as you did in those days. How did it come about?

"Well, I always had a natural knack for catching the ball that was coming over my head. That's a tough catch for a lot of people. It wasn't for me. So we began practicing it at training camp. It got to be like a contest. Could I outrun the quarterback's arm? Bob and Norm would throw the ball awfully high and I'd run under it. We just happened to have two guys who could throw the hell out of the ball. Then, Red Hickey was our end coach. He taught me fakes. And the two together just seemed to work out. Pretty soon, it seemed like an awfully easy way to score."

It couldn't have been quite that easy, could it?

"Well, the makeup of the rest of our offense had a lot to do with it. We had a tremendous set of running backs—guys like Tank Younger, Dan Towler, Dick Hoerner, Glenn Davis, V.T. Smith —so if they waited for the pass, we'd run them to death. Then we had Tom Fears playing the other end. There was no finer end in football when it came to running the buttonhook and sideline patterns. And he had deceiving speed. I think we all kind of complemented each other."

Would your offense still be as effective in today's more specialized game?

"I think so. In fact, I'm sure it would. One of our Ram teams still has the all-time passing yardage record for a game. And I still hold one record for yardage in a season. If it's broken, I'm going to demand an asterisk. We played 12-game seasons back then. Not 14 games."

Could you have done this much damage against a zone?

"Maybe not me personally. But I think our team could have. Offense is still a matter of personnel. And we had tremendous personnel. We had the balance it takes to move the ball consistently. We were able to take what the defense gave us. And with all our talent, they had to give us something. It would be the same today. If the zone stopped our long passing attack, we'd still be able to run like hell. The game doesn't change that much."

Just how fast were you in your prime?

"I ran a 4.4 40-yard dash. I was always able to get off the line quick. Once I got further down field, I started to wobble. That's where the nickname came in. My left foot points out farther than my right even when I walk. I guess it does look kind of funny. But, really, football is a game of short dashes. The only time you run 100 yards is when they introduce you before the game."

How many patterns did you run then?

"I never ran any patterns, as such, until Sid Gillman became our coach. Before Sid, it was all mostly individual stuff. They'd just call wide post and they knew where I'd end up. The moves

were up to me. Under Sid, I had more trouble. He wanted the patterns precise and he wanted them called by number. So all of a sudden, they'd call the blocking formation and then say 92. It was really a tough thing for me to adjust to. I'm not sure I ever really did."

After your great success in 1951, for example, what were opposing defenses doing to try to stop you?

"Mostly, they'd work me over at the line. They'd either rotate their defensive backs or put one deep and one nose up on me at the line of scrimmage. That was okay, though, because when they did that, it left a wide open situation on the other side. After awhile, they started shifting linebackers over to bother me. But even that helped us. We ran a lot better with that linebacker out of there."

Players in that era had a great reputation for being dirty. Ed Sprinkle of the Bears was one. How much of it was fact and how much fiction?

"I know Sprinkle was attributed to be a dirty player. But I can't say he was from personal experience. He never made an overt act toward me. A lot of the less publicized players were rougher than anyone realized. The late Gene Lipscomb is one who comes to mind. He was a lot tougher than Sprinkle."

What about playing conditions? What were they like?

"As a whole, they were good. But there were some tough places to play. I guess Wrigley Field was the worst. You name it, and it happened to the Rams at Wrigley Field. Late in the season at Wrigley, you'd be in a huddle by the end zone and everyone in the second deck would be throwing snowballs or ice down on you. Our punters would be practicing before the game and people would run out and steal the footballs. After about 20 minutes, we'd actually run out of footballs. It got so, when we had to play a game in Chicago, we just figured that when we started

the game we were behind by fourteen points."

Were the Bears your fiercest rivals?

"Not really. I think the 49ers were. Our series with them was something. It seems like every game was real tense. You could throw form out of the book. Basically, I think we were the superior team, but when we played them up there, we only won about 50 percent of the time. We always had trouble at old Kezar Stadium. I remember the low point up there. We walked off the field at half leading something like 20-7. We were still ahead by a point or so with two minutes to go and they were 80 yards away from the end zone. They threw a screen to McElhenny and he went about 70 yards. Then Gordy Soltau kicked into the bright sun. We swear the field goal missed by three feet but the official couldn't see because of the sun. He called it good. Oh, how that one hurt. You have no idea."

What about the loss to the Browns in the 1950 championship game?

"That was even worse. That was the low point of my life. Those Brown teams of that era were so great. They had tremendous personnel and Paul Brown had them extremely well organized. Otto Graham was a great passer who could scramble. They had excellent ends and Marion Motley was a terrific power runner. But it was a very simple offense. They just executed perfectly. They were a lot like the Vince Lombardi Packer teams. I honestly think they'd still be a great team today. Anyway, here we were beating them for the championship. Then, in the last 19 seconds, Lou Groza kicks a field goal to beat us. After we had led the whole ballgame. It took me an entire year to get over that one. It wasn't until the last play of the championship game in 1951 that I felt better."

What happened on the last play?

"Well, we had gone ahead in the fourth quarter when Fears ran a helluva pattern and Van

Brocklin hit him right on the button with a bomb. With a minute and a half or two minutes to play, we were hanging onto the lead and Cleveland got the ball back. They put me in as an extra safety man and on the final play of the game, they threw a long pass. Two or three of us went up and we were able to bat the ball down. Then the gun went off. I couldn't believe it. We were world champions."

Yet, that was the only time the Rams won the championship. With so much talent and personnel, why weren't they able to build a Packer or Brown-type dynasty?

"We were close to it. From '49 through '55, we either won our division every year or finished right up there. The Browns were part of it, of course. They had a great team the same time we did and maybe they had a little better balance. If we lacked any one thing in all those years, it was a super tough defense. But then, the emphasis wasn't on defense in those days. The goal was to outscore everybody. And we usually did."

What was your greatest thrill in football?

"You're not going to believe this, but it was being introduced before the College All-Star Game in 1946. I was scared to death and we were playing against the Rams. They darken the whole stadium and two spotlights come out on you. You run out of the tunnel by yourself and between the posts, you look up toward the open end and you see this huge American flag they had stretched out there. Boy, that was a thrill. I'm telling you, it was something. The fact that we won the game 16-0 in a great upset and I was voted most valuable player only added to the evening. But still, that introduction remains the biggest thing. It's just something you never forget."

You always wore No. 40. What was its significance?

"It was issued to me at Wisconsin in 1941 and

I just always kept it. I wore it at Michigan and when I was in the service I asked for it. When I joined the old Chicago Rockets, their numbers went from 80 to 100 and something, so I had the equipment man sew No. 40 on the inside. Not that I was superstitious, or anything."

You retired twice. What made you come back after the first one?

"I quit after the 1954 season. I hadn't had a good year, although I felt good physically. I was going to make a movie that year and I had this television job working, something waiting for me to go into. Anyway, the club really experienced some injuries that season. I think Skeet Quinlan, the No. 1 flanker, was hurt in the final preseason game. Tex Schramm called me and asked me to come back. I was glad I did. We won the title, even though I didn't have what I felt was a real good year. I went on to play 1956 and 1957 and then I hung it up for good."

What about your movie career?

"It was a good experience. Naturally, I liked the football film best. The others were hard work. I still get kidded a lot about it, but it's something I can look back on and it was an exposure to a completely different atmosphere. People come up to me and say 'I saw your movie on TV last night and it stunk.' You know what I say to them? I say, 'Oh yeah? How many pictures did you make?' It makes me feel better, anyway."

Perhaps the most important single person in the development of the Los Angeles Rams was Dan Reeves. What was your opinion of him?

"He was probably, all-around, the finest man I've ever known. I worked 10 years in the front office without ever signing a contract. We just had a handshake agreement. He had never been known to break his word. And I mean never. He probably had faults just like anyone else. But he was like a father, a consultant and an

His duties as athletic director at the University of Wisconsin keep Hirsch so involved on football weekends that he rarely sees a professional game in person. He's an avid television fan, however. He still retains the robust good looks that made him an idol of fans in the '50s.

employer all in one. Honestly, I just don't have the proper vocabulary to describe the guy."

Why, then, would you leave the Rams and Reeves to accept a job as athletic director at the University of Wisconsin?

"Well, I'd kinda gone as far as I could go with the Rams. All the major decisions pertaining to the club were up to Dan, which is the way it should be. I came to Wisconsin for the interview with sort of a negative attitude. I didn't think I'd ever take it. Then I saw the problems, a lot of people talked to me and I got caught up in the thing. When I went back to see Dan, all he wanted to know was one thing: What's it going to take to keep you here? I told him it wasn't a matter of money. Then he sat down with me and listened and I told him all about it. When we were finished, he said, 'You know, I think it would really be a good thing for you.' And it has been. We've got 50 problems a day here. But I'm involved."

Do you miss living in a big town?

"Not really. We thoroughly enjoy a town this size. It's very active. Something's always going on. We've got two beautiful lakes. We have a boat on one of the lakes and my daughter has her own horse. We really have a wonderful life here."

Do you still watch pro football?

"Never miss a game on Sunday or Monday. Television allows me to keep up. I haven't seen a pro game live in three years. It just seems like my schedule is too tight to make it over to Green Bay or Chicago in just one day. During football season, my job is a six-day thing. When that day off comes, you don't feel like leaving the house."

Looking back, do you feel there is anything in pro football you've missed?

"Yes."

What was that?

"The pension."

Don Paul

Position: Linebacker
Years played: 1948-55
Height: 6 feet, 1 inch
Weight. 230
College: UCLA

In an era when glamour quarterbacks and fleet wide receivers dominated, Don Paul was an exception. He was a Los Angeles Rams star on defense. A brutal linebacker who was flattening ballcarriers before anyone had ever heard of Dick Butkus. Paul led the unit that might have been the first defense ever to receive a standing ovation. Anywhere. In 1954, Detroit's Leon Hart paid Paul what Don still considers one of his greatest compliments. "Don Paul," said Hart, "is the dirtiest player in the league." The Ram season ticket holders didn't see him that way. They were infatuated with him and showed their appreciation in 1954, when they honored him and Elroy Hirsch in a special on-field ceremony. They presented him with a new car, and, to this day, Don Paul says that tribute was "one of the greatest things that ever happened to me." Paul, 48, is owner of a restaurant in the San Fernando Valley and does the color on the taped telecasts of Ram home games.

Even today, you are still remembered as one of the roughest and/or dirtiest players in the history of pro football. Did you deserve such a distinctive label?

"I've relished what Leon Hart said all my life. But I always felt there was a great deal of difference between being dirty and being rough. For instance, in all my years in football I never bit anybody. But I was bitten."

You mean actually bitten by another player?

"Certainly."

Is that the worst thing that ever happened to you?

"No."

What was?

"Once I had my helmet ripped off and then was hit over the head with it. Can you imagine that? My own helmet."

Who did it?

"I'd rather not mention names. But the guy is now a good friend of mine. In fact, we get to-gether, talk and laugh about it all the time."

Did you wear a face mask in those days?

"As far as I know, I started the trend toward face masks. What happened was that Bill Granholm, our equipment man at the time, made me one of those special bird cage things when I suffered a broken jaw. Then, in 1949, Joe Stydahar demanded that everyone wear a mask."

You were noted for your, uh, unorthodox tactics. What were some of them?

"What I tried to do was use them as gamesmanship. Many times, I was physically incapable of doing something. So I had to try something else."

For instance?

"Well, if a halfback comes up the field faking like he has the ball, you can just lay him out. Then when he does have the ball you give him something to think about. It was the same way with receivers. You laid a guy out, it gave you a better chance the next time if the guy turned out to be a timid soul."

So you still claim you weren't that dirty?

"Yes. There were guys like Gil Mains in Detroit. He'd come into you on a kickoff feet first. Other guys without my reputation did things that I'd never think of doing. I wouldn't have stooped so low. But I got tagged as a dirty player and that's the way people thought of me. To be honest, I really didn't mind it that much."

Was the game actually rougher then?

"That's awfully hard for someone who isn't playing today to say. But from what I can see, it's about the same. We had big, strong, fast, hard-hitting gorillas just like they do today."

What other players around the league were known as being unusually rough or dirty?

"Well, Ed Sprinkle was one, of course. He had such fantastic manueverability, he could get around a quarterback, and he loved to hook them with one arm. It was perfectly legal, too. Ed was about 210 pounds and he could really move. He

117

also had tremendous determination. The funny thing is, Ed is maybe one of the kindest souls in the world. You ever met him? He's quite a guy. You'd never pick him out in a crowd. You'd never know that he had that kind of reputation as a player."

You sound like you have kept in close contact with several players of your era. Have you?

"Oh yes. That's the great thing about football in our era. There was a tremendous bond among all guys from all the teams that played back then. There weren't that many of us. So today, you can run into someone who had been your most violent opponent, and you sit down and buy each other a couple drinks and have a great, old time. And then, of course, the associations and memories collected with the Rams will never be forgotten by any of us."

I guess there is no need to ask you where you got the idea for the name of your San Fernado Valley restaurant, "The Rams' Horn," is there?"

"It is rather obvious, isn't it?"

What did playing for the Rams mean to you?

"Those are the fondest memories I have. I've always felt very lucky to have even had the opportunity. Listen, there were only 12 teams back then with 36 players on a team. It wasn't easy to make one of those clubs. I remember thinking my first year or two how nice it was that I wouldn't have to worry about running out of eligibility like I did in high school and college. As it turns out, I was wrong. Old age made up for it and finally caught me."

Still, by today's standards you retired young, didn't you?

"I was 30."

They would consider you in your prime now, wouldn't they?

"I don't know. Things were different then. I had put in eight years, and most of that time was on the actual field. I was among the leaders in the league in longevity. In my eighth year I

knew I had to get something going quick and I was fortunate enough to get a business started. There was this nice contract sitting on my desk, waiting to be signed. So I signed it. I don't regret the decision. I regret only that I didn't start a year earlier with the Rams. If I'd have known how much fun it was, I would have gone in as a junior. I was drafted No. 2 as a future, you know."

What was the best Ram team you ever played on?

"This will surprise you. Most people expect you to say the 1951 club that won the world championship. Well, that was a good team. But my own personal favorite was the 1952 team. We stumbled at the start and lost 3 of our first 4 games, as well as our coach. The guys got together after that and vowed to win eight straight and we did, ending up in the playoffs, only to lose a real tough game to Detroit."

Was that the year the defense took charge?

"Well, that was the first year the defense began to get cheered. I think we broke the league record for interceptions. Night Train Lane had something like 14 all by himself. But those standing ovations were something. It was quite a thrill for us nuts and bolts and broken nose guys."

Defenses were generally accepted to be much simpler then than they are today. Was this team different?

"I think it was. I know they say the defenses in the '50s were less sophisticated. But a lot of the teams would come out in five, six or seven different types of coverage. We had different lineups and shifted around a lot. Sure, there were teams that got in the old 5-4 and just stayed in there. But much of the defenses were not as simple as some people like to think."

Can you elaborate?

"Well, take the zone, for example. I get a great kick out of the way people have been ooh-

ing and ahhing about the zone the past few years. Heck, I watched the Oakland Raiders playing Baltimore, I think it was, in the playoffs last year and there was Daryle Lamonica having all sorts of trouble with the zone. Finally, when the game already was lost, they put in George Blanda, a guy who's been around for over 20 years, and he promptly picks the zone apart. You know why? Because we were playing zone defenses back when Blanda was a young quarterback. He learned how to beat them then and he hasn't forgotten. Zones were all we used to combat the bomb. Teams started getting killed by long passes when they were covering man-to-man, so they had to do something. What they did was go to the zone. The difference today—maybe the only difference—is that now everyone is using zones and complicated coverages. Back then, not all teams were going with it. But the stuff you see being used today is hardly brand new."

You sound like one of those former players who refuses to admit that athletes are better today. Is that the way you feel?

"No. All teams have great athletes today. They're bigger, stronger and faster. They're everything but hungrier, and that's not their fault. It's because of what has happened in our world. I was a lot hungrier than my kid is today. But I can't complain about it, because that's what I'm working for. I can't tell my kid he can't swim in our swimming pool because I didn't have a pool when I was a kid. The lack of hunger is just a sign of the times. Otherwise, I'm the first to admit how much better today's athletes are."

Who were some of the best athletes of your era? For instance, who was the best blocker you ever played against?

"Tex Coulter, the guy from Army. He was easily the best lineman I ever faced."

What about runners? Who was the toughest guy to tackle?

"I have to list two. Steve Van Buren and Hugh

Paul roamed the field from sideline to sideline, and when
he made a tackle, it was usually one the runner would
remember. At left, he runs down Bill Osmanski of the
New York Bulldogs. Don played under five Rams' head
coaches. The most astute of the five? Hamp Pool, he
says, who used techniques which other head coaches in
football did not adopt until years later.

McElhenny. Van Buren was a great one. But McElhenny, he was something else. He could put chills down your spine when you saw him coming at you.''

What made McElhenny such a great runner?

"Well, to begin with, he was a hurdles champion in high school. And besides his natural speed and gait, he had what was probably the finest coordination and balance of any back I've ever seen. He was a threat anytime he touched the ball, running from scrimmage, handling kicks or catching passes. He could score from anywhere. I'd say the only player of recent years who could compare with him would have been Gale Sayers. Except that McElhenny wasn't hurt as often as Sayers.''

What about the great players on your own team? Let's talk about some of the Rams. Bob Waterfield, for instance. How good was he?

"The only word you can use to describe him is fantastic. He was some kind of athlete. He could play baseball, basketball, football, any sport. You know he did the best defensive job ever on Don Hutson? He was the only rookie ever to take a team to a pro championship when he did it with the old Cleveland Rams. I go way back with Bob. I played on his team in an East-West game when he was a single wing tailback. Naturally, his team won the game.''

What about Van Brocklin?

"Along with Otto Graham, he was the best pure passer I ever played with or against.''

He was and still is a controversial man. How would you categorize his personality?

"He's one of the nicest guys who ever walked the earth. Really, he has a heart as good as gold. It's just that he's spent 47 years hiding it. He gives that bad guy impression on purpose. There's no more honest man in the world. He never lies, never tries to hide an emotion and maybe that gets him in trouble some time. But you can't ask anyone to be more straightforward

or more honest with you than Van Brocklin is.''

What do you remember about Elroy Hirsch?

"He was one of the guys who really wanted to play. He'd play today if he thought he could get away with it. You know, he came to camp in 1949 as a three-time All America halfback and had to sit it out. Then they watched him in 1950 and one day they walked up and asked him how he would like to play end. He jumped straight up in the air and said, 'Which one?' Now no one remembers him as a halfback, anymore. I remember those fantastic hands, the good, gliding moves and those catches. Even today those catches would be tremendous to see. If you ever put together one big highlight film on Elroy, you wouldn't believe it. Off the field, I never knew anyone who didn't like Elroy. He was a real fun guy.''

How about Tom Fears?

"If Fears had played defense, he'd have had my kind of reputation. They would have called him dirty. He was a squirmer who kicked and scratched and crawled for every inch. He could catch the short pass, he could block or he could go deep. We were co-captains at UCLA together. As a guy, he was much more serious and intense than Elroy. He liked to have fun. But he wasn't the gregarious type.''

Almost all players of your era speak fondly of Dan Reeves. You gave the eulogy at his funeral and were obviously very close to the man. What about him do you remember most vividly?

"I've never met a finer gentleman than Dan Reeves. If I were to make a list of people of integrity, his name would be at the top of the list. I think what people tend to forget is all that the man contributed to the game of pro football. No one came up with more new ideas. For instance, he was the originator of the great scouting system that brought in more and more top players for the Rams to look at. We always seemed to draft more people and make more trades than anyone else. It was a big part of the season we had so much talent. Then take something like his free football for kids program. I think he started that back in 1947, or something. It's still going today. How many of those kids do you think have grown up and are season ticket holders today?"

Did the Ram organization change after Reeves became sick and couldn't spend as much time with the team?

"Well, being only an announcer and not working full-time with the club, I wouldn't know for sure. But I could never see where the organization changed. Maybe Dan didn't have as much impact as when he could work 12 to 15 hours a day with the team. But he trained the people and made them learn his system. Even when he became seriously ill and had to be in a New York clinic as an out-patient, the club was still run à la Reeves."

Who among the coaches was your favorite?

"In my eight years in pro ball, I served under five head coaches and it seems like 200 assistants. To me, the most astute of them all was Hamp Pool. He was the best technical coach I ever ran across. He had charts broken down in those days that some teams are just starting to use today. Everyone likes to talk about how hard head coaches work today. Let me tell you, no one ever worked any harder than Hamp and those on his staff."

In your opinion, what is the toughest position to play in football?

"I have to go along with the majority and vote for quarterback. It's certainly the toughest position to learn. After that, I'd say defensive cornerback. You have an awful lot of responsibility at that spot."

For most of your career you played outside linebacker, didn't you?

"I played what you would now call outside linebacker, yes. Until the end of my career.

Then I moved over to middle linebacker."

Did you like the middle better?

"I'll say. I never had so much fun in my life. I only wished they had gone to the 4-3 defense sooner."

What made it more fun for you?

"You're always right where the action is. It's almost as if you should be benched if you don't make 70 percent of all the tackles. The whole thing is set up for some big gorilla to get in there and do all the cleanup work. If you'll notice, the middle linebackers are all about the same size. They're 6-1 or 6-2 and weigh anywhere from 220 to 240 pounds. That hasn't changed much sizewise. Look around now. Who are the linebackers who receive most of the publicity? Guys like Willie Lanier of Kansas City, Dick Butkus of Chicago, Mike Curtis of Baltimore and so on. That hasn't changed, either. The middle 'backer has been the glamour guy ever since they switched to the 4-3. Sam Huff of the Giants started all that. Then there was Bill George of the Bears, Joe Schmidt of the Lions and all kinds of guys after that. Really, it's a great position to play. I'd only wished I could have been moved there six or seven years sooner."

What are the Ram games you rank among your most memorable?

"Well, naturally, you have to begin with the 1951 game. I'll always remember that Van Brocklin to Fears pass because it won the ball game and brought us our first world championship. I also remember Groza trying a long, long field goal in that game. I remember I was laughing so hard it was difficult to call the defensive signal. And then he went and put the ball right through the uprights."

What about the championship game the year before?

"Please, don't mention it. That's one we never should have lost. We gave up two touchdowns after we'd already had the game under control.

Leon Hart, the man who made Don Paul famous when Hart called him a "dirty player" in a magazine article. In eight years in the NFL, Paul made some enemies . . . and he left a lot of memories at the Coliseum. Later, he was a Rams' assistant coach and a TV broadcaster. "Football is something special to me," he says.

On the first play of the game Waterfield hit Glenn Davis for an 80-yard touchdown. We had that play called for two weeks. I guess I never really forgot that game. The next year I was so ready to play Cleveland you couldn't believe it."

Was that the highest you've ever been for a football game?

"No. I was more up for my last game. That old stuff about getting old and just going out and doing a job is a lot of crap. That's for guys who don't like to play. I got up more for each game I played. I was much more emotional my last year in the league than I was my first.

Are there players around today who feel the same way about the game?

"I'm sure there are."

As many as you had then?

"That I couldn't tell you."

Do you think today's players are overpaid?

"No, I don't begrudge them their salaries. At least I don't begrudge those who deserve them. I want to emphasize that word—deserve. I don't think a guy should automatically get $50,000 or $60,000 coming right out of the draft. I think he should have to prove his worth. He's certainly going to have to prove it when he leaves football."

Was there anything in the game you feel you missed?

"I don't know what. I was in four world championship games, three playoffs, two East-West games, a Rose Bowl and two Pro Bowls."

Is there a way to describe what it really meant to you?

"No, I don't think so. The way I'm talking to you now, you just can't talk to other people like that. Unless it's another ex-player, you know the guy won't understand. I don't even bother trying to tell them anymore. Football is something special to me. Very special. It's also very personal. And it's something that will always be that way."

Hamp Pool

Position: Head coach
Years coached: 1952-54
Height: 6 feet, 3 inches
Weight: 225
College: Stanford

Hampton Pool coached the Los Angeles Rams for three years. They were three good years. Although the team finished a notch lower each season, beginning with second place in 1952, the interest in the club was climbing to new heights. Pool's teams were exciting and colorful and Los Angeles adopted the Rams the way they had USC and UCLA in earlier eras. The Coliseum became the mecca where pro football fans came to worship and, yes, it was also where they came to boo. Hampton Pool was an innovator, an offensive genius who might have been several years ahead of his time. The theories that were laughed at then are being utilized now. And Hampton Pool smiles and sighs. He is now 58, the director of QUADRA, a scouting service that serves Dallas, San Francisco, Los Angeles and San Diego. He sits behind a desk and does paper work, but he enjoys it because he is still involved with the game he loves.

How would you describe the football team you coached for three years in Los Angeles?

"It was a very good team. A team gifted with a great deal of talent. We had excellent passers, excellent receivers and outstanding ballcarriers, in my opinion. I think the records, at least offensively, bear that out."

How did it happen that all of this came together on one team?

"I think it was a result of the farsighted scouting program we had under Dan Reeves. You see, we were doing it long before other teams. The Rams, at the time, were way ahead in the number of scouts working on the road. Reeves was the first to put full-time scouts to work. This gave us a tremendous advantage. It allowed us to create a backlog of talent that enabled us to trade for even more draft choices. Year after year we went into the National Football League draft with higher choices than anyone else in the league. Consequently, we were able to look for more blue chip players than anyone else. Once you get your talent to a certain level in pro football, the procedure more or less snowballs. You can parlay your choices for talent and vice versa. Dan Reeves really got a kick out of the scouting end of our business. In fact, I think that's where he got most of his thrills in football. He really enjoyed it. It was something he spent a great deal of time working on. He realized its importance and he realized it sooner than anyone else in the game."

What did you think of Dan Reeves?

"It's awfully hard for me to describe all my feelings. We were very close friends. I have an extremely high regard for him personally. I not only think he was way ahead of his time in pro football, but I respected him because he was one who never at any time interfered with the technical end of the game. I can never recall him having a negative word to say to anyone connected with the football end of it."

You were noted as one of the game's great innovators. For instance, you were the first coach to install the three end offense that today has become the basic pro set. How did you come up with that one?

"Well, really Clark Shaughnessy was the first coach to split his receivers out in the late '40s. What I did really was make a running back into a flanker. Before that, they often would send him into motion and utilize him as a receiver. But we put him out there from the beginning. I guess what made me do it was our personnel. It seemed made for it. We had a bunch of guys who were equally adept catching the ball as they were running with it. People like Glenn Davis, Tommy Kalmanir and Vitamin T. Smith."

You were also one of the first, if not *the* first, to come out in a zone defense. How did an offensive oriented guy decide to start zoning?

"Easy. Our success with our offense made most of the teams in the league go to the same thing. So now we had to figure out a way to

125

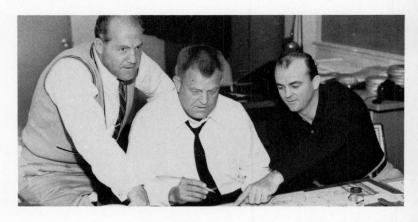

stop it. We had to find a method to combat the bomb. Everybody had been covering strictly man-to-man and that's what made our offense so effective. You couldn't stop our receivers with just one man. Like Elroy Hirsch. One man just couldn't stay with him. So we experimented with the zone in the early '50s. We used three men deep, things like that. Everybody else went to it gradually after that. The irony is that little by little, the zone took the bomb away and that took a lot of the excitement out of the game."

Are you saying the defenses have caught up with the offenses?

"No, not completely. It's also a matter of the talent being spread out so much thinner. Remember, we only had something like 12 teams in those days. Everyone on every team had outstanding passers and receivers. It made for a truly thrilling sport. Now it's different. Now, with expansion, some teams have it and others don't."

What was your basic theory of coaching?

"To keep ahead of everyone else offensively and defensively, whenever possible."

What do you mean, keep ahead?

"With new formations and innovations. I didn't like to stick with the same old pattern. They go with more of a simplified offense these days. They rely more on technique and execution. To that extent, sometimes I think maybe I went too far. If I had to do it over again, I'd drill more on basics and techniques and keep the offense and defense more simplified."

Some of your innovations created quite a bit of trouble for you, didn't they?

"You'd have to say that. For instance, I began using performance charts in which I would grade every player on every play. It was my personal opinion that we could eliminate errors by pinpointing the breakdown of plays to individual responsibility. This way, we had the breakdown of each play signaled out in rating form. Naturally, this created quite a furor among our players and then it was brought out in the press which was my undoing and eventually cost me my job."

Don't most teams in football now grade their players this way?

"I believe there are a lot of teams now using my system, yes."

What about personality tests? Didn't you try those, too?

"I don't know whether we actually started that. But we did use them. I felt it gave a coach a better understanding of an individual on his team. It made it easier for a coach to treat him as an individual and to understand him better."

Was Los Angeles a difficult town in which to coach?

"Well, there was a lot of pressure. We had a great number of metropolitan newspapers at the time, and the competition for stories was much more severe. The reporters in those days were out to get any information they could. I think that added to it, certainly. In the early '50s, as an assistant coach, I didn't have that pressure. Looking back, I know I enjoyed coaching so much more then. After you become a head coach, you are taken out of much of the coaching end of it. You have to rely more on assistants. It's not as much fun. You're thrust into a situation in which handling administrative details becomes more important than the technical part of the game. It isn't nearly as satisfying, either. The game is fun when you're devoting all your time to the technical aspects of it. Being a head coach is comparable to running a bluff in poker. It's satisfying, but you're not wholly involved, anymore."

Do you miss coaching?

"Yes, I miss it. To a degree. I think anyone who's been in it misses it. Especially the technical part. In my present job [Director of QUADRA] we're basically a fact-gathering or-

Pool brought an inventive nature to his work, and he had an abiding interest in the tactics of offense and defense. At left, he works on the Rams' play book with assistants Vic Lindskog (left) and Tom Fears. Pool was one of the first coaches to use a "three-end offense" (right), splitting Tom Fears and Elroy Hirsch out wide, and putting another receiver out with them. Glenn Davis and others played the "slot" position for Pool.

FEARS   HIRSCH

DAVIS

ganization. I'm not involved with the technical aspect of the game at all. I know very little of what's going on in football right now, as far as techniques are concerned. When I watch a game, I'm usually concentrating just on a particular individual. I'm not even aware of what's going on offensively or defensively."

How about when you're watching a game on television? Do you find yourself doing a little second guessing?

"Very little. I just don't get into it that much anymore. This job has its rewarding aspects. It's a highly fascinating business. A real challenge. Nobody—no computer, even—has figured out how good a football player is really going to be in the pros. Nobody will ever figure it out, either. Everyone still searches for the right keys, though. We're all trying to eliminate as many mistakes as we can. Still, everybody makes mistakes in scouting. That's why it's so fascinating. We're trying to be perfect when, in reality, we know we can't be."

Getting back to your Ram teams, who was the most valuable player on your squad over three years?

"Wow, it's tough to single out one. We had so many fine players. Certainly our quarterbacks were tremendous factors. You couldn't get better passing than we got from Van Brocklin and Waterfield. I used to stand out there at practice and just marvel at their accuracy. As for receiving, ours was tremendous with Hirsch and Fears. I suppose if you really forced me to make a pick—and I hate to do it—I guess I'd have to go with Elroy Hirsch. He simply had an uncanny ability to get open and catch a football."

Did pro football de-emphasize defense in the early '50s?

"I think so. Those things go in cycles. At that time, most coaches spent very few hours on defense. In the '40s, it was even worse. When I played with the Bears, we had a simplified man-to-man coverage system because it was very easy. All you did was point to someone and say 'I've got him.' Gradually, it became evident that everybody had to find a way to stop the bomb. And soon people realized more and more that teams able to stop their opponents had the best opportunity to win."

Are you sorry the Rams didn't devote more time to defense?

"I think we could have concentrated a little more on it. Definitely. If I could do it over, I would concentrate more on defense. But I'm still basically an offensive-minded guy and I still get more kicks out of offense than I do out of defense."

What about the reputation that led your team to be called the "Hollywood Rams?" Was there anything to it?

"I'll tell you this much: they were far from playboys. We got that reputation because so much of the scoring was done the easy way—with bombs, reverses, fake runs and passes, etc. We had a flashy style, sure. But then, the main thrust of our offense was passing, so we had to do things in a way which would best utilize the talents of the players we had. Maybe that's why we gained that reputation. But these guys were certainly far from playboys when it came to hard work. And I never had any problem as far as partying and night life was concerned during that period."

Were Waterfield and Van Brocklin the dominant personalities on the team?

"They were certainly among them, although each was dominant in his own, different way. But they weren't the only ones. Certainly, Don Paul was a real leader on defense and Hirsch and Fears were also very important. Another one who must be mentioned is our center of that era, Leon McLaughlin. He was a dominant person as long as he was with the ballclub."

Pro football salaries have skyrocketed in the

Hamp Pool's two great quarterbacks: Bob Waterfield (left, watching a teammate score against the Bears) and Norm Van Brocklin.

past few years. **Were players of your era paid enough?**

"Not all of them. You know, it's funny. But one thing my performance chart was trying to do was help that situation. My one big goal was to rate each and every player so that at the end of the season we could come up with a factor that would tell us who did the most in contributing toward winning. And we would pay players accordingly. It would be a very fair salary scale. At the time, a lot of players who were sitting on the bench were drawing higher salaries and contributing much less. I wanted to make it commensurate with performance. It seems ironic, but in trying to be fair I upset a lot of people and got in trouble. Maybe not all of them wanted anyone to know what they were really worth."

Does any one game stand out in your mind as the greatest the Rams played during your tenure?

"Well, let's see. We had a lot of good ones. But I guess that game we were down 28-6 to Green Bay and came back in the fourth quarter to win it. That was certainly a thriller. I guess that ranks as the best comeback I've ever been involved in."

What about the toughest defeat?

"All of them are tough. Seriously, I guess that playoff loss to Detroit would rank right there. There was a 49er game at the Coliseum in which Gordy Soltau caught a pass in the corner of the end zone right at the end of the game to beat us. That one really hurt. In 1953, we lost three ball games by a total of eight points. So you can see I had lots of experience in tough losses."

The game had a reputation for being rougher, or dirtier, if you will, in the '50s. Did it seem that way to you?

"I don't believe so. I think the game is rougher now than ever before. We oldtimers hate to admit it, but the athletes of today are faster, bigger and stronger. Through strength programs, special diets and other factors, they're improv-

ing all the time. The result is that when collisions occur now, they're that much more dangerous and more explosive."

What is professional football's most demanding position? Most people say quarterback. Do you agree?

"I know we demanded more of our quarterbacks than anyone else. And, yes, I think it's still that way. Without a capable quarterback, you're in serious trouble in pro football."

Could your Ram team have been a contender today?

"I honestly don't know. I don't think you can make a valid comparison. At least I don't see how anyone can. The talent today has been diluted, don't forget. The players who made our team in those days were truly outstanding. I mean, we cut some great players. There just wasn't enough room for all of them. Now it's different. There are 26 teams and the talent has been spread out. It's not as concentrated. By the same token, the players of today have gained so much in all facets of the game. They're bigger, stronger and probably come into the game a bit sharper mentally. Don't forget, these kids now coming up have been watching football for a long time. They get coached every week in front of their television sets. Before they even get to the college level they know how to run patterns and when to blitz a quarterback. So, as you can see, it's practically impossible to make a valid comparison. How would the Rams, say of 1951, have done against the Vince Lombardi Packer teams, for instance? Or even the Dolphins of 1972? I'd love to find out. Unfortunately, I don't think we ever will."

You were known for going into hibernation right before the season. It once was written that you rented a trailer and drove to the mountains to be alone and spend the solitary hours thinking about football. Is this true?

"Actually, I just liked to go camping. I think

the rest of that story has been magnified a little. But I did like to go off by myself for a few hours every week during the season. It helped me get my thoughts organized and allowed me to concentrate solely on football. I was able to get myself prepared technically this way. I would try to anticipate all situations so I could act on them more sensibly."

You were not noted as a man able to keep his composure on the sidelines. Did you get upset a lot?

"I don't think I had any serious problems along those lines."

Just how demanding is coaching a pro football team?

"Very demanding. You have to be able to put everything into it, both physically and mentally. I honestly don't think it's a job for an old man. You must be young and willing to put in those long hours. It can sap your strength and make you feel older than you are. But it's a lot of fun."

You were very big on having a weekly motto for every game. You even had these slogans mimeographed and distributed to all your players. Things like: "The 49ers are Ready! Are you?" and "Rush Em! Ram Em! Ruin Em!" Do you really think they helped?

"I guess I did at the time. It was just something different, something I hoped would keep the players thinking and give us some kind of small edge."

Were the players of that era less sophisticated than they are now?

"No. I don't think so."

Bob Oates, presently of the *Los Angeles Times*, once wrote that your theories ". . . as soberly recited to the press, were so intricate and so progressive that no one short of a football coach could understand him. He was under suspicion very likely because he didn't sound like a football coach, couldn't murmur the familiar inanities and generalizations, wouldn't tell stories. Never more than partially understood, he was assailed throughout his career by the people he had studiously tried to keep informed." Do you feel that's an accurate statement?

"I know that I never felt that way. I always had the feeling all of my players absorbed my theories thoroughly. I must admit, however, that I was not good at communicating with the press. I probably didn't spend enough time on it. It's something I'd concentrate more on if I were to go back and coach again. At the time, it was a matter of not having enough hours in the day. Some coaches can find the time to spend hours with writers. I couldn't. To me, there wasn't enough time between games, as it was. You know, two of the people who had the most influence on me in the Ram organization were Tex Schramm and Pete Rozelle. And as I think about it now, I can remember both of them criticizing my failure to have better rapport with the press. They stressed it and said it was important. I didn't listen very well. I wish I'd paid more attention now. I really do. Those two guys knew what they were talking about. It was no surprise to me to see them go on to their recent success. Both were very well schooled under Dan Reeves. Schramm had an awful lot to do with the Ram scouting setup and he was Dan's righthand man for a long time. I never did think he got all the credit he deserved. But he's one of the big reasons the Cowboys are doing so well today. He knows how to run a football operation. Rozelle was the same way. It was a pleasure working with both men. My only regret was that I didn't listen to them more."

Your contemporaries have described you as something of a stubborn man. Take your two-quarterback theory, for example. You remain one of the few football people around who still believe it can work. Why?

"I believe in the two-quarterback system. I

Pool today is head of QUADRA, a scouting bureau representing the Rams, San Francisco 49ers, Dallas Cowboys, and San Diego Chargers. QUADRA's headquarters are in Palo Alto, California.

always have. But then, I had two who were so expert at the position they both had to play. The Waterfield-Van Brocklin alternating thing worked out great for us. Both knew before the game exactly who would start and when the other would come in. And we'd stick by that no matter what. If, however, one went in at the start of the second quarter and had trouble, and the other had done well in the first period, I'd quickly go back to the hot hand. I'd say the only bad part of it may have been that, because of the intense competition, we probably threw a few more long bombs than we should have. But that kept things exciting, anyway. I'll tell you this much, I felt lucky to have two such tremendous quarterbacks. There are a lot of coaches around who never have one. I had two. They were something."

Your enthusiasm for the game certainly hasn't diminished. Would you ever like to take another shot at head coaching?

"I don't think so. Football has passed me by so many years it would be impossible for me to compete with the coaches of today. They have learned so much since I quit coaching. There's no way I would be able to catch up. They have advanced in their thinking and in their overall ability as much as the players. I don't think there's any way a coach can stay out of it as long as I have and walk back in and not be behind."

You mean you never even get a twinge to try it again? Not even once in awhile?

"Well, I have to admit it sounds exciting. But my better judgment tells me no. Coaching is a young man's game. Unless you're in your prime it's too demanding physically. The game changes very fast. The average fan doesn't notice it but it does. The techniques are different and the strategy is different. It almost changes game-to-game. I just think the odds would be too much against me."

131

Bob Waterfield

Position: Quarterback
Years played: 1946-52
Height: 6 feet, 2 inches
Weight: 200
College: UCLA

To a young boy growing up in Los Angeles in the early fifties, there was only one name that really mattered. Bob Waterfield. He was the first major league hero the town ever had, and on the field and off, he was like someone out of a storybook. He was even married to a glamorous Hollywood movie star, Jane Russell. There are those who still insist that, as a pure football player, Waterfield may have been the most versatile of them all. He was the complete professional. He ran, he passed, he kicked, he even played defense. And as a leader, his former teammates unanimously voted him No. 1. *Los Angeles Examiner* sports writer Vincent X. Flaherty once wrote: "No other athlete ever embodied so many different football skills and qualities. Waterfield is the finest all-around football player of the generation, and perhaps of all time."

The first thing anyone mentions when your name is brought up is your all-around skill. Did it come naturally?

"I don't know. I'll tell you this much: I wasn't a very good high school player. Not until my senior year, anyway. In fact, I didn't start at Van Nuys High until I was a senior."

How big were you then?

"I think I was a mighty 155 pounds."

Did you receive a scholarship from UCLA?

"No."

How did you suddenly manage to become an All-America?

"Well, I got bigger and I worked hard."

When mentioning your versatility, everyone brings up the time you played defensive back against Don Hutson. Some say you did the best job ever on him. How did you do it?

"Well, first, let's be honest. Hutson was about at the end of his rope at the time."

But he could still play. What do you remember about him?

"He was quick, I'll tell you that."

Did you go in with any special plan?

"We watched a lot of film on him and we knew what he usually ran under certain circumstances. And, of course, we doubled him."

For someone who barely started in high school, did you feel confident going to Cleveland to play professional football?

"I felt a lot better once I looked around and saw all the talent we had out there. You know, like where have these guys been all my life?"

You mean you didn't expect to see good players?

"I guess I did. But I had never seen receivers and runners like that before."

Who made the biggest impression on you when you first walked in?

"Probably Jim Benton. I looked up on one play and saw Benton 25 yards from everyone and I wondered, hey, what park am I in?"

Just what kind of receiver was he?

"He was all moves. He had no speed. He used to get caught from behind all the time."

What kind of moves did he have?

"Any kind you wanted to see."

Did the two of you develop a good rapport?

"Sure. I didn't call the plays. He did. He'd tell me what he was going to run and I'd say okay."

You mean you never told him what to do?

"No, not quite. But usually he'd tell me he was going to get open on a hook, a corner or an out. And I believed him. When I got ready to throw, sure enough, he was open."

How would you rate him with some of the other great receivers you had?

"He'd have to rank right there with Hirsch and Fears."

Do you remember your first game as a professional?

"Yes. It was in Buffalo against Pittsburgh. We won 21-0. Afterwards, I began to think I could play up here. I even thought we could win the championship."

Turns out you were right.

"Yes, but not by much. We beat Washington and Sammy Baugh, 15-14, in 3 below zero weather. We should have scored more, but in that weather, anything could have happened."

Didn't you throw two long touchdown passes in the game?

"Yes."

What did you think afterward, after you had won the world championship as a rookie?

"I was a little amazed. Then I was lucky enough to be voted the most valuable player in the league, the only time anyone ever won it unanimously. You could say I got off to a pretty good start."

After your success in Cleveland, were you disappointed when Dan Reeves suddenly moved the team to the West Coast?

"Are you kidding? I loved the idea. I was going home."

It was in Los Angeles, in 1946, that Reeves signed Kenny Washington, the first black ever to play professional football. What was the team's reaction?

"There was never any problem. Not one. It's incredible when you look back on it. And we had a lot of Texans on the ballclub in those days. Those guys just all believed in one another. They were aware that we had all good players and you had to respect them."

You are described as one of the dominant figures on those explosive Ram teams of the early fifties. How good were those teams?

"Well, I don't know of any club that scored more points. I know we set an awful lot of records in 1950 and '51, some that still stand. And don't forget, we were playing 12 games, not 14."

What was it like as a passer to have a pair of receivers named Fears and Hirsch?

"It was fun."

How would you describe them?

"Hirsch had that great quickness and tremendous moves. He could go deep very well. Fears was big and strong. Both were excellent runners after they caught the ball. When it was third and three, you'd go to Fears. When it was first and 40, you might go to Hirsch."

Did you have any basic philosophy because of the makeup of this particular team?

"Yes. We tried to score every time we got the ball."

You must have felt you could get to the end zone from anywhere on the field.

"We had good reason to feel that way. We proved we could."

You had more than good passers and receivers, though. What about the runners?

"Well, we had the Bull Elephant backfield of Dan Towler, Tank Younger and Dick Hoerner—three really big backs."

How good were they?

"Plenty good. That is, if you like big guys who can run that fast and block that well. They could all even catch the ball. They were good people, too."

How would you like to play today and have that backfield behind you?

"Boy-oh-boy, would I!"

Are you saying it might be even more effective today?

"I think so. All coaches today are looking for the big, fast back. Well, we had three in the same backfield. I don't know of any team that could keep any of them from playing."

What was it like in the days when Norm Van Brocklin and you were both playing quarterback for the Rams? Was there any animosity between you two?

"No, I don't think so."

There had to be a lot of competition, though?

"That there was. We really had competition. Especially in practice. We would have a two-hour passing drill in the morning, and when someone would drop a pass or get overthrown, it was like a big check mark against you."

Of the two quarterbacks on Rams' teams of the early '50s, Waterfield (far left) was a better runner than Van Brocklin. Waterfield was a triple-threat; he could run, pass or kick. Van Brocklin was a superb punter, too, leading the league twice in that category. At quarterback, however, he was more at home dropping back and throwing, or handing off the football.

But did you two get along personally?

"I thought we did."

Would you have preferred a one-quarterback situation?

"All I know is our situation worked out well. I think the competition actually helped both of us. It made us work that much harder."

Was there any particular procedure that was followed in games?

"Yes, I started almost all games. I'd come out at the end of the first quarter and go back at the start of the third. Norm would play the second and fourth periods. Unless one of us was off. Then the procedure would be altered."

The fans naturally had their favorites. Did their reaction to you ever upset you?

"No. I don't think they bothered either one of us."

Did anything bother you two?

"Well, we both had our pride. And we both naturally liked playing as much as possible. But under the circumstances, I think it worked out very well."

How would you classify Van Brocklin as a passer?

"He was probably one of the very best, if not *the* very best passer who ever played this game. He was a good leader and he had great timing on all his balls, long and short. Much better than you generally see nowadays."

People still talk about his accuracy. Just how accurate was he?

"Well, he won three passing titles in an era of some pretty good passers. I think that makes him pretty accurate."

Has the job become more difficult for quarterbacks today than it was in your era?

"Well, we probably didn't have to read as many defenses as they do now. We did do a lot of audiblizing, though. An awful lot. Defenses in those days were primarily man-to-man, which made it great for the Rams because we had all those excellent receivers on our side."

Did any one team bother you more than the others?

"Philadelphia always seemed to give us a hard time. They were one of the first teams to start using zone defenses. For some reason, it seems like they were always beating us."

You were part of a golden era of quarterbacks. Who was the best you ever saw?

"I won't try to answer that one. It's too tough. There were so many good players around, guys like Sid Luckman, Johnny Lujack, and, of course, Otto Graham."

It seems like quarterbacks in your day ran more than they do today, although more runners are beginning to appear in pro football now. Does that seem like a correct statement?

"All I can answer is for myself. I never did run that much."

You did run more than Van Brocklin, though?

"Yes. A little more than that."

You sound like you don't advocate running quarterbacks?

"I don't."

Why?

"The more you run, the more sore passing shoulders you're going to get. A quarterback's primary responsibilities should be calling signals and throwing. He should only run when he has to. Otherwise, you're going to need a whole sack full of quarterbacks on every team."

In other words, you don't foresee the Wishbone making a big impact on pro football?

"Not unless you try it with about a half-dozen quarterbacks who are comparable in ability."

You were just one of the quarterbacks in your day who also handled placekicking and punting. That seems to be a vanishing breed of football player. Why?

"I don't know, unless it's because kids specialize more today. Back then, we did it a little out of necessity, I guess. The more you could

do, the better chance you had of sticking around."

Did kicking come natural to you?

"I liked it. But I also worked at it."

Who was the best placekicker of your era?

"It wasn't even close. Lou Groza. By far. He had range, consistency and anything else you want to mention."

As a quarterback who also had to kick, did you find your concentration impaired?

"No. On the contrary, I think it works out better. The placekickers today walk up and down the sideline worrying every time it gets to third or fourth down. If you're playing, your mind has been somewhere else. When the time comes, all of a sudden you realize you have to kick. You haven't had to worry about it for a half hour. I think this was especially true at the end of a game."

How about during the week in practice? How were your duties split up?

"I usually didn't worry about practicing my placekicks until the last two or three days before a game. Like I said, I think every kicker should get in a little contact here or there. It's good for his concentration."

There sure aren't many quarterbacks like that around now, are there?

"No. I guess Dan Pastorini down in Houston is about the closest to it."

You mentioned Groza earlier. That must have been some kind of championship game in 1950. When Groza won it with a field goal in the last few seconds, what went through your mind?

"I remember thinking that I owed every guy on our ballclub $750."

What do you mean?

"I missed a short field goal earlier and $750 was the difference between the winners' and losers' shares in those days."

I think your teammates knew they would never have gotten to that game without you. Didn't you open that game with a play that had been planned for weeks?

"Yes. We felt, looking at the films, that they'd be keying off our fullbacks. So on the first play, we sent Glenn Davis swinging out of the backfield. I hit him deep and he went right by their linebacker. He could really fly."

Who were the best defensive players of your era?

"It would be hard to mention them all. Guys like Chuck Bednarik and Joe Schmidt, etc."

What about defensive backfields. Does any one unit stand out in your mind?

"Yes. The one in Detroit. They had Jack Christiansen, Yale Lary, Jim David and that bunch. 'Chris' Crew,' I think they called themselves. They were the best group I've ever seen."

How many dirty players were around in your day?

"I never played against one. I played against some who could hit, though. There's a difference. Take Deacon Jones when he was with the Rams. He got a lot of licks in. But I would hardly classify him as a dirty football player."

In most pictures, you were seen without a face mask. Why?

"I just never used one."

Did it ever cost you?

"Oh, maybe a few teeth. But that's all."

Your durability record was amazing. How did you do it?

"I don't know how, except that maybe I accepted injuries as part of the game. I must have been a little lucky, too. All I ever suffered was a separated shoulder or two. In my entire career, I missed only two games. One complete game against New York and one game against Detroit in the Coliseum when all I did was placekick."

Isn't the casualty rate today a little higher?

"I guess so. But there are quarterbacks around who have done pretty well injury-wise.

Two of the best linebackers Waterfield faced were Chuck Bednarik of the Philadelphia Eagles (left) and Joe Schmidt of the Detroit Lions.

Roman Gabriel of the Rams is one. He hasn't missed many regular season games. But any quarterback is bound to get nicked a little here and there."

How old were you when you quit playing?

"Thirty-two."

If you could do it over again, would you play longer?

"Yes. I know I could have hung around longer, although I didn't regret it at the time. But I think I could have played another four or five years. I wouldn't have wanted to go as far as George Blanda, though."

What made you decide to try your hand at head coaching?

"I just figured as long as I'm doing it part-time, I might as well stay with it. I felt I knew the game better than anything else."

Your coaching record is not what you could call distinguished. Looking back, what do you feel was the primary reason?

"I think we just had an awful lot of young kids then. Heck, that was 1960, and a lot of those guys are still playing, people like Gabriel, the Deacon, Merlin Olsen, Joe Scibelli, Joe Carollo."

Did coaching appeal to you?

"Sure. I liked it. But there was a great deal of hard work involved and the hours were long."

How about the rewards?

"It's not too rewarding if you don't win."

What was your quarterback situation?

"Well, beside Gabriel, we had Billy Wade with us. I didn't want to hurry Gabe. He knew that and I think appreciated it at the time."

Is Los Angeles a tough town in which to coach?

"They're all the same. If you win, fine. If you lose, you're a bum."

Did you find yourself frustrated at not being able to win?

"Anything done poorly is frustrating."

You've been exposed to just about every aspect of the Rams. What is your opinion of the Los Angeles organization, particularly Reeves' role ?

"I don't know how it could be any better. Mr. Reeves' leadership was always the outstanding part of it and I think it's being carried on today by the people he trained, even though there has been a recent change in ownership."

What was Dan Reeves really like?

"He was a great man. Of course, he created the draft as we know it today. He was way out ahead of everyone for a long time. The rest of football has caught up now, but I think the game learned a great deal from Dan Reeves."

Is scouting itself a drudgery?

"Well, I don't like scouting. I like players and I like games. And I hate to be away from home so long. But, overall, I must think it's worth it or I wouldn't have done so much of it."

Have you specialized in scouting any certain types of players?

"Yes. Primarily quarterbacks and also receivers."

On a scouting mission, what do you look for in a prime pro quarterback prospect?

"Well, No. 1 he has to be able to throw straight. He must be able to zip it short or hang it out there when throwing long. Most teams call the plays for their quarterbacks in college, so you can't really judge them on that. But you do look for courage and poise. Those are two extremely important traits."

In your years of watching college quarterbacks, who is the best one you've seen?

"Jim Plunkett, I guess. He's big, strong and he throws very well. He's got all the attributes, even if he isn't the greatest athlete in the world."

Isn't Archie Manning a better athlete?

"Manning is like Roger Staubach. Both are likely to spend considerable time recuperating in the hospital."

What do you look for in a receiver?

"You begin with their moves. Then you try to study how they read defenses."

Waterfield was a member of the Rams' family for over three decades: star quarterback of a championship team in 1945 in another city, Cleveland; head coach in 1960-62 (left, with his quarterback, Bill Wade) and more recently a scout. During Waterfield's years as head coach, several players who would later become stars were added to the team. Among them were Roman Gabriel (right) and future greats of the defensive line Deacon Jones and Merlin Olsen.

I'm not sure most people realize that receivers have to read defenses almost as much, if not more, than quarterbacks.

"I think you're right. People don't realize it. But receivers do. And they've got to be reading that defense coming off the line of scrimmage. They have to pick out where that zone is weak or strong."

How does a kid in college learn to read defenses as a receiver?

"It isn't easy. It's a combination of coaching, study and hard work, all of which can't help you unless you have the speed and quickness to begin with."

Who is the best receiver you've seen since you've been scouting?

"Oh, I don't know. Maybe Chuck Dicus when he was at Arkansas."

Is football, in general, being played better now than it was when you were active?

"I think so. I think basically because of the size and speed of the players. The combination of better coaching and better facilities has a lot to do with it, too."

Has the game changed in any one area more than another?

"I think on defense. That's where the kids have gotten so much bigger and faster. The offensive players are basically the same size, although I guess some of the linemen are bigger now, too."

If the Ram team you played on in the early '50s were together today, how would they do?

"They'd be Super Bowl contenders."

Are you saying most teams in your era could compete?

"No. As a whole, the teams today are much better."

Why is it, when looking back at those great Ram teams, people tend to express disappointment that they weren't more successful? That is, why didn't they win more world championships?

"All I know is that I played in four world championship games. That's not too bad."

So you think the Rams played up to their potential in those good years?

"Yes. I know there was a lot of talk about all that Hollywood bunk. But that's just the way people liked to think. The rumors were fun for people to knock around. None of it was true."

You are the same as most Ram players I've talked to. You remain fiercely loyal. Is there any reason for the feeling?

"I'm not sure. I just know that I'm awfully glad I played with the people I did."

Even today, there is no badmouthing of one another, is there?

"No. In that respect, I think our team was unique. I can honestly say that we didn't have any enemies among us. At least if we did I didn't know about them."

After being involved with the game so long, do you think you could ever leave it now?

"It would be pretty hard to do. It's been my whole life. I've always been happy in it and I hope to keep it that way."

Looking back, is there anything you're sorry you missed?

"Yes. A couple of field goals."

Seriously, does a player of your magnitude look back with any regrets?

"I can't knock anything about the game. It was good to me. I think I did just about all I could do. If I missed anything, I don't know what it could be."

If Bob Waterfield, the versatile All-American from UCLA, were just coming into pro football today, would he still be a quarterback? Or would he be better suited at another position?

"No, I think I'd still be a quarterback. A pretty rich one, too."

Paul Younger

Position: Running back, linebacker
Years played: 1949-57
Height: 6 feet, 3 inches
Weight: 226
College: Grambling

Paul Younger, better known to friends and opposing tacklers as "Tank," arrived in professional football about the same time Jackie Robinson was roaring across the color line in major league baseball. Tank wasn't the first black man in the league. But he was the first from a black school, and all you need do is look down the rosters of most teams in pro football today to realize he qualified as a full-fledged pioneer.

He also ranks as one of the greatest two-way players the league has seen. He was a savage linebacker and a fullback who combined speed and power as a member of the "Bull Elephant" backfield. Maybe George Halas said it best. Once, after a game, he ran up, put his arms around Younger and said, "Tank, you're the greatest, dirtiest, best football player in the league. I just wish we had you." Younger, now 45, has been a full-time Ram scout since 1966.

When did the Rams first contact you at Grambling College?

"It was after a bowl game my junior year. Eddie Kotal walked into the dressing room and said he wanted to talk to me."

Were you surprised?

"You better believe it. It wasn't very common down there in those days. I can't really tell you what my reaction was. But I do remember he only stayed a few minutes. Then he left and said he'd be getting in touch with me."

Obviously, he kept his promise.

"Yes, I heard from him first through the mail. He sent me a questionnaire. Detroit contacted me also. So did the Yankees of the old All-America Conference."

Where did you actually negotiate with the Rams?

"It was back home in Grambling after my senior year. Dr. Ralph Jones, who has been president of the school since 1936, practically raised me. He, coach Eddie Robinson and the school publicity director all got in a car with Ed-

die Kotal and we drove to the hotel where Eddie was living. I can still remember it. We sat in front of that hotel and Dr. Jones, who is my godfather, negotiated with Eddie, while the rest of us listened. It was raining. Raining hard. I wound up signing for $6,000."

Was that your bonus?

"Bonus, hell. That was my first year's salary."

Coming from a small school like that, did you think you could make it right away in the pros?

"This may sound silly, but at no time did I ever doubt my ability. In spite of the fact I knew the odds were long. The only blacks in the league at that time were Emlen Tunnell, Bobby Mann and Mel Triplett. Mann and Triplett were with the Lions."

Did that fact bother you?

"It really didn't. Maybe I was too stupid to think about it. Maybe it was just the fact I had this supreme confidence in myself."

Were you an outspoken rookie?

"Hardly. In fact, I'm not too sure I opened my mouth at all."

Were you the only black in camp?

"No, they had four others that year."

Did you think about the racial situation much?

"Really, the only time I was aware of it was when the press mentioned it. As far as the players and the organization were concerned, they always treated me as just another member of the ballclub."

Were you surprised by that?

"No. It's always been that way with me. I never have believed in not getting along with people. It's never been a hang-up."

How about around the league the first time? Did you run into any racial incidents?

"A few. In Green Bay once, they turned a black cat loose on the field."

What did you do?

"I just kept running the ball."

Any others you remember?

"In San Antonio for an exhibition game, they wouldn't let Willie Steele, a black rookie from San Diego State, and myself through the gate. We were with George Trafton, an assistant coach, and Trafton almost had a fit. It took a long time, but we finally convinced them."

Were there blacks in the stands then?

"In San Antonio, they let them in, but they had to sit in the end zone."

What happened in that particular game?

"Funny you should ask. We were playing the Boston Bulldogs and Bobby Layne was their quarterback. Well, Layne was an All-America from Texas and they had promoted him big. Once, he went back to pass and couldn't find a receiver. He decided to run and as he headed out of the pocket, I moved over and tackled him. I hit the hell out of him and pried him loose from the ball. Then the catcalls started. It got so bad, Clark Shaughnessy had to take me out of the game. I didn't know why. I was concentrating on making the ballclub. I didn't hear any of that stuff. So when I got over to the sidelines I asked Mr. Shaughnessy what happened. He told me. I told him I didn't care. So he let me go back in and I played the rest of the game. The catcalls never did stop."

Were you worried about making the team that first year?

"You had to be in those days. I think the roster limit was 32 at the time. I had confidence, but not that much confidence."

When did you get the feeling you might make it?

"Well, we were playing our last exhibition game in Omaha, Nebraska, and we had just come in after warmups when Shaughnessy said the same team would start that started last week. Except at right halfback. Then he said, 'Big Boy, you'll start at right half.' He always called me Big Boy. I don't think he ever really knew my name. I saw him six months before he died and he still called me Big Boy. Anyway, just

prior to kickoff that night, Shaughnessy called the starting backfield together. It was Bob Waterfield, Elroy Hirsch, Dick Hoerner and myself. He put his arms around us and said: 'I think this is the greatest backfield in the National Football League. They can have that dream backfield in Chicago (Pat Harder, Paul Christman, Elmer Angsman and Charlie Trippi). I'll take you guys any day.' That's when I figured I had a pretty good chance to make the ballclub."

How did you do in that game?

"I wound up the leading ballcarrier and played the last half on both offense and defense. Once, when I was trying to break for a touchdown, my shoe busted in half. It was my last pair. I only had two when I got to camp. After the game, I was talking to Emlen Tunnell, who caught me at the six-yard line on that particular play. I was kidding him. I said, 'Here I am trying to make this club, and you have to go and tackle me like that.' At that point, Shaughnessy came by, patted me on the back and said to tell the equipment manager to order me a new pair of shoes and to have the bill sent to him. Tunnell turned to me and said, 'They're not going to buy you a new pair of shoes to send you home.'"

Did you finally feel safe at that point?

"I have to admit, that's when I thought I had it made."

Did you always play both ways?

"Well, I did at Grambling."

How big were you?

"About 6-3 and 225 pounds."

Did you prefer offense or defense?

"I guess I was like anyone in those days. The glamour was on offense. Now it doesn't make any difference. You can get just as much publicity by playing linebacker."

Did you realize what an accomplishment it was to make the team?

"Not right away. Then the writers started talking about it and I read some of the stuff in the

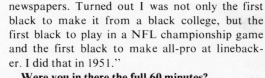

newspapers. Turned out I was not only the first black to make it from a black college, but the first black to play in a NFL championship game and the first black to make all-pro at linebacker. I did that in 1951."

Were you in there the full 60 minutes?

"Not quite. Let's say 55."

Didn't it take a lot out of you?

"Sure. But like the man said, youth is a special commodity. There are a lot of things a guy can do when he's young and enjoying himself."

And you enjoyed it?

"I'll say. Money was never really a big issue with me. When I got to the point where it wasn't fun anymore, I quit. Even though I think I could have hung around on my reputation for another three or four years."

When did other blacks from black schools come into the league?

"It took about three more years before guys like Willie Davis started making it."

When did the big transition take place?

"I guess it was in 1951, right after the old leagues merged. The All-America Conference brought in quite a few blacks. Afterward, the influx began."

Kenny Washington was the first black pro football player after the war, wasn't he?

"Right. The Rams signed him in 1946, before Robinson signed with Brooklyn. Dan Reeves could have made a big thing about it, but he didn't go for the publicity like Branch Rickey did with Jackie."

What was it like for a kid from Grambling playing his first game in the Los Angeles Coliseum?

"I was nervous, I'll tell you that. I wasn't in the starting lineup, but even when I ran out of that tunnel and the announcer said here comes the rest of the Rams, the place went wild. I heard that yelling and screaming and wondered what the heck was going on here."

When did you get into the game?

"The old man put me in during the second quarter."

Do you remember what happened?

"Yes. Sammy Baugh was the Washington quarterback. We were in a defense where a linebacker had to cover the back to his side. The guy I had to cover had run the kickoff back some 90 yards. Baugh came out, looked up and saw me over there. I could almost feel him calling a switch. Sure enough, here comes this guy around the horn. He was easing away from me so I just tackled him. Naturally, they called me for it and the team was penalized. We held them the next three downs and when I came off the field Shaughnessy proceeded to read me out. I let him finish and then told him I just did what he told us to do in practice. He always said if you're going to get beat, tackle the guy. A penalty is better than a touchdown. Shaughnessy hesitated and then said, 'You're right.' And he told the trainer to wipe my face off and get me ready to go back in."

What do you remember about the "Bull Elephant" backfield?

"Well, Frank Finch of the *Los Angeles Times* gave us the name. And, to be honest, I rather enjoyed it. We thought we were unique. I remember Karl Hubenthal, who's now with the *Los Angeles Herald-Examiner,* did a cartoon on us we all liked very much, too."

How big were the other two runners?

"Dick Hoerner, Dan Towler and myself were all about the same size, between 225 and 230 pounds. We were about similar in speed, too, although Dan was probably a bit faster. He could run about a 9.8 100. We could all go inside or outside, and we could catch a forward pass. When we were in there, our offense was not in the least restricted. One of us was usually spread out as a flanker, just like in the usual pro set."

How would a backfield like that fare today?

"What do you think? We'd be even more effective. We'd make ourselves some money, too."

You gained a lot of yards for the Rams. Is there any one run that stands out in your mind?

"Yes. We were playing San Francisco, I think it was 1952 and I broke one for 97 or 98 yards and a touchdown. I had gained a lot of yards already that day. Only one thing was wrong. They called the run back. When I got to the end zone, I saw the flag back there and I got awfully mad. But I was too tired to argue. Turns out, the pictures dispute the call. I would have gotten my money's worth in, I'll tell you that."

It must have been fun to play on the Ram offense in those years.

"It was. We were so explosive that a game never was really over as long as we had a couple chances left. We never got excited or panicked if we fell behind by a couple touchdowns. We always knew we could get them back."

If the game was so much fun, why did you quit so young?

"I was 30. That wasn't considered young in those days. The game began to change for me. Guys began to talk about players' unions and business matters. That stuff wasn't for me. It took a lot out of it and made me think that I didn't want to stay around any longer."

I'm going to put you on the spot now. If you had to start a pro football team tomorrow and could only pick one player on offense, who would it be?

"Bob Waterfield. He was simply a great all-around football player and a great leader. He's the one guy I'd want. I never saw him get excited, and yet, in that quiet way of his, he really could fire you up. He could chew you out and you wouldn't get mad at him, either. He could make you put out, I'll tell you that."

What about defense? Who's the one guy you'd want there?

"Dick Huffman. He's as good a defensive lineman as I've ever seen. He was also great of-

Clark Shaughnessey (left) always called Tank "Big Boy." But then, that's what he called just about everybody else on the team. Once, when Tank stopped a pass play by tackling the intended receiver, the team was penalized. After Shaughnessey scolded him for it, Tank reminded his coach, "That's what you told me to do." And he was right.

fensively. If he were around today, he'd rank right there with the best."

You didn't start scouting with the Rams right away did you?

"No. I was in business and worked some for them on the weekends. Finally, I decided I might as well go full-time with them in 1966."

Your specialty now is the black schools, isn't it?

"Yes. It's satisfying to know you help paved the way for some of these kids to get a chance now. And a lot of people down there still know me. Most of the schools have coaches I either knew then or played against. I usually get a pretty good reception when I go down there."

What do sports mean to a black youngster in a small black school?

"The sky is the limit. It can mean instant economical success. I like to think that blacks have three big problems. Employment, housing and education. If they can sign a pro contract, they get two of the three things—housing and employment—instantly. And if they attend a school for four years, they should already have the third. So that's it. They have all three, where the average guy takes five or six years to make it, if he ever makes it at all."

Does it do anything else for him?

"Sure. It affords him a chance to meet important people. It puts him into a place in society where, under normal circumstances, he never would be. A president of a college doesn't meet some of the people a football player gets to meet. It's a great opportunity."

Yet, some players don't take advantage of it, do they?

"There are always some like that. There are white kids the same way."

Who are some of the players you've brought into the league?

"Well Willie Ellison and Isiah Robertson are two. Willie made me awfully proud in 1971 when he ran for 1,000 yards with the Rams and set that one-game record of 247 yards against New Orleans. And Isiah made Defensive Rookie of the Year that same year. That made me happy. But the one player I'm probably closer to than any other is Harold Jackson of Philadelphia."

Why Jackson?

"Well, I strongly recommended him. Still, we drafted him down low. He wasn't very big, but he had as outstanding a training camp as any rookie I've ever seen here. But George Allen wasn't too big on rookies, as you know. So Harold got traded to Philadelphia, and he's had some big years there. I think he's on the verge of becoming a superstar. He's a great kid, too. He calls me a lot and whenever he's in town, he comes over to the house and is practically a member of the family."

Tank, you're known throughout the Ram organization for your sense of humor. Do you have a story that's your personal favorite?

"Well, I think the funniest thing I ever saw with the Rams happened in either 1953 or '54. We drafted this defensive back from somewhere in Florida. He was All-Everything. I don't remember his name. Anyway, this kid plays in the College All-Star game and reports the next day, on a Saturday. The first day there he spends most of his time listening to Hamp Pool explain all the coverages. You know, complicated stuff, like what you do in the 5-4 Eagle defense. Things like that. Well, Hamp takes some 30 minutes to explain all these details, covering everything from the man-in-motion to who knows what. Finally, he asks this guy, 'Do you understand?' We're all standing there, now. The kid says no, except for one thing. He says, suppose the quarterback gives the ball to the right halfback and the guy slips past the line into the defensive backfield. So, says Hamp, you tackle him. 'That's just it,' says the kid. 'I can't tackle.' I laughed so hard I thought I'd die. Hamp sort of stammered and said, 'Well, then do the best you

Younger was a tenacious linebacker and charter member of the Rams' famous Bull Elephant Backfield. At 226 pounds, he was hard to bring down when he got up a head of steam. He gained 3,295 yards in nine seasons with the Rams. In more recent years, he's had just as much success as a scout, bringing such stars as Willie Ellison, Harold Jackson and Isiah Robertson into the league.

can.' Then he walked away and headed for the sideline. I don't know what he said, but I think he told someone to get the kid's plane ticket ready. Because he didn't make the ballclub.''

Those Halas quotes are special to you, I know. How and when did he say that to you?

"Well, we were playing in Chicago one day. I was at linebacker and Johnny Lujack went back to pass. He got hemmed up back there and started to run. This was right in front of Mr. Halas' bench, mind you. I moved in for the tackle and right then he jukes me. Now I'm out of position and he's about to run by. So I stuck out a hand and necktied him. He goes down, slams his head to the ground and gets kayoed. Mr. Halas comes out on the field and yells at me: 'Tank, you SOB, we're gonna kill you.' Then he puts Sid Luckman in at quarterback and the next three plays they come right at me. Stan West, the linebacker playing next to me, yelled over, 'It's time to grab grass and growl.'' Somehow, I managed to weather the storm, and after the game, Halas runs out on the field and puts his arm around me. That's when he said, 'Tank, you're the greatest, dirtiest, best football player in the league. I just wish we had you.' And then he walked off.''

How did that make you feel?

"Very proud.''

Over the years, what has the Ram organization meant to you?

"I don't think I can put it into words. I know that probably sounds corny. But I mean it.''

Can you elaborate a little?

"Well, just working with some of the people down through the years. Men like Bill John and Johnny Sanders. I look back now and I don't know how I could ever have worked for anybody else. I like to think that I'm part of the Rams. A real part of it. Somewhere in the middle of that R-A-M-S.''

The Other Years

His name is Bob Snyder and he is best remembered as the Rams' coach whose personal instruction had turned Bob Waterfield into one of the game's great quarterbacks. In an early preseason game in 1948, the team had played so badly in the first two periods, the coach stood up to make his halftime address. "There had better be a change this second half," he said, "or some of the guys in this room will not be here tomorrow."

The statement was prophetic. The next day Bob Snyder was gone.

It was to become a pattern for the professional football team in Los Angeles. Except for the all-winning years of 1949-55, this was an organization beset by controversy and change. The tone was established, in fact, before the club even moved West.

It was in 1937 that the National Football League first granted a franchise to a gentleman named Homer Marshman in Cleveland. Previously, the professional team in Cleveland had belonged to the American Football Association, founded in 1921. That club was known as the Indians. When Marshman was awarded the NFL team, he and his general manager, Buzz Wetzel, set out to find a new name. "There is one college team that has a name I really like," said Wetzel. "The Fordham Rams." Marshman agreed immediately. "That's wonderful," he said. "That's what we'll call them. The Rams."

The new Rams didn't exactly break in spectacularly. They finished fifth in a five-team division of their league in 1937, and fourth the next three years. They did, however, produce their first authentic all-pro, a fullback named Johnny Drake, and their first productive forward passer, tailback Parker Hall. A syndicate of sportsmen actually shared ownership until Dan Reeves made his move in 1941.

Hugo Bezdek was the head coach through that dismal 1-10-0 1937 season. Assistant coach Art Lewis took over three games into 1938 and man-

aged to win three of his last seven. Earl (Dutch) Clark assumed control in 1939, with Lewis staying on as an assistant.

In 1941, Reeves and Fred Levy Jr. made their purchase, installing Billy Evans, a former sports columnist and American League umpire, as general manager.

The Rams played their 1941 opener in the Akron, Ohio, Rubber Bowl against Pittsburgh. Reeves and Levy were interested spectators, having just shelled out some $125,000 for the franchise. Rams halfback Dante Magnini parked under the opening kickoff, caught the ball and promptly returned it all the way for a touchdown. Levy pounded Reeves on the back, almost knocking him over. "Is it this easy?" he laughed. It wasn't. The Rams won that game and their next one. But they didn't win any more. They finished the 1941 season with nine losses in a row.

Charles (Chile) Walsh was the new head coach in 1943, the year the club suspended operations because of wartime difficulties. Walsh was promoted to general manager the following season and appointed Buff Donelli as coach. A 4-6 season wasn't enough for Donelli to keep his job and Chile picked his brother, Adam, to be the new coach.

It was under the two Walsh brothers, Chile and Adam, that Cleveland rose to impressive heights in 1945. A third-round draft choice as a future became their new T-formation quarterback and as a rookie led the Rams to a 9-1 season and the world championship. For his accomplishment, Bob Waterfield was named the league's most valuable player.

That was an important year for the future of both the Rams and the National Football League. Waterfield's emergence and the efficiency of the team provided Reeves with the confidence to make his unparalleled move to California. And Dan quietly hired a gentleman named Eddie Kotal as chief scout, a move that would turn out to be al-

The champion Rams were moving to a glamorous new town in 1946, and they would show the fans in Los Angeles an exciting backfield: (left to right) Bob Waterfield, Kenny Washington and Tom Harmon.

most as important to the team as the move West.

Bill John was hired as business manager of the Rams in 1944. A year later, he was asked if he would like to move with the club to Southern California. Startled, he eventually agreed. He was, however, a little late in arriving in Los Angeles. There was a slight problem of how to get rid of tons of straw. To soften the field in Cleveland's icy Municipal Stadium for the championship game with Washington in 1845, John purchased enough straw to fill six boxcars and part of a seventh. It worked out well, except after the game, John was forced to solicit stables and farmers, trying to sell a bale or two at a time. That's when he got the news. the team was moving to Los Angeles. John still had six boxcars of straw left. "I thought I'd never see California," said John. "But eventually a circus came to town and bought me out."

The voyage was not made, of course, without first surmounting several major problems. Reeves found the other NFL owners less than overjoyed at the prospect of the higher costs they would incur traveling cross-country to play the Rams. But he stood his ground. At one point, in fact, in the face of strong opposition, he told the league that if it did not approve the switch, then the Rams would no longer be playing members. He stalked out of a conference room and was followed by several worried owners who managed to calm him down in a nearby hotel suite. They did not, however, change his mind. It was the league, not the Rams, that finally gave in on the point.

"I remember how strongly he felt about the West Coast," recalled Art Rooney, president of the Pittsburgh Steelers. "Some of the owners, including myself, reacted to a West Coast franchise as if Indians were still lurking on the other side of the Mississippi. Dan clinched the deal when he offered to pay, out of his own pocket if necessary, $5,000 over the existing guarantee when NFL

teams played against his team on the Coast."

The next assignment was to convince officials of the Memorial Coliseum in Los Angeles to allow professional sports inside its hallowed walls. Originally built for the 1932 Olympic Games, the Coliseum had long been considered a sanctuary for amateur sports. Both USC and UCLA, along with the rest of the then Pacific Coast Conference, were not enthralled by the possibility of new competition.

Reeves, though, was already ahead of them. Even before leaving Cleveland, he had contacted influential George Preston Marshall of the Washington Redskins and persuaded him to sign a contract that helped provide the keys to unlock the *Los Angeles Times* Charities, Inc. It was a contract that helped provide the keys to unlock the Coliseum gates.

So it was that in 1946 the Los Angeles Rams made their debut. Waterfield was at quarterback with two familiar names, Kenny Washington and Tom Harmon, providing added glamour. The receiver wasn't as well-known, but Ram historians still maintain that Jim Benton was the Raymond Berry of his era. Although the personnel was excellent, the club could finish only second. Chile Walsh was so upset he fired his brother, Adam, as head coach. That was not enough to satisfy Reeves, who then fired Chile.

And that's the way it started. The Rams have not always been successful. But they rarely have been dull.

The site was a posh Beverly Hills hotel. The occasion a 1961 dinner honoring champions of all sports. The toastmaster, Art Linkletter, introduced Jim Phillips, the Rams' talented wide receiver who had led the National Football League in receptions the previous season. At the dais to receive his award, Phillips was asked a serious question. "Do you think," wondered Linkletter, "the Rams will trade you now?" Phillips grinned and said, "No, I'm not good enough yet."

The fall of that famous empire in Rome may not have been covered as well or analyzed as much in depth as the deterioration of the professional football team in Los Angeles. The coaches and the success of the club varied from 1949 through 1955. But, overall, the tone was a winning one and the popularity continued to spiral.

If one year has to be pinpointed as the beginning of the slide, the start of the downfall, it would be 1956. It was one season after the Rams, under rookie coach Sid Gillman, had captured their fourth Western Conference championship in seven years. There was little reason to suspect a sudden slump. Especially, when one glanced over the roster.

The quarterbacks were Norm Van Brocklin, Bill Wade and Rudy Bukich. Ron Waller had made all-pro as a rookie running back. Duane Putnam was an all-star guard, Don Burroughs a standout in the defensive backfield and Larry Morris, after an emergency year at fullback, was returning to his best position, linebacker. Defensively, there were two more all-pros, Andy Robustelli at end and Bud McFadin at tackle. Frank Fuller was a rising, young star opposite Robustelli and there was a tackle of immense potential, Gene (Big Daddy) Lipscomb. The draft also had produced its usual cluster of talent. Leon Clarke was a big, rangy end from Southern California. Ken Panfil of Purdue appeared ideally suited to play professional tackle. John Morrow was a good-looking offensive lineman. Hugh Pitts was an All-America linebacker from Texas Christian. And Jesse Whittenton was judged a promising prospect at cornerback.

Seven years and several losses later, all the above players were still active and very successful in professional football. But none were with the Rams. How could something like that happen? What caused the breakdown? There are many theories, none of which was ever proven.

It is agreed, however, that the difficulties began that summer in 1956. When they opened training camp, the Rams seemed strongest at quarterback. Van Brocklin had been the motivating force behind the conference championship captured the previous season. He had finished either first or second in the National Football League passing statistics for five straight years. He was a proven quantity. Or so it seemed.

Wade, a No. 1 draft choice from Vanderbilt, was young, eager and talented. He was also inexperienced. Bukich was a quarterback of some potential from USC who had gained most of his reputation by throwing a pass that beat Wisconsin in the Rose Bowl.

When the preseason started, Van Brocklin appeared uninspired. His passes lacked their usual zip. His arm didn't have the sure strength of previous seasons. His rate of interception was alarming. Wade, meanwhile, sensing an opportunity, was performing as well as he ever did in Los Angeles.

Still, the feeling was Van Brocklin would play himself into shape in time for the start of the league schedule. So, on opening day against Philadelphia, the Dutchman was at quarterback. On the Rams' second offensive play of the day, he threw a pass. It was intercepted. The Eagles went on to score and, on the sideline, Gillman seethed. He could take no more. He benched Van Brocklin and ordered Wade to take over. Los Angeles recovered to beat Philly 27-7, but in the dressing room afterwards, reporters were less concerned about the game and more interested in the quarterback situation.

The incident became a cause celebre and said much for the personalities of the two strong-minded men involved. "It looked like a lousy pass to me," Gillman said later. "I asked the Dutchman at the time if he's been rushed. He said no, so I had no choice." Van Brocklin, who would not make an excuse even if he had one, also described it as a poorly thrown ball. The films, however,

With the Western Conference championship of 1955, the great era of success that the Rams had known came to an end, and the next year the fortunes of the team began to decline. Quarterback Norm Van Brocklin had either led the NFL in passing, or finished as the runnerup, for the last five years. He had a disappointing training camp in '56, however, and was replaced by Bill Wade (far left). For several games that season, Van Brocklin did nothing but punt. After a mediocre '57 season, Van Brocklin retired. Los Angeles then traded him to Philadelphia. Guard Buck Lansford (right) and safety Jimmy Harris came to the Rams in the trade.

showed Philadelphia defensive end Tom Scott hitting Van Brocklin's arm as he threw. Gillman issued a statement to that effect later in the week.

If the interception was blown out of proportion, the problem wasn't. It remained and even festered as the season progressed. The fans and the press were quick to leap in and offer their own suggestions. Naturally, opinions were divided. As it turned out, so was the team.

The Coliseum would rock with regular chants. "We want Van Brocklin . . . We want Van Brocklin . . ." When Van was in the game, and especially when he was doing poorly, the opposition party could be heard, "We want Wade . . . We want Wade . . ."

Gillman seemed as confused and befuddled about the situation as everyone else. One Sunday, he'd start the veteran. The next week he'd go with Wade. "We're going all the way with Bill," he'd remark. But then Wade would falter and after making the switch, Gillman would say: "You've got to go with experience. Van Brocklin's the boy."

Following the Philadelphia win, the team lost five straight games, won one, then lost three more. Wade was at quarterback the majority of the time, establishing Van Brocklin as the highest paid punter in football. In four of the first 10 games, in fact, all Van did was kick.

The Rams were popularly described as disgruntled, returning from a disastrous road trip that saw them lose in Chicago, 30-21, get slaughtered in Baltimore, 56-21, and embarrassed in Pittsburgh, 30-13. Yet, 51,037 curiosity-seekers came out to see the Rams' rematch with the Colts at the Coliseum. Wade opened at quarterback, but was badly off form. He threw only three completions in his first 12 attempts, although the team was winning, 14-7, when he left. Van Brocklin's sudden appearance brought a tremendous roar from the crowd. And on that warm December afternoon, he was brilliant. He kept his passes to a

minimum, but completed seven of 10. More important, his play-calling was masterful. The Rams won, 31-7, and the controversy at quarterback was over. Temporarily.

Against Green Bay the following Sunday in the final game of the season, Van Brocklin was even better. He hit 17 of 22 for 289 yards and three touchdowns, including a pair of identical 56-yard bombs to Bob Boyd, and the Rams breezed, 49-21. It was an encouraging finish to a depressing 4-8 season, but also one that led to some obvious speculation.

Where, people wondered, had Van Brocklin been the rest of the year? Why was the team forced to suffer with Wade when a quarterback with Van's ability sat on the bench?

The reasons for Van Brocklin's ineffectiveness in the preseason games were never advanced. But it did seem clearly to have upset Gillman. Van's rally in the final two weeks, however, at least made the decision the following year simple. The Dutchman would be the Rams' quarterback in 1957.

The Billy Wade Fan Club had plenty of opportunity to chant, but little chance to cheer in 1957. Wade threw only 24 passes in the 12 games. Van Brocklin was responsible for 20 touchdowns and 21 interceptions. He had a decent year and the Rams rebounded enough to finish at .500. Their 6-6 record earned them fourth place. But the breach that had been opened the previous fall between coach and quarterback continued to widen. Gillman felt he should call the plays. Van Brocklin thought responsibility should be his.

Finally, in December, the Dutchman made a decision of his own. He announced his retirement from football. It turned out, of course, to be a retirement only from the Rams. Los Angeles traded him to Philadelphia for offensive lineman Buck Lansford and defensive back Jimmy Harris.

While all this was going on, things were not going well in the front office, either. A controversy,

much of it unpublicized, was fomenting among owners Reeves, Ed Pauley, Fred Levy and Hal Seley. It was developing into a full-blown feud, and it made matters even more difficult for Gillman. When the coach needed guidance, he did not know where to turn. He was not sure who his boss was and not positive how any of them felt about his quarterbacks.

Clearly, the problems on and off the field resulted in considerable damage. But none of it came at the box office. At least not in 1957. The fact that the team could break even only in 12 games did not temper the enthusiasm of Ram fans who apparently enjoyed booing as much as cheering.

In one game, against San Francisco, the Rams drew 102,368 people, a National Football League record. And club officials claimed 10,000 more were turned away at the gate. It was an extraordinary year at the gate. These are just some of the records set:

TOTAL ATTENDANCE (19 games, preseason and league)—1,051,106.
HOME GAME TOTAL (10 games, 4 preseason and 6 league)—711,924.
LEAGUE GAME TOTAL (6 games)—455,766.
LARGEST SINGLE GAME TOTAL—102,368.
AVERAGE ATTENDANCE HOME GAMES (10)—71,192.
AVERAGE ATTENDANCE LEAGUE GAMES (6)—74,296.

So in Los Angeles in 1958, the most popular team in professional football also became the most discussed. Gillman, who had been used to the quiet atmosphere of a small college town in Ohio, was now being placed under the microscope in a huge, football-crazy city.

Van Brocklin's departure had brought with it the usual divided opinion. But if nothing else, it at least established Gillman as the man in charge.

And it settled his quarterback dilemma, temporarily anyway. The job was Wade's, although a young strong-armed mathematician from Rice named Frank Ryan had been selected No. 1 in the draft.

Van Brocklin was not the only front-line player who would be missing from the Coliseum, though. The colorful Elroy Hirsch, who may have been the most popular of all Ram performers, also decided he'd had it. And this time he meant it. Tank Younger was another. One of the fine power runners in the league, Tank might have enjoyed an even more distinguished statistical career had he been able to concentrate on offense. As it was, he is remembered as perhaps the best two-play player the Rams ever had. His contributions, as well as his sense of humor, would be missed.

Gillman's new-look 1958 team would set the tone for Ram squads in the late '50s and early '60s. Always, there would be a generous number of flashing offensive backs . . . the Jon Arnetts . . . Dick Basses . . . Tom Wilsons . . . and good receivers like Del Shofner and Jim Phillips. But the personnel would get thin up front on both units, and the defense backfield would begin to show cracks.

Seeking to discover the story behind the eventual Ram decline, Philadelphia's Hugh Brown quoted "a disgruntled ex-Ram" thusly: "They collected more top draft choices than anybody else in the league and what has it gotten them? Nothing but dissension and jealousy. The Rams can only play three backs at a time, so the result is they have great runners like Tom Wilson and Joe Marconi warming the bench most of the time. The Rams have concentrated so much on names, they've neglected the diggers of wells and the hewers of wood. Meaning that their offensive and defensive lines are second-rate."

In Wade's first year to himself, he played capably. In fact, he threw for more yardage than any quarterback the club has had, then or since. He completed 181 of 341 attempts for a spectacular

2,875 yards. He had 18 touchdown passes, but also threw 22 interceptions. Arnett ran for 683 yards. Del Shofner, who had been drafted out of Baylor as a defensive back, was switched to wide receiver and developed into one of the best in football. He speared 51 passes and averaged over 21 yards per catch.

The Rams won eight of their 12 games and finished in second place. After Gillman's horrendous 4-8 season in '56, the team appeared to be making solid progress, improving to 6-6 and then 8-4. Characteristically, though, instead of seeking blockers or pass rushers in the draft, they once again decided on a running back, one who had another year of collegiate eligibility, no less. Dick Bass, from College of the Pacific, was their choice on the first round.

It was later, a few weeks after the 1959 draft, however, that they made even more startling news.

"The Los Angeles Rams," said the television sportscaster, "may have made the biggest trade in their history today. They have acquired running back Ollie Matson from the Chicago Cardinals in exchange for nine players. In return for Matson, one of pro football's most exciting players, Chicago will receive Glenn Holtzman, Ken Panfil, Frank Fuller, Ed Hauser, Don Brown, Larry Hickman, John Tracey, a player to be named during training camp and a high 1960 draft choice."

The trade was stunning only if you failed to understand the Rams' belief that a star was always required. After years of prospering with Waterfield, Van Brocklin, Fears, Hirsch and the rest, their galaxy was disappearing. Arnett was a great draw because he grew up in Los Angeles and was an All-America at the University of Southern California. He might, in fact, have been the best broken field runner in football since Hugh McElhenny was at his peak. But Arnett was not a big man and remained somewhat injury prone. Wade, while exciting and unpredictable on the field, did not have the charisma of past Rams

quarterbacks. But Matson . . . ah, Matson. Here was a man who could appeal to the multitudes. The irony was that the Rams had turned down an opportunity to pick Ollie in the 1952 draft, the year they had the bonus selection, the year they went for Wade. Now, seven years later, Matson, who said he always wanted to play in Los Angeles, would get his chance.

"I don't know how the Cardinals could have traded him," wailed George Halas of the Bears. "He's a 'wonder player' and you just don't trade away your 'wonder players.' There are too few of them in the league—Brown of Cleveland, maybe Arnett of Los Angeles, certainly Matson. There isn't any value really great enough to make you give them up."

Ollie Matson arrived in the National Football League from the University of San Francisco, where he had been an All-America, and from the 1952 Olympics, where he had finished third in the 400 meters and also had run on the relay team.

He was more than just another fast running back. He was a breed unto his own. He was 6-2, 208 and could run 9.6. The league had never seen a runner of his dimensions who could move that fast. It was his misfortune to land in Chicago, which, as it turned out, wasn't his kind of town.

Not that the Cardinals didn't try to utilize his vast talents. Unable to spring him from conventional sets because of a lack of adequate blocking, they experimented with just about everything else. One year, they went to the split-T, hoping Ollie would get the room he needed on pitchouts. But opposing defenses didn't fall for it. They tracked Matson and forgot about the rest of the Cards. Frank Ivy, the Chicago coach, then came up with what he called his "double slot" offense. It worked briefly, but once teams realized Ollie was running laterally behind the line of scrimmage, they keyed on him, and that was that. Frequently, they sent him in motion to the right, then tossed him a pitchout as he tried to circle end. That one didn't

General manager Tex Schramm (left) left the Rams in 1957 for an administrative position with CBS Television. His replacement as GM: former publicity director Pete Rozelle (right). Three years later, Rozelle was the surprise choice to replace Bert Bell as commissioner of the National Football League. Rams' owner Dan Reeves re-acquired control of the team in 1962, purchasing the interests of three co-owners, and a year later a new ownership group was formed that included, left to right, Paul A. O'Bryan, Reeves, Gene Autry and Bob Reynolds.

work because Ollie was beating his own blockers to the line of scrimmage.

Frustrated in their failures to get him in the clear from the line of scrimmage the Cardinals schemed to break him into the open with a pass. They tried to isolate him on one defender, and although it didn't succeed consistently, sometimes they were able to manage. In one game against Pittsburgh in 1952, the Cardinals were losing 31-7 in the fourth quarter. They shifted Matson from left half to right end and started throwing to him. He scored three touchdowns in six minutes and reduced the Steelers' advantage to 34-28 before time ran out. In his final year with Chicago, the Cardinals managed to complete 33 passes to him. He scored on three of them and, although most were screens or short swings, he averaged 14.1 yards per catch. His speed for 100 yards varied, according to whom you talked. "The first time I ran a 'hundred,' said Ollie, "I did it in 12 flat." His best recorded time was 9.6, but Matson insisted he had been clocked unofficially at 9.5 "a couple of times."

In the NFL, they talked of his speed as if they were awed by it . . . Clark Shaughnessy, who had been an assistant coach with the Bears, remembered the day the Cardinals slaughtered them, 53-14. "If you watched them carefully, you could see it was the *fear* of Matson as much as Matson's running ability that beat us. We had two men waiting outside—so far outside that it opened a big hole between tackle and end. Matson kept pulling us outside and Johnny Olszewski kept running off tackle through those holes to hurt us. I've never seen Matson flinch from a tackle, no matter had bad his team was being beaten. I've never seen him fold up."

Bob Konovsky, a Cardinal lineman, described the joy of having Matson on his side. "Sometime watch him when he doesn't get a kickoff," said Konovsky. "He takes off down the field like a highspeed truck and bangs into those big linemen like they didn't outweigh him by 40 or 50 pounds. When he gets up his speed, boy, there's nothing that'll match his momentum. He's got just enough weight to knock those linemen flying on kickoffs. It's a real thrill to watch him." Ray Prochaska, a Cardinal assistant coach at the time, put it this way: "Ollie doesn't have the finesse of Arnett or Frank Gifford of the Giants. But they don't have the tremendous speed that he has." Prochaska used the analogy between a P-47 World War II fighter plane and what was then a modern jet. "The P-47 can outmaneuver the jet in any particular space, but it'll never keep up with the jet in any test of speed."

When Gillman and the Rams' cool, young general manager, Pete Rozelle, consummated the trade, they realized that of the nine people they were giving up, three would leave the largest gaps. Panfil was a fine offensive tackle and Fuller was, at times, the best defensive lineman on the team. Holtzman played both offensive tackle and defensive end, and he proved accomplished at both positions.

"Our immediate concern," said Gillman, "is in replacing Panfil and Fuller. If Matson can run as well as we think, those losses will not be as great as they ordinarily would be. It is possible that Ollie will leave a little to be desired from the power standpoint, but we think he will give us enough power, plus his added speed."

The second-guessers, of course, immediately went to work. They could not understand the need for Matson on a team that already owned an Arnett, a Tom Wilson and a Joe Marconi. As it was, there had not been enough playing time for all three. Now there would be even less. Still others felt the Rams had traded their way to a quick championship.

"At Los Angeles," wrote Chicago's Bill Furlong, "Matson will have the benefit of the passing of Billy Wade. He will also have the benefit of the pass-catching threats of Del Shofner, Jim Phillips,

Wilson and Lamar Lundy. For it is not simply what Matson brings to Los Angeles but what Los Angeles contributes to him that provides the challenge and the opportunity. The speed of Matson can only supplement—not replace—the agility of Arnett."

Matson would, in time, become the focal point of Ram misery in the ensuing seasons. He would be the scapegoat, although he was hardly at fault. In 1959, his first year in a Ram uniform, he ran for 863 yards, the third best total in the league. But the figures that attracted more attention were the ones in the won-loss column. From 8-4 without Ollie, the Rams fell to 2-10 with him.

It may have been the most disappointing season of all in Los Angeles. The expectations had been so high, the predictions so promising. Unfortunately, the feeling was not completely shared by Matson's new teammates, some of whom resented his presence, not to mention his salary. It was like a Hollywood leading man being asked to suddenly share top billing. Also, the Rams who had been traded had made many close friends. The buddies they left behind did not hide their feelings. Openly, they criticized Rozelle for making the trade. And some writers in town felt a couple of linemen deliberately refused to block when Matson carried the ball.

After that, the situation only got worse. A year later, Matson, a fullback all his life, was switched to the defensive secondary. He played well, but the Rams weren't satisfied. In 1961, he became a slotback. For awhile, they even deployed him as a safety man on kickoffs. Finally, in 1963, they announced that he would be given another "trial" at fullback.

It was the spring of 1963, and Ollie Matson, now 32, was trying to express his feelings. He had threatened to play out his option in Los Angeles, then changed his mind. "I've been very disillusioned since I joined the Rams. I never felt I was given the opportunity to perform as I had in

Chicago. This winter, I did a lot of thinking about what it might be like to play somewhere else. I'm fond of Los Angeles. I called Dan Reeves. I've always had a lot of admiration for him. We talked it over and came to the conclusion I should spend the rest of my football days here."

On August 21 of that same year, Ollie Matson was traded to the Detroit Lions in exchange for one football player, a 32-year-old offensive guard named Harley Sewell.

"In the Ollie Matson story," wrote Bob Oates, "the most awesome fact is not that he was traded for nine players in 1959 but that Pete Rozelle made the trade. And Rozelle is a man who does not have to be introduced. As the NFL Commissioner, he is set apart from all other commissioners and indeed executives of sport by the unfailing wisdom of his decisions.

"So this is the man who, in his 1959 capacity as general manager of Los Angeles, determined that Matson was worth nine Rams, including four starters, two of them the anchors of the defensive and offensive lines.

"It was apparent at once that Rozelle was right. Pro football in its first 53 years has turned up few if any with Matson's versatility; he could have made the Hall of Fame as a fullback, halfback, defensive back, tight end or simply blocking back if he had specialized in any of these positions. He was seldom allowed to settle down, however, because he had the bad luck to spend most of his pro career in harness with journeymen.

"The record of the teams for which Matson played does not support the notion that he was an all-time all-pro. You had to see him to know it; and if you saw him you knew it . . . ."

The effects of Matson's first year in Los Angeles, however, could not be shaken. When a team loses its last eight games in a row, some action must be taken. Gillman and his assistants saved them the trouble. On the last day of the 1959 season, the coach and his staff resigned.

In 1960, general manager Pete Rozelle become commissioner of the NFL, Elroy Hirsch replaced him as GM, and Bob Waterfield became head coach. Waterfield's staff included (kneeling) Jim David, Don Paul and Tom Fears and (standing) former head coach Hamp Pool and Vic Lindskog. A 1961 trade brought the Rams a No. 1 draft choice, which they used to draft Merlin Olsen (in foreground at right). Los Angeles' other first choice that year was Roman Gabriel (number 15 in the photo made at the All-Star camp in Chicago).

Thus, a Great Search, similar to the one prior to Gillman's selection, was organized again. Only this time the eventual choice did not come as any large surprise, although the gentleman had been out of pro football for awhile. Bob Waterfield's name still had some of that old magic. It was the hero coming home to try and patch things up. The man who had proven he could win on the field would now try to do it from the sideline. The years hadn't changed him much. He was still lean and hard. The only sign of age was a slight graying at the temples. His conversation was short, maybe a little terse, and as frank as ever. On the night of his appointment, he was asked about assistant coaches. Calmly, he named names and said, "These are the men I want. I hope they're available." In every case, the assistants hired were the men Waterfield mentioned that evening. Tom Fears, Don Paul, Jim David, Vic Lindskog and, yes, Hamp Pool, joined the staff.

It was a time of change in Los Angeles. Never, perhaps, had the Rams experienced so many people coming and going, so much transition. Ths death of Bert Bell left the league without a commissioner, a vacancy that eventually would be filled by Rozelle, the Rams' young general manager. That left Reeves without a man in charge in the front office. He rectified that by hiring one of his all-time favorites, Elroy Hirsch, as the new general manager.

But while the change in leadership was surprising, the turnover in personnel was startling. Maybe embarrassing would be a better word. The players let go by the Rams would have formed an excellent team, an all-star team, some would say. Van Brocklin, of course, was first. He was followed by defensive end Andy Robustelli, who would guarantee his eventual Hall of Fame enshrinement by becoming one of the dominating players for the New York Giants for a half dozen years. Billy Wade and Rudy Bukich both became quarterbacks with the Bears. Wade, a regular, called the signals for Chicago's world championship team in 1963. Don Burroughs, the skinny safetyman known as "The Blade," joined Van Brocklin on the Philadelphia championship club. Larry Morris became a standout linebacker with the Bears. Gene (Big Daddy) Lipscomb was acquired by Baltimore for the $100 waiver price. Big Daddy would quickly develop into the best known defensive lineman in football. Bud McFadin, seriously wounded in an off-season shooting incident, was another who had decided he no longer wanted to play for the Rams. The Denver Broncos were another matter. Sure, he said, he'd play for them. So for two years McFadin was the best lineman in the American Football League. The list hardly stopped there. Night Train Lane became a perennial all-pro in Detroit. Jesse Whittenton became a fixture in the Green Bay secondary. Billy Ray Smith moved in as a solid regular in the Baltimore front four. Lou Michaels became a terror on and off the field in Pittsburgh. Jimmy Orr was to become one of John Unitas' favorite receivers with the Colts. Dean Derby and Jack Morris won starting spots in the Minnesota defensive backfield. The list seemed endless.

Ironically, perhaps the Rams' most publicized "goof" turned out to be a successful move. In 1961, they traded Wade, Del Shofner and John Guzik. In return, in this three-team deal with the Bears and Giants, Los Angeles received Lindon Crow, Zeke Bratkowski and a 1962 first-round draft choice, giving them two picks in the opening round. It appeared as if Los Angeles had been robbed. Shofner, who had fallen out of favor with the Rams, had been perhaps the best deep receiver to come into the league since Hirsch. In New York, with Y.A. Tittle getting him the ball, he quickly re-established himself as an all-pro on a championship team. "In return," one writer angrily explained, "the Rams got a No. 1 draft choice to stick up on the bulletin board." The draft choice turned out to be Merlin Olsen, who would become

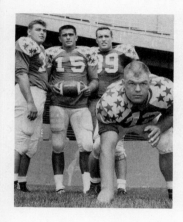

one of the great defensive players of his generation. The Rams' other No. 1 draft choice that year was a quarterback from North Carolina named Roman Gabriel.

For all their celebrated problems, the esteem with which the Rams' organization was held throughout the league was evident in the selection of Rozelle to the sport's highest office. The Pete Rozelle success story is something right out of a Hollywood scenario.

Rozelle started as a part-time assistant to the late Maxwell Styles when Styles was the Rams' publicity man in 1946. His first actual assignment in professional football was to paste pictures of Ram players on cardboard for a montage art layout in the program.

Progressing from a job on campus at the University of San Francisco to become the school's press agent, he was then hired as a member of the Rams' public relations staff in 1952. His reported salary was $6,500.

One of the first official functions in Rozelle's new position was to invite the Joe Stydahars over for dinner. Stydahar was the Ram coach at the time. Rozelle had furnished his apartment in the Crenshaw district of Los Angeles, promising to pay $140 eventually for all three rooms. At the little dining room table, Stydahar sat down comfortably and told a couple stories about the good, old days with the Chicago Bears. Always known for his strong appetite, Stydahar soon inquired about seconds. "Please pass the potatoes," he asked, just about the time he disappeared from view. "I looked down," said Rozelle, "and there he was on the floor—on a pile of kindling, my ex-chair. It just disintegrated. What a great way to start a career in pro football."

In 1954, Rozelle moved to San Francisco where he spent two years in private business as a public relations specialist. When he returned to the Rams, it was as their general manager in 1957. Typically, he was the right man for the right job at the right time. In 1957, three of the Ram owners, Reeves, Pauley and Levy, weren't saying much to each other. The incumbent general manager, Tex Schramm, was a Reeves man, a fact that did not please Pauley and Levy. So Schramm left the Rams to accept an executive position with CBS-TV Sports. Rozelle was his replacement.

One of Reeves' great talents was in picking employees. It is one reason for the number of ex-Ram executives now working in the front offices of so many National Football League organizations. "I think part of the reason," explained Rozelle, "is the training we received while working for Dan. For example, I was very lucky as a public relations man in that I was given an opportunity to learn a lot about the organization. Dan would have you involved in scouting and even researching players on service teams. I spent a great deal of time tracking down some of the better players in service ball and eventually signed quite a few. Tom Wilson and Big Daddy Lipscomb were just a couple. I learned something about all phases of the business from Dan. He wanted to use his personnel to the maximum. When the Rams would make a trade, he'd bring you in and evaluate it for hours, writing names on a blackboard and even projecting the way it would look in two or three years." Rozelle made the most of his opportunity and applied the lessons he learned early.

One year, after the Rams had lost a couple of exhibition games, general manager Rozelle called in Gillman, his coach and a man 16 years his senior. "We're paying for a telephone that you're not using," said Pete. "It costs us $15 every Sunday to run a direct line from your bench to your assistants in the press box. How can I justify this expense to the owners when you never pick up the phone?" From then on, Gillman conferred with his assistants in the press box.

Although he enjoyed a good rapport with the players, Rozelle could be tough when the situa-

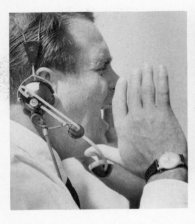

tion called for it. On one Rams trip, Rozelle ordered Duane Putnam, an all-pro guard, to "take off your shoes and go to bed." The order was given at midnight. Putnam refused. Rozelle shipped him back to Los Angeles on the next plane.

His appointment as commissioner was hardly expected. He was, after all, just 33 years old, hardly an age when men rise to such heights. As it turned out, he was the compromise candidate, a man acceptable only after several others could not be agreed upon in 22 rounds and five days of balloting. Reeves always maintained that Marshall Leahy of San Francisco would have been elected if George Halas "had kept his word" to vote for Leahy if and when the San Francisco attorney had received eight other votes.

"Halas put a condition on the election that he would not vote at all unless and until a candidate received eight other votes and Halas' would mean the ninth and electing vote," said Reeves, afterwards. "He had guaranteed Vic Morabito he would vote for Leahy as soon as Leahy had eight other votes. It got to that point three times. Each time Halas went back on his word and still refused to cast the vote that would have elected Leahy. Halas felt the vote on the commissioner might upset the balance of expansion and he considered expansion the more important of the two subjects.

"The issues in this meeting," Reeves said, "went beyond the people involved. The whole thing was startling. I've never seen more revelations of character, strengths and weaknesses. Out of it all, we got closer together. We got to know each other better. It was a great meeting. Wellington Mara of the Giants was a very strong figure and a very sound one. Paul Brown, who in the past had been mostly bored with league meetings, took a very active and a very important part in this one. These are the men who are moving to the front in our league. This league has for many

years been dominated by Halas and George Preston Marshall, to a lesser degree each year. This is a complete reversal of form."

Rozelle, it turned out, was first suggested by Mara and Brown as the compromise choice. Ironically, it was Carroll Rosenbloom of Baltimore who actually nominated him. Twelve years later, Rosenbloom, a longtime friend of Reeves, would buy the Rams after Dan's death.

Rozelle's name first came up as a candidate for commissioner at a noon recess. Pete didn't hear about it until the owners began interrogating him, one by one, during the afternoon. Thirty minutes before the announcement would be made, Rozelle had been dismissed and had taken refuge across the hotel lobby in the men's room. When reporters and others wandered in, he'd turn away and nervously wash his hands. He once confided that he must have washed them 27 times. The man who brought him the news was, once again, Rosenbloom. He smiled and said, "Good evening, Commissioner." Pete bumped into some reporters as he emerged from the rest room. "I am taking the job," he said, "with clean hands."

"I think the Rams have had a serious loss," said Reeves, after the news became official, "one that will hurt us now. But in the long run, the election of Pete Rozelle will help Los Angeles, the Rams, the West and pro football. The Rams are going to feel that loss, at the start, much, much more than the average man realizes. It's going to hurt deep. He was the cellophane of the organization. He kept things together. This is an amazing tribute to a young man of 33. Pete is going to have troubles at first. But he has all the qualifications to be a great commissioner—and one for life."

"Look at it this way," a friend told Reeves, "you're not losing a son, you're gaining a father."

When Rozelle headed East to confront his new

Harland Svare (far left) become one of the youngest head coaches in football when he took over the Rams' fortunes in 1962. The early 1960s produced few moments of elation for Rams' fans, but two exceptions were the 105-yard kickoff return by Jon Arnett against the Lions in 1961 (left, note the makeshift press box hung in the Coliseum tunnel for the baseball Dodgers), and Dick Bass' heroics in 1962, when he gained 1,033 yards (right) for a team that had a 1-12-1 record.

problems, he left some old ones behind. The heir to the Ram confusion was Hirsch. Crazylegs had not really been trained to work in a front office, but he was personable, projected a good image and, perhaps most important, was the least offensive of any of the candidates considered. His biggest obstacle was a lack of complete authority. If a fast decision was required on a trade, Elroy first would have to go to Reeves and then to Pauley, Levy and Seley for the okay. "Sure, it was bound to hurt us," confessed Reeves, later. "Hirsch was powerless. And the players were bound to feel it, too."

The balance of power seemed to be the No. 1 issue in Los Angeles in the early '60s. No one really knew where it was located. Even on the field, the leadership seemed to be split.

Waterfield improved the record to 4-7-1 in 1960. But in 1961, in the wake of the controversial Shofner trade and an expanded schedule, the Rams fell back to 4-10. Not surprisingly, the players began to stir. A full-blown rebellion was exposed in December of '61. The target was Pool, the assistant who already had been fired once from the organization. Pool had too much authority, some players claimed. He was working them too hard. Waterfield, meanwhile, was described as a "figurehead." The players said they needed to know who was boss. "We need leadership from a single owner to a single coach," said one veteran, who asked to remain anonymous. He did.

None of the rebellious players were ever identified. But among the most dissatisfied Rams of the era was perhaps their best player, Jon Arnett. Frustrated in part because his great running talent could not be fully utilized behind a weak offensive line, he threatened to bolt his contract because of a salary dispute. "I'll quit," he said, "if Merlin Olsen gets more than me." Joe Marconi was another who was upset and Tommy Wilson, who never got a chance to play full time,

was preparing to play out his option and move on.

The year it all erupted was 1962. Off even slower than usual, the Rams won just one of their first five games. It got only worse after that. The final record was 1-12-1, though Waterfield was no longer around. He resigned after the eighth game. Harland Svare, a one-time Ram who had been a starter on the New York Giants championship teams, was named to replace him on an interim basis. Svare joined the staff at the start of the season as defensive line coach, replacing Don Paul.

The year's most important decision, however, was made behind closed doors. The scene, ironically presided over by Commissioner Rozelle, could have been described as the Great Ram Poker Game—except that the stakes were unusually high, even by Nevada standards. The winner of the game would have control of the professional football team in Los Angeles. It was a sealed bid auction, with the high bidder automatically declared the winner among Reeves, Pauley, Levy, Seley and Bob Hope.

Typically, Reeves was ready. His bid was so shockingly high that he won going away. The headlines of December 27, 1962, screamed the news: "Reeves Buys Rams for $7.1 Million."

What it meant was that it would cost Reeves $4.8 million to buy up the shares his partners had acquired for $1 each a few years earlier. But Reeves, the financial expert, worked it out so that he emerged as owner of 51 per cent of the club for an outlay of $1,028,422. It happened this way: First, Dan came up with the $1,028,422 for 51 per cent of the property. Second, he sold 49 per cent to seven new associates for $2,450,000. That left a balance of $1,300,000 on the total due the Pauley faction. Third, to raise the $1,300,000, Reeves organized a new corporation, the Los Angeles Rams Football Co., Inc., wholly owned by himself and his seven new partners. The company borrowed the money and

pledged to retire the loan before declaring any dividends. So that portion of the purchase price would be paid out of Ram profits, a standard business device.

The new ownership structure was rather complicated. In all, 12 men were involved. Reeves, with 51 per cent, was president and general manager. But five others, with seven per cent each, held offices on the board of directors. They were Gene Autry and Robert O. Reynolds, vice-president; lawyer Paul A. O'Bryan, secretary; and Leonard K. Firestone, treasurer. The other four board members were nonowners. But they were all close friends of Reeves, helping to insure 5-4 votes for the president. Their names were R.A. Corroon Jr., W.A. (Bill) Barnes, A.A. (Buddy) Gillespie and W.C. (Bud) Duffy. Three more nonowners were added to the board from the Los Angeles Angels syndicate, in which Autry, Reynolds and Firestone were involved.

The reaction at the Rams' office was a happy one. Practically every National Football League team sent warm greetings of congratulations. Reeves was deeply moved. "The way people have reacted is a tremendous feeling," Dan told Mal Florence of the *Los Angeles Times*. "There are many nice people in the world."

Jack Dwyer, a former Rams halfback with a sense of humor, sent a wire that read: "Can you loan me $2, Dan, or shall I call Ed?" Norm Van Brocklin said: "Now I know there is justice in the world. I'm going to start going to church." Publicist Jack Teele had been waiting hours to hear the news. When he learned that Reeves had won, he ecstatically rushed out to give the news to the media in the area. He phoned Jerry Wynn, the current San Diego Chargers publicist who was then covering the Rams for the Long Beach newspapers. "Jerry . . . Jerry," blurted the excited Teele, "it's Dan . . . it's Dan . . . ." "Oh," said Wynn, matter-of-factly, "hello, Dan."

Florence, in his story in the *Times* the next day, related further details of the auction. The opening bid by the Pauley faction had been made at $6.1 million. Reeves raised it to $7.1 million. Under the rules agreed upon, the next bid would have to be 20 per cent higher. That would have been approximately $8.5 million. After a half hour's deliberation, the Pauley group declined.

Obviously happy afterwards, Reeves wisecracked that the auction conducted at the Bel-Air Hotel was like a wake. "Everyong wore dark suits," he said. Someone asked how he could pay $4.8 million for what originally had cost $4. Dan replied, "I guess I value money lower than some people." A reporter wondered how the transaction would affect the future of the Rams. "Probably all that will happen," said Reeves, "is that we will make the same mistakes a little more efficiently."

The rest of the National Football League certainly was hoping that wouldn't be the case. As early as the fall of 1961, NFL owners were concerned over the slump in Los Angeles.

"Not so many years ago, an Eagles trip to Los Angeles was worth $95,000," said Philadelphia general manager Vince McNally. "Even the preseason trips there were financial plums. But no more. On our last preseason game there in '59, the attendance was about 35,000." McNally was asked if that meant the Rams might have to venture East for their preseason games. "Could be," he replied. "If the gates keep shrinking, who's going to go out there?"

Reeves' new plan appeared to be one of gradual improvement, rather than immediate success. Svare, his new head coach, was 32, the youngest in professional football. His staff was even more youth-oriented. His six assistants were Ray Wietecha, Don Heinrich, Bob Schnelker, Pat Summerall, Jack Patera and Lindon Crow. The oldest was 36.

The choice of Svare was questioned by some

because of Harland's defensive background. In his first three games as Ram coach at the end of the 1962 season, he started three different people at quarterback. Some writers in town wondered if he were experienced enough to provide this team with offensive direction. Clearly, it needed some kind of boost. Once the most imaginative and explosive team in football, the Rams suddenly had forgotten how to score. In 1962, they finished 14th in a 14-game league in total yards and points.

Several theories for the failure were advanced, such as one in the *Los Angeles Herald-Examiner,* whose large headline read: "Ram Demise Laid to Rozelle." Actually, the writer defended Rozelle, even calling him "one of the three or four great NFL general managers of his decade." A later paragraph in the story analyzed it this way: "Spelling it out, a ballclub torn by the dissension of fighting owners could not surmount the losses of four first-string linemen and three high draft choices, including Louisiana State's Billy Cannon, in an era which introduced a controversial athlete, Matson, who was never fully accepted by the players."

That was the situation as Svare began to build. His foundation included Gabriel, Olsen and an obscure rookie defensive end from South Carolina State, David Jones, whose nickname came to be Deacon.

From the beginning, Reeves liked Svare's style. "He has confidence without being cocky," said Dan. They called Svare "Swede" because of his Norwegian ancestry. But he really was a farm boy from Washington State who went Ivy League in New York. He lived well, ate well and dressed well. Svare was trained by Jim Lee Howell, who helped develop a number of fine coaches, including two named Vince Lombardi and Tom Landry.

While trying to be optimistic, the new coach glanced over his roster and admitted some sad

truths. "These are players who don't know how to win," he said. "And you have to win the close ones in this league. That's what the game is. Of course, we would like to develop a winning attitude, a winning habit, a confidence such as the Giants have had. But to get that, you have to win some games first. I believe this club has the potential to win some games. When we get to that point, we can go on from there. I don't expect miracles. I do expect consistent progress. I'm not concerned with the troubles the club has had in the past or the mistakes it has made. I'm concerned that I have only a one-year contract. In this league, you try to win every ballgame, right here and now, anyway. I have the job for a year, and if I do it well, in my own way, the future will take care of itself."

The future was more difficult than Svare realized. After an 0-5 start in his first full year, the coach inserted Gabriel as his regular quarterback. The Rams rallied strongly under Gabe, going 5-4 in the last nine games to finish 5-9-0. But that was not the end of Svare's quarterback dilemma. Zeke Bratkowski was around, so was an expensive Heisman Trophy winner named Terry Baker. Another fine looking young passer out of Utah State named Bill Munson soon entered the picture in 1964. Munson was poised, almost unshakeable, and many likened him to a young Bob Waterfield. He took over in his rookie season after an early injury cut down Gabriel. Munson performed brilliantly in a losing effort in the rabid environs of Baltimore Memorial Stadium. So Gabriel vs. Munson became, for awhile, a latter-day Waterfield vs. Van Brocklin or Van Brocklin vs. Wade. Only this time the delicate problem was never solved. Svare finally committed himself, more or less, to Munson. Meanwhile, new players were constantly moving in, bringing promise, but little experience. In '64, the club finished 5-7-2. The following season the Rams fell to 4-10.

Defense was George Allen's game, and he assembled one of the best around him in Los Angeles. Jack Pardee (left, stopping Brian Piccolo of Chicago) was one of the linebacking stars; he was joined by Maxie Baughan and Myron Pottios. Eddie Meador and Richie Petitbon were outstanding safetymen. And the line was superb, led by the two greats on the left side, Merlin Olsen (74) and Deacon Jones.

The Rams signed a new 10-year contract to play in the Coliseum in 1964. The new design featured a "stadium-within-a-stadium," bringing in bleacher-type seats at the peristyle end, moving more people closer to the action. It also provided fans with new theater-type seats. "We want to be sure," Reeves said, "that our fans suffer in comfort."

In public, he joked. In private, Reeves failed to see the humor in the Rams' losing record. After the 1965 season, Svare had been on the job three full years and part of another, and although he captured three of his last four games against top teams in each division that year, and had put together a promising, young defensive line, he was fired at the end of the season.

The year 1966 probably was the most tumultuous in pro football history. It was the year of the merger, the year the entire scope of the game changed. Naturally, Reeves was in on it from the beginning. Talks actually had begun months in advance. Just how willing and how far Reeves and fellow NFL officials were prepared to go was revealed by Tex Schramm, who learned his football under Dan and had since advanced to a prominent position in the Dallas front office.

Schramm, one of the leaders of the merger, a man who was quick to attack, recalls some of the discussions:

"My original plan was to get Oakland out of Oakland and the New York Jets out of New York. I talked with Ram owner Dan Reeves in Los Angeles first. To give up New York, there had to be a major city available for the person who had the Jets. Werblin had been with MCA and was close to the Hollywood picture scene. Los Angeles and Hollywood would be an attraction to him. I talked to Reeves about moving out of L.A., to either San Diego or Phoenix. At that time, San Diego was not successful and it, in turn, would move to Phoenix or be assimilated. I didn't get into that, because things took a dif-

ferent turn. There were other options.

"Under certain circumstances, Reeves indicated there was a possibility of moving out of Los Angeles or leaving the team there and he'd take over the San Diego franchise. Werblin would have assumed the L.A. team, with the Jets moving elsewhere, perhaps to Miami or New Orleans. Or the Jets would move to Los Angeles and the Rams move somewhere else. Under certain circumstances, it was understood Werblin would be willing to move from New York. I did not speak to him personally, though. But I did speak with Reeves and he liked the idea of the merger. It had to be done. I always thought that money could be obtained to compensate for what had to be done. If you could reduce the problem to money, it would be easy."

Fortunately, none of those drastic measures ever was required. The merger was completed with Rozelle, the Reeves-trained commissioner, acting as chief diplomat, tying all loose ends together and soothing bruised prides and egos.

For the Rams, though, the year of transition was just beginning. The next step was to hire a new coach, and again, the speculation started. It was silenced when the announcement arrived that George Allen, a one-time Los Angeles assistant, and the man behind the Chicago Bears' amazing defensive team of 1963, had been hired.

There was, of course, one slight roadblock. Allen had signed a three-year contract with the Bears in 1965. And George Halas, who could never be described as a longtime friend of the Rams, was not happy about Los Angeles coming in and luring one of his most talented assistants away.

So Papa Bear filed suit in Circuit Court for a permanent injunction to restrain Allen from taking the job. Things happened fast after that. Contacted for his opinion, Commissioner Rozelle said he saw "no cause" to interfere with the Rams' hiring of Allen. "It has been traditional

with the NFL and throughout sports that assistant coaches are permitted to take advantages of opportunities for advancement," Rozelle said. "It is hoped that the matter can be amicably resolved by the two clubs." Halas, of course, had an answer: "I agree with Pete Rozelle that this is a matter between two clubs and is not of league concern. It is for that reason that we filed our suit. The suit stands."

The actual complaint charged Allen with "willful breach of a three-year contract executed June 22, 1965, in which Allen's salary was set at $19,000 a year. The Bears further alleged that Allen, during his seven-year tenure with the club, obtained information on Bears plays, scouting reports of other teams and players and a variety of other information which would be detrimental to the Bears if disclosed.

"Unless he (Allen) is restrained," the complaint read, "he will use this information in coaching the Rams against the Bears." Which, of course, was the idea all along.

Halas went so far as to cite examples, however. He said Allen possessed the Bears' defense manual, defense textbook and numerous motion picture films. If Allen were allowed to leave the state of Illinois and move to California, the complaint pointed out, he would then be beyond the jurisdiction of the Illinois court. The complaint revealed that Allen addressed a letter of resignation to the Bears. It read as follows:

"Dear Coach Halas,

"No man has ever owed more to another than I do to you for all you have done for me. No one has ever had a more agonizing experience in arriving at a decision than I have had in bringing myself to this final act of resignation.

"The opportunity which has been offered to me to become head coach of the Los Angeles Rams is one I feel I must accept. The job of realizing this ambition is marred only by the regret of leaving a team, and an association with you, which has given me the most rewarding years of my life.

"In accepting the challenge to take over the Rams, I do so with deep humility, knowing that my opportunity has come about only because of my personal growth which has occurred under your leadership during the past eight years.

"It is more than difficult to even imagine myself in competition with the Bears. Yet, I shall attempt to compete with you and with the other NFL teams with the same spirit which you have most exemplified.

"Most sincerely,
George Allen"

Already in Los Angeles, Allen told the press he was aware of the suit brought by the Bears and said he could not believe Halas "would stand in the way of somebody getting a better job." Allen said he was "flattered" Halas considered him so essential. "I didn't realize I was that important," he said.

Finally, Halas released Allen and George set out to put together a staff. The men he picked were Jack Patera, Ted Marchibroda, Ray Prochaska, Howard Schnellenberger, Tom Catlin and Joe Sullivan.

The Rams had changed coaches again, the merger had been accomplished and a new era was about to begin. But one old and familiar friend would not be around to join in on it. Bob Kelley, the voice of the club since its inception in 1937, died in September 1966. To longtime fans, many of whom did not attend games in person, the Rams would never again be the same. Dick Enberg, Kelley's eventual successor and the present play-by-play man, is an excellent announcer, extraordinarily gifted in a variety of sports. But for the purists in town, there would never again be anything to match Ol' Kell's emotional description of a dramatic Rams touchdown.

It didn't take long for fans, writers and em-

ployees to learn about George Allen. Here was a man who was dedicated to being dedicated. Success was his purpose in life, and because little else occupied his mind while striving for it, he would often seem insensitive.

A Ram employee picked up a telephone one day and was informed his apartment had just burned down. As far as he knew at that moment, everything he owned had been lost, his clothes, his furniture, everything. His face was ashen as he hung up the phone, and George Allen walked into the room. "What happened?" inquired George. "You're all white." The employee explained. Allen offered a few quick words of sympathy, then said, "Do you think you can have this stuff ready for me later this afternoon?"

Allen's job in Los Angeles was not to become the most popular man in the Rams' organization, though. He was being asked merely to win, something he managed to do from the beginning. His methods, familiar now throughout football, were the same then. Immediately, he set out to trade every draft choice he could lay his hands on for veterans. "I like men with bald heads," he'd say. "I want to win today, I don't want to wait for tomorrow."

"The future is now." If there is one quote that will identify the Allen philosophy, that's it. The future was not quite yet for the Rams, however. It took Allen time to establish things, to find out who his best players were, to get old, hard-bitten football players to believe his message. Among the first and most important moves he made was to recognize the potential of Gabriel at quarterback. A large, somewhat shy, introverted young man with a powerful arm, Gabriel had taken over the job late in the 1965 season when Bill Munson suffered a knee injury that required surgery. Recovery was slow for the promising passer from Utah State, compounded by a toe fracture that failed to heal properly. Munson also suffered a series of severe virus at-

tacks in the summer and fall of 1966. Finally, at the end of Allen's first year, Munson was completely recovered. But his job was gone, never to be regained again. Gabriel, Allen and a revitalized defense combined to produce an 8-6 season and the Rams' first winning record in eight years. A year later, Munson, tired of being a benchwarmer in Los Angeles, asked to be traded. His wish was granted. He was dealt to Detroit. Gabriel, improving rapidly, made a statement Ram quarterbacks and coaches of the past could well have heeded:

"It's necessary to have the confidence of everyone involved," he said. "The people who surround you, the coaching staff, the players . . . that's 40 men. If you're the quarterback, that means that 39 other players must have confidence in you. If just one guy doesn't . . . well, it could be the start of dissension."

The quarterback problems that plagued Gillman and Svare never hindered Allen. Gabriel's greatest asset was his physical strength, and he was rarely hurt. Gabe was to become the prototype of the modern quarterback, the type for which all scouts would soon look. A man tall enough to see over the increasingly large defensive linemen and one big and courageous enough to absorb a pounding.

By 1967, Allen's building program was ready for fruition. He would not wait for the regular season to begin. "You must win early to establish a winning attitude," Allen said during the summer. The statement would serve as an inspiration to the Rams all through the 1967 season.

The Rams opened with a victory over New Orleans, then routed Minnesota 39-3, intercepting four passes from three Minnesota quarterbacks. The following week it was a 35-13 victory at Dallas. Gabriel masterminded the win with scoring drives of 80, 72 and 93 yards and scored two touchdowns himself. Cowboy rushers were

If Allen specialized in defense, that is not to say that he ignored the offense. He surrounded Gabriel with a tough, experienced corps of offensive linemen (left): center Ken Iman, guards Tom Mack and Joe Scibelli and tackles Bob Brown and Charlie Cowan. Scibelli (right) was the co-captain and leader of the unit.

stifled, picking up only 51 yards on 24 carries.

Los Angeles' next game was at the Coliseum against the 49ers. The 49ers got off to a quick start, mainly on the passing arm of John Brodie, and built a 20-0 halftime lead. But the Rams came back with three third-quarter touchdowns for a one-point lead and had a 24-20 advantage in the fourth quarter. Brodie, however, sealed the decision with nine minutes left, hitting Sonny Randle in the end zone for a 27-24 49ers victory. It was the Rams' first loss of the season. It also would be the last time Los Angeles would lose during the regular season.

But the Rams didn't win the next two weekends, either.

Los Angeles traveled to Baltimore to meet the Colts in the season's fifth week. The Colts were 4-0, the Rams 3-1 in the Coastal Division race. In the fourth quarter, Baltimore held a seemingly safe 10-point lead at 24-14. Then Bruce Gossett kicked a 47-yard field goal to narrow the margin to one touchdown. Next, Maxie Baughan stole a John Unitas pass, setting up Gabriel's scrambling 16-yard touchdown pass to Bernie Casey for a 24-24 tie. The Rams continued to trail the Colts by one game, a situation that would not change until the season's final weekend.

Playing the Washington Redskins at home the following week, the Rams built up a lead, then watched the fabulous passing of Sonny Jurgensen eradicate it. Jurgensen's arm earned the 'Skins a 28-28 deadlock.

Without a victory in their previous three games, the Rams won their next seven, capped by the Coliseum win over the Packers, which gave them a chance at the Coastal Division title.

Baltimore was still a game in front, but a victory by the Rams would give Los Angeles the Coastal title since the Rams would win the season series from the Colts.

Over 78,000 fans jammed the Coliseum for the rematch. Rarely, if ever, have the Rams played a better game. Gabriel skillfully moved his team to a 17-7 halftime advantage, and the Rams' defense contained both Unitas and the Colts' running game. The Rams' pattern was precise: three points in the first and third quarters, 14 in the second and fourth. The result: a 34-10 rout in which Gabriel completed 18 of 22 passes for 257 yards and three touchdowns. Green Bay, whom the Rams had defeated in southern California, was next, in the Western Conference title game. The rematch was held in the Arctic air of Wisconsin.

Allen, ever the perfectionist for detail, moved the Rams to Green Bay early so that they might become acclimated as much as possible to the cold weather. His decision was not universally accepted by the players. Most resented being away from their families, and several were openly disdainful of the Rams' ability to adjust quickly to a condition as common to the Packers as sunshine was to Los Angeles.

Nonetheless, the Rams started quickly. Gabriel threw a touchdown pass to Casey, and fumbles thwarted two Green Bay drives. Then Chuck Lamson intercepted a Bart Starr pass and the Rams were in a position to take a 10-0 lead on a 24-yard field goal try by Gossett.

One play turned the game around. The momentum was on the side of the Rams as Gossett lined up. The snap was perfect, but the kick never had a chance. Dave Robinson blasted through the Rams' line to bat it down, and from that point, the momentum—and the game—shifted to the Packers. Bart Starr completed 17 passes in 23 attempts and Green Bay eased to a 28-10 victory.

"Winning," said Dan Reeves that year, "makes life more pleasant but it makes it more difficult, too. In football, you're allowed 24 hours after a win to enjoy it. Then it becomes time to worry about the next game. In a way, when you're winning, there is more pressure on you, if you're going down to the wire every week, every minute, every play. Of course, it's not the sort of pressure you

really object to, but after awhile, it gets to you."

It was a hint of things to come. Despite the winning and the surging attendance figures, all was not healthy with the Rams. Allen continued to create animosity among those in the front office. "The Green Arrow," they called him. "Compared to Allen, Vince Lombardi is Santa Claus," said one employee. Reeves, of course, had pioneered scouting in its modern form. He believed in building with draft choices. Allen would get a sick look on his face when you'd mention draft choices. Reeves liked to run his own operation. Allen slowly tried to assume more and more control, making decisions people in the front office weren't sure he should be making. If George knew the team operated under a budget, he never acknowledged the fact. He liked to encourage players quietly, like offering bonuses. And when the Rams were successful, Reeves wanted to enjoy it, to celebrate, for instance, after a game with his coach. Allen could care less about celebrating. After a game, he began thinking about the next game. His only libation was a dish of ice cream.

Following a 1968 game in San Francisco that ended in a tie, Allen openly criticized the Kezar Stadium playing surface, describing it as the worst field he had seen. Reeves, who didn't like alibis, called a sportswriter and rebuked his own coach, claiming Allen was out of line for knocking Kezar. Allen was very upset. So was Reeves, who appeared in the locker room after the next week's game, approached Allen and said, "George, how was the field today?" Allen was stunned. "Dan," he said, "you had no right to criticize me in the paper. You embarrassed me and my family. Here I am working 16 to 18 hours a day, trying to build our team into a winner, and you make a fool out of me." Allen walked away. Reeves called after him, "George, you come back here." Allen didn't. Other Ram officials scurried the owner out of the room, trying to avoid a further scene.

Though Allen and Reeves continued their feud

in private, it did not deter George from his primary mission: winning.

The 1968 Rams won 10 games, lost three and tied one, a figure that in most years would have been good enough to win the division. But 1968 was the year Baltimore set the NFL ablaze with a 13-1 regular season record.

Nonetheless, it was a productive year for Allen's team. Attendance in Los Angeles soared over the million mark and the Rams set an NFL record for fewest yards allowed.

Three games crystallized the Rams' season. The Rams won their first six games and held a one-game lead over the Colts when they met Baltimore for the first of two meetings, this in Memorial Stadium.

The Colts had been upset the previous week by Cleveland and after Gossett kicked a field goal, the Colts' offense, led by Earl Morrall for the injured John Unitas, struck for two first-quarter touchdowns.

Meanwhile, the Colts' defense contained the Rams all afternoon. Gabriel was sacked five times and Rams runners had only 70 yards to show for their efforts, compared to the Colts' 159. Morrall passed 44 yards to Jimmy Orr in the second period and Baltimore took a 20-3 lead at halftime, en route to a 27-10 victory.

With the division tied, the Rams won two straight before a 20-20 tie with San Francisco dropped them a half-game behind Baltimore. The standings remained unchanged when the Chicago Bears came to the Coliseum the next-to-last game of the season.

The Bears were in the midst of a so-so season. The Rams had two alternatives: a victory would force a showdown with the Colts in the final week; a loss would mean the season was over.

The Rams' offense had been in high gear in a 31-3 victory at Minnesota the previous week, but against the Bears, Los Angeles could do little offensively. Chicago took a 3-0 first quarter lead

and held a 17-7 advantage in the third period. Faced with a fourth down deep in their own territory, the Bears' Bobby Joe Green went into punt formation. The snap was high, too high for Green, and the ball bounced into the Bears' end zone as a host of Rams gave chase. Dave Pivec, a seldom-used tight end, got to the ball first, a split-second after it rolled out of the end zone. Instead of seven points, Los Angeles had to settle for two and trailed by eight, 17-9.

Inspired, Gabriel marched his team to a fourth-quarter touchdown. Gossett's conversion brought the Rams to within a point and no one in the Coliseum audience of 66,368 doubted the Rams could get the ball back and attempt the winning field goal.

The Bears tried a ball-control approach, but with a half-minute to play, the Rams had the ball at the Chicago 32. On first down, Gabriel faded to pass. It was incomplete, but of more importance was a penalty flag near the line of scrimmage.

The referee signaled that a Rams interior lineman was guilty of holding. The ball came all the way back to the Bears' 47, out of Gossett's range, but the Rams still had a chance, however slight.

On the ensuing play, Gabriel passed incomplete again and glanced at the sideline marker. It read third down. Gabriel did not notice anything wrong. Nor did the Rams' bench. High in the press box, Mal Florence of the *Los Angeles Times* did. When the Rams were penalized, the chain gang signaled a second-down play coming up, when the Rams should have had a first down with 25 yards to go after the penalty.

What should have been second down was actually third. The Rams threw incomplete again. On fourth down, Chicago took possession of the ball, holding on for a 17-16 victory.

The Rams' season had come to a frustrating end. The following week's game with Baltimore was meaningless and the Colts won, 28-24. The "lost-down" game would be remembered by

coaches, players and fans for years to come, though it was a newspaperman's story which brought the error to light. By then it was too late. The Rams would experience another winter of discontent—on several fronts.

Meanwhile, the gap widened between coach and owner. In New York, Reeves, afflicted with Hodgkin's Disease, was undergoing regular treatment at a clinic there, missing most of the Ram games. Allen claimed he didn't talk with Reeves again after the flareup at the Coliseum. The next time he heard from him was at 8 o'clock in the morning on the day after Christmas 1968—the day Allen learned he'd been fired.

"He began rambling," Allen told reporters afterward, "and he rambled on and on. He told me I was a great coach and that I could get a job any place and that I shouldn't worry about money. He would take care of me. But he said that he was unhappy and I had to go.

"I told him we should meet with each other in person and talk this thing over. But he said his mind was made up. And, basically, that's about all there was to it."

Not quite. The news reverberated like one of Los Angeles' famous earthquakes. The Ram switchboard lit up like the control panel of a 747. Newspapers in town were flooded with phone balls. Pickets soon appeared in front of the club office on Pico Boulevard. Many of the Ram players were shocked and disappointed. Twelve of them showed up at a press conference with their coach, who by this time seemed like a martyr. The tears flowed, the flashbulbs popped and the cameras rolled. It was all very dramatic.

The town could talk of nothing else for days. Everyone connected in any way with the situation was interviewed by reporters who appeared to be enjoying the part they were playing.

Etty Allen, George's wife, commented freely on the case. "It was brutal," she said. "It was so unexpected, too—but the brutality, that's what hurt.

So different than Paris. Before going to the guillotine, they always gave a man a cigaret and the chance to say a few prayers."

Contacted for specific reasons for his action, Reeves accused Allen of high-handedness and of trying to establish complete autonomy. He also said George was somewhat extravagant.

"When you pick up a losing team," argued Allen, "and you try to get going, you can't have static. You must have control. Shula has it, Gillman has it, Sherman has it and Lombardi and Al Davis and many others have had it."

Allen was asked if he thought Reeves might reconsider. "I doubt it," he said. "I think he will make it stick. Reeves is a charming man and he has fooled the press, which protects him more than it should. For years, writers have blamed Ram failures on everyone except the owner. If Dan didn't like the way I was doing things, he could have sat down with me and the two of us could have discussed it like mature men, setting up ground rules by which we could live. But he didn't try to talk with me. He picks up the phone and fires me at 8 in the morning, rambling on in a way I could hardly understand. On my record in Los Angeles, I think I deserved better."

It was on New Year's Day that Dan Reeves gave in. Public sentiment had been so overwhelming, something had to be done. Clearly, firing Allen seemed to be a horrifying public relations mistake at that point, and the pressure on his successor would have been monumental. So Dan called George and asked him to come back. Allen did not give an answer immediately.

"We're still giving it a great deal of thought," said Mrs. Allen, three days later. Allen reportedly had received two new offers to coach, one from each league. "George is not so much interested in doubling his salary," said a friend, "as he is in getting more security than he has with an organization that could call him up after a 10-3-1 year and say, 'You're fired.' "

"If he hadn't been fired," said his wife, "he would have worked 12-hour days straight through the holidays getting ready for next year's team. You have no idea how he loves those 40 players of his. He goes around the house talking about Merlin Olsen and Lamar Lundy and Roman Gabriel as if they were his own children. And the first thing he told me after the season was that 1969 was going to be a championship year for the Rams. The firing has not changed his feeling for his players. That love affair is still on and those are the players he wants to lead to a championship—but it is still five months till summer camp. If he's ever going to stop and take stock, this is the time. Would you blame him for thinking there's still a sword dangling over his head? It simply isn't fair to ask him to come back under the same conditions."

The Allens lived in a Palos Verdes Estates house valued at between $150,000 and $175,000. "We'd like to stay, of course," said Mrs. Allen. "But we had a nice home in Chicago, too, and we left that. We prefer to make our homes our principal investment. We'll leave it if we have to because we think of it as an investment—and George's job comes first. But somehow, I think we'll be staying. It would be such a waste if a good coach and the players he likes so much were separated."

It was later reported that Dr. Jules Rasinski, the team physician, acted as an intermediary in the case, convincing Reeves that Allen's only wish was to return to the Rams. Finally, on Jaunary 6, the coach and owner appeared in public together, briefly, announcing that Allen was returning to coach the Rams.

The press conference was held at the plush Century Plaza Hotel, where the ventilation system is excellent. But observers said they felt a definite chill in the air. Reeves appeared to be the more relaxed of the two. "There is no change in George's contract," said Dan. "It has the same monetary value." By the time Reeves got to the podium,

though, Allen was no longer around. He left after reading the following statement:

"From the meetings which Dan and I have had in the last few days, it is clear that we have each, unintentionally, hurt the other. These discussions have, however, been greatly beneficial in establishing communications between us, and thereby enabling us to view our problems with clarity, and to resolve them with dignity.

"I am, therefore, very happy to be returning as Dan's coach. Aside from my family, my sole interest for the past three years has been the Rams, and I want very much to return to my players and finish the task to which I dedicated myself. I owe this to the players, and the fans who have been so loyal to me.

"Since we have resolved our differences, it is my conviction that a public airing of them would serve no useful or healthy purpose, but would harm the individuals, the players and the franchise. I have, therefore, asked Dan to permit me to be excused at this point."

Reeves said, "Thank you George. Can we do this?" The owner extended his hand. The coach hesitated, then accepted, while the two posed for pictures.

"The handshake," wrote Bud Furillo in the *Herald-Examiner,* "seemed to pack all the sincerity of a marital vow by Zsa Zsa Gabor."

"A week ago tonight Dr. Rasinski called me," explained Reeves to the press. "He told me that George said there was nothing he would rather do in life than return to the Rams. I said, 'Doctor, there is no chance.' Then I thought about it. If a man has that kind of dedication, maybe I should reconsider. One of the biggest blocks was the attitude of the players. I commend them for backing their coach, but players can't run a franchise.

"It is difficult for me to get through to George Allen. He works 14 hours a day. He doesn't care that much about anything else. He is single minded of purpose. Of course that's what makes him a great coach. We are both going to make a great effort physically to meet once a week. If we agree there is something wrong we'll get to it immediately and not let it fester."

Asked if he had been moved by Allen's tearful press conference with the players, the president smiled and said: "I thought it was well done."

So that is how the Rams entered the 1969 season. In the front office, Elroy Hirsch, who had been with the club for 20 years as a player, general manager and then assistant to the president, left for the University of Wisconsin, where he accepted the job as athletic director. Jack Teele, the team's public relations director, took his place, with John Sanders becoming assistant general manager.

Of all the Allen years in Los Angeles, 1969 was probably the best, but it, too, was filled with frustration. The team sprinted away to its best start ever, winning the first 11 games of the schedule, the first club to do that since the Chicago Bears in 1942.

Suddenly, inexplicably, the Rams' fortunes shifted. Minnesota snapped the streak with a 20-13 victory in the Coliseum. Then Detroit inflicted a 28-0 shutout. With the Coastal Division title already clinched, the Rams then lost their final game, 13-7, to Baltimore. Allen attributed the late-season losses to other factors, but many believed the Rams were a tired team.

The Rams never really got a break in the playoff schedule under Allen. For winning the Coastal championship, their only reward was a date two days after Christmas with the Vikings in Minneapolis. The chill factor could not have helped a team accustomed to playing on sunny California Sundays.

Nonetheless, the Rams took early command of the game. Both teams scored first-quarter touchdowns, but Gossett kicked a 20-yard field goal and Gabriel passed to Billy Truax for a touchdown. The Rams led 17-7 at halftime.

As the fourth quarter opened, the Rams held the lead (17-14) but the Vikings had the momentum. The Minnesota defense reamined as stout as ever, but Joe Kapp finally had his offense rolling. With a couple minutes left to play, Kapp ran two yards for the go-ahead touchdown and Minnesota had a 23-20 victory. The Rams, and Allen, once again were denied the big game.

There were those who thought that in the steamy disappointment of the Ram locker room that day, much of Allen's mystique evaporated. Players began to question the coach's methods, wondering if the extra effort extracted from them was really worth it. After all, they had nothing tangible to show for the sacrifices they made.

In 1970, Allen's Rams seemed to be sliding the other way. They were still winning, but the age factor appeared to be creeping in more and more. And with most of his draft choices traded away and few first or second year players on the roster, there was genuine concern for the future.

George Allen walked into his weekly breakfast meeting with the press and paused momentarily to look at a battered table nearby. "See that," the coach said, his eyes twinkling. "See that table. That's my kind of table. It has experience. You can see it. It's been through a lot. Most people would rather have a shiny, new table that's never been used before. Not me. I want to know what I'm getting. I want a table just like that."

Allen's relationship with the press was, for the most part, a good one. He was, after all, good copy. He'd talk about old tables, his blackberry brandy and his penchant for ice cream, and then his face would twist into a serious expression and he'd lecture reporters on the importance of giving your best, the old 110 per cent. At the same time, though, he never understood the newspapers' function. He honestly believed that they should have been an extension of the Rams. He didn't want reporters, he wanted rooters.

"You can help us this week," Allen told the writers covering his team one day in 1970. "We're playing a San Diego Chargers team Sunday that has a lot of ability. People don't realize how good they are. You have to tell them. Let the public know that this is one of the best teams in football." The writers laughed it off and wrote their usual stories, not paying any attention to Allen's plea. The Rams won the game easily, 37-10, and at their next weekly meeting with the coach, the writers walked in to find footballs autographed by the entire team waiting for each of them. "Those are your game balls," beamed Allen. "You guys deserved it. You really helped us this week. We couldn't have beaten the Chargers without your help."

The Rams remained in contention until the final weeks, when Detroit arrived in Los Angeles for a Monday night game. The Lions, with a gifted, young quarterback named Greg Landry beginning to realize his potential, were finishing as fast as anyone in the league.

The Rams appeared to get a break early in the game when Mel Farr, the running back with all-pro ability, dislocated a shoulder in the first period. But Steve Owens, the Heisman Trophy rookie from Oklahoma, was there to take his place. Owens had been injured much of the season, but was now ready and eager to prove he could play in the National Football League. He proved it to the Rams. He ran well, particularly inside, and caught his share of passes. The Lions opened up a lead, and although the Rams made a run at them, they could never get close enough. Detroit won 28-23 and now Los Angeles needed help to win the division championship. A win in New York against the Giants the following Sunday wouldn't be enough. Oakland would have to beat San Francisco, too.

Rumors flew in the late weeks of the season. Allen's chances of keeping his job after his contract ran out were not supposed to be good. There was still a matter of incompatibility. The people in the

Ram front office were Reeves people. Allen knew it, and although both factions often tried hard to get along, most of the time they failed miserably. It was simply a matter of conflicting personalities and philosophies. Reeves and Allen were not working together. In fact, they practically never saw or talked to one another. When the Rams were in New York for the final game of the season, the coach and owner did not meet.

The Rams flattened a Giant team that had played unusually well that season. They won, in fact, so easily that it was almost embarrassing. The final score was 31-3, and Allen and his team rushed into the dressing room to watch the telecast from the Bay area. They rooted hard for the Raiders, but it didn't help. The 49ers were playing for money. The game meant little to an Oakland team that already had been assured a spot in the playoffs.

The pilot of the Rams' chartered jet announced the final score from California, and it received little response. The Rams knew already. Their season was over. Probably more than that, an era had ended. Allen sat in the front of the plane with his confidant and assistant coach, Joe Sullivan. "I haven't even thought about the future," said George. Three weeks earlier, in the emotional atmosphere of a winning dressing room at San Francisco, he had shouted that he already had several new job offers. "And they're all for a lot more money than I'm making with the Rams," he said.

The announcement came December 30. Calling from New York, Reeves told his Los Angeles office to make it official. George Allen's contract, which would expire on the last day of the year, would not be renewed. "As soon as it can be done," said Reeves, in his statement, "we will arrange a press conference. I have no statement concerning a new head coach at this time except to say that I will do everything I can to provide the best possible field leadership to our players and our fans."

Allen, meanwhile, hastily arranged a press conference in a park fronting the Beverly Hills Hotel. Not all writers in the area were contacted. Allen asked only a selected few. Later, in a magazine story, he would claim his favorite writer in the area was Joe Hendrickson of the *Pasadena Star-News*. He described all the others as "gutless."

Allen revealed he got the news from Reeves the same way he got it two years earlier. "It was a cold conversation, no gratitude, no appreciation," he said. "Yes, I'd like to coach in the NFL again but after this experience I wouldn't take a position unless the general managership went with it."

"George recently stated that we have different theories of operations," said Reeves, from New York. "This is true. It is therefore unrealistic to continue. I have discussed this with our stockholders, and they are in full accord with this action."

The reaction this time was different. The town no longer was shocked. Allen had turned the team into a winner, but in his five years with the Rams, they never won a playoff game. The players, too, seemed more solemn about it. None showed up to stand behind the coach at this press conference.

"I think George Allen is a good coach," said guard Joe Scibelli. "But Mr. Reeves owns the ball club and does what he thinks should be done. I can't say whether he's making a mistake. I know I'll be back as long as the new head coach wants me. I think we have enough material to be a contender."

Some of the divergent opinions of George became public after he was released. A player told Bud Furillo that Allen tried to whip the team up before the 1968 game in San Francisco by telling them that Reeves had telephoned to say the players were a bunch of washed-up old men who couldn't win. "We knew he hadn't spoken to Reeves for 11 months," the player said. "But it amused us that he would do anything, even that, to try and win. We knew George would steal the

Trades that George Allen, as coach of the Washington Redskins, negotiated with the Rams produced three important members of the Los Angeles defense for 1971. They were linebackers Marlin McKeever and Isiah Robertson (left, bringing down a Denver ballcarrier) and safety Dave Elmendorf. McKeever was traded by Allen from the Redskins to the Rams. The draft choices which Los Angeles used to get Robertson and Elmendorf were included in the same trade.

other guy's playbook if he had to, but that's how he is. And he's a winner."

"George is a player's coach," said Merlin Olsen. "He makes you feel like he's doing it for you. His strength is in organizing and unifying a team in its defensive strategy. He works hard to establish trust between himself and the players. Then after awhile you find out that George just doesn't tell the straight story. He's always got some gimmick. After awhile you get so you just sigh and say, 'Well, George wants us to get up for another game.' The man will pay any price to win. But after awhile the unfortunate, negative influences started to come out. George would say one thing, the front office another. It was hard to pin down. All you could think was that it was just a shame. But the pressure, from within and without, became continuous and the stimulus of caring about winning just became mechanical. A team gets to where it just wears out."

Allen won 49 games, lost 17 and tied four in Los Angeles. He lasted five seasons, tying him for the Rams' longevity record with Sid Gillman. Reeves now set out to find his 10th coach in 25 years.

And so the name game started all over again in Los Angeles. John McKay was the first one that popped out. One report, a few months earlier, even indicated it was all set. The University of Southern California coach would take the job for a multi-year contract that would run into six figures. That rumor ended shortly thereafter when, to go with his coaching duties, McKay was elevated to athletic director at USC. Tom Fears, an old Reeves' favorite, was available. Members of Allen's staff such as Ray Prochaska, Tom Catlin and Marv Levy were mentioned. When Joe Paterno, the Penn State coach, stopped to visit in the Rose Bowl press box, everyone rushed up to ask him the obvious question. Paterno laughed and said, "No, I'm not the man." Who was? No one knew. The only part of the secret that leaked out

was that the Rams were talking mostly to college coaches. Ray Willsey of California was reported to be a prime suspect. Finally, as the suspense heightened, a press conference was called for Saturday, January 2.

The afternoon papers got the call early that morning. "You'll never guess who it is," said a sports editor to his staff. "Prothro." No one could believe it. A slow-talking southern gentleman, J. Thompson Prothro was a highly-regarded coach at UCLA, one of the best. But somehow, he never was seriously considered as a candidate by anyone in town. Not because the Rams wouldn't consider him, but because he wasn't expected to consider the Rams.

"We promised to try to find the best possible man for our players and our fans," said the statement from Dan Reeves. "It is my conviction we have done just that and that Tommy will prove it." Prothro signed a long-term contract of undisclosed length for a salary that was estimated at $75,000 a year, plus bonuses. Residuals, some said, could push the amount over $100,000.

Those who knew Prothro explained that this was a man who enjoyed challenges, whether he was sitting across from a world class chess player, playing bridge or trying to upset the No. 1 football team in the country.

"Maybe you people in the media influenced me as much as anyone," explained the Rams' new coach at his first press conference. "I've always felt that college football was bigger than anything, but in my six years here, the media, which creates and reflects public opinion, has convinced me that pro football is bigger than college football."

Prothro admitted that he violated what had been a long-standing rule with him. "That's the fact that the Rams under George Allen were big winners. I always felt that a coach, if he's going to move, should do it where a team was losing, not winning. That way, when you bring up something, there's a better chance your players will say, 'Hey,

you know, he may have something' and accept it. I guess why I went against the way I've felt is that a lot of people believe a college football coach can't handle a pro job.

"Let me say I have real respect for Allen as a football coach, but I'm going to work my own way. Anyone who tries to be anyone but himself is going to get into trouble. I know I've got a real selling job to get the Ram players to accept anything new I might project. But I think they're mature enough to do that. I know I've dealt only with college players, but I've treated them like men until they've shown me I shouldn't. I'll do the same thing with the Rams."

It didn't take Prothro long to put his own stamp on his new team. In his first National Football League draft, he unloaded a bomb. He completed a major trade with the Rams' old friend in Washington, George Allen. He gave up linebackers Jack Pardee, Myron Pottios and Maxie Baughan and defensive tackle Diron Talbert. In return he received linebacker Marlin McKeever and a satchel full of draft choices, including a No. 1 selection that turned out to be Isiah Robertson, the 1971 defensive rookie of the year.

That wasn't his only deal of the off-season. He also acquired players such as Lance Rentzel, Travis Williams and Harry Schuh.

Training camp opened quietly enough at Cal State Fullerton. Most of the Ram veterans were waiting, witholding judgment of their new coach for a few months. Prothro was accepted easier than a few of his assistants, who not only were young, but determined to teach new techniques. Players who had been blocking and tackling one way for 10 or 15 years suddenly were being asked to change by men who never had played professional football. Some conflicts were inevitable. But Prothro and his low-key attitude helped. He was patient. He knew the transition would not come easily.

Two weeks into camp, the head coach turned

51. His new team did not let the day go unnoticed. The Rams presented Prothro with a carton of cigarettes and a case of Coke at breakfast. The gifts were accompanied by a proclamation suggesting, among other things, that the players be given the day off to help celebrate. "Well," drawled Prothro, "it's the thought that counts."

The brief morning ceremony seemed, to some, more significant than it looked. It appeared to be the veterans' way of expressing their official acceptance of the man who replaced George Allen. The short trial period seemed to be over. "I've been very pleased with both the practices and the reaction of the players," said Prothro. "Overall, they're being very cooperative."

It was a reaction that would have pleased Dan Reeves. Hiring Prothro had turned out to be his last major decision as owner of the football team he loved so dearly. On April 15, 1971, Reeves died. His five-year battle against Hodgkin's Disease and two other forms of cancer led to several operations. The seriousness of his illness was kept out of the public print. The Rams' employees knew about it. So did most of the town's prominent sportswriters. Nothing was written, however. "Dan Reeves never wept in public," wrote one Los Angeles columnist. He did not complain in private, either. And he maintained full control of the Rams until his final day.

After Reeves' death, William A. Barnes, a close business associate of Dan's, took over as president. He had been in charge of Reeves' brokerage firm, and he admitted that he was far from an expert in football. He was there to manage the business, while at the same time, keeping the club on the open market until the right offer came along.

In their first year without Reeves, the Rams continued to prosper. Burdened with probably the most difficult schedule in the league, Prothro started slowly. Unlike Allen, who was as fanatical about preseason games as he was about regular season games, Tommy used the summer games

Tommy Prothro (far left, giving instructions to Marlin McKeever) had more than a few frustrations in his two years as coach of the Rams. Happier moments occurred when Willie Ellison gained a league record 247 yards in 1971 against New Orleans (left, on an 80-yard touchdown run that day) and in games against San Francisco (right). Prothro's teams swept the 49ers in 1971 and 1972.

to experiment, to look at his new players and to rest his older veterans. The Rams looked bad in several games, and some of the season ticket holders began to squirm.

In the regular-season opener in New Orleans, the team looked even worse. Roman Gabriel, who suffered a rib injury during the summer, was badly off form, and Archie Manning, the young New Orleans' rookie quarterback, scored a controversial touchdown on the final play of the game to win for the Saints.

Fortunately for Prothro, Gabriel's condition improved and so did the Rams. They were in the race all the way. It was, in fact, almost a duplicate of Allen's final year. The Rams needed a victory on the final Sunday and the 49ers had to lose. Again, both teams won. And again, it was a Monday night television game in Los Angeles that killed the Rams' chances. This time, though, to make matters even worse, the opponents turned out to be George Allen and his new team, the Washington Redskins.

It was an unusually cold night in the Coliseum. The home team opened fast, with Kermit Alexander intercepting a Bill Kilmer pass and returning it 82 yards for a touchdown. But after that, the evening belonged to the Redskins. Roy Jefferson and Clifton McNeil romped unabashedly through the Rams' secondary and the Los Angeles receivers seemed unable to hold Gabriel's key passes. As the score mounted, Allen's jubilation on the sideline only made defeat more difficult to accept. The final numbers on the Coliseum scoreboard read Washington 38, Los Angeles 24.

Joe Scibelli, the veteran guard, sat in his dressing room cubicle after the game and tried to make some sense of it. "I used to think that maybe George Allen was the jinx," he said. "Maybe he was the reason we always seemed to blow the big game. Now I think maybe it's me or someone who's been here all along. There's got to be

some reason for it." He wasn't the only baffled one.

It had been five years of disappointing finishes for the Rams, and they were beginning to wonder when it would all end. For Prothro, this was just the start, though. He had been the only one among the three recently hired college coaches (Dan Devine at Green Bay and John Ralston at Denver were the others) able to keep his team in contention during his rookie year. Prothro made many personnel changes. He had traded away several of the more experienced, older players and was building for the future. There were those on the club who still didn't fully agree with many of his theories. But, overall, the most important by-product of Prothro's first year was the feeling of harmony that existed between the front offices and the field. The critics from the Allen Era were missing. So was the constant badmouthing. The Rams started the Prothro Era working together. They finished it the same way.

Longtime Ram watchers knew, of course, that the waters could not remain that calm for long. Soon the news that the club was being sold began to reappear. The Rams couldn't have just completed a routine sale. Not them. They seem to do everything a little more flamboyantly. This was no exception. Early in his second training camp, Prothro was not sure who he was working for. Finally, in mid-July, the announcement came.

Typically, it was extremely complicated. Baltimore Colts owner Carroll Rosenbloom, Reeves' old friend, the man who had nominated Pete Rozelle as commissioner, had talked two midwesterners named Robert Irsay and Bud Kelend into buying the Rams from the Reeves' estate for $19 million, a National Football League record. Then Rosenbloom swapped teams with Irsay and Kelend, chipping in $3 or $4 million to equalize the value of the Baltimore franchise with the more valuable Rams property.

Rosenbloom is a vibrant man who could pass for being 20 years younger than 66, his actual age. He started in professional football 20 years ago, investing an original $13,000, a sum he never had to pay because in their first year of reorganization in Maryland, the Colts sold $300,000 worth of season tickets. Eventually, Rosenbloom bought out his partners for $1 million. So in 19 years, his $13,000 investment was turned into his $19 million.

He was equally successful in running his team in Baltimore. He was there when a free agent quarterback was hired, a young man named John Unitas. He also proved to be shrewd in his selection of head coaches. The three he had handle the Colts were Weeb Ewbank, Don Shula and Don McCafferty. Over a period of 15 years, Rosenbloom's team was the winningest in the National Football League.

Rosenbloom also was loved by his players. He was, and still is, known as "The Godfather" to his employees. "Everybody has trouble," he has said, "and almost everybody has some kind of financial trouble. If you're an athlete, you can't play your best football if you're worrying about money today—or when you retire. We encourage the players to come to us for loans so they can get started in business. When Gino Marchetti retired, we helped him get a $50,000 loan. Gino turned out to be a good businessman. He ran the $50,000 into a million, and today he's a multimillionaire. So is Alan Ameche. They're exceptions, of course, but our objective is to help all our players invest their money well. I don't believe the bromide: 'The only good ballplayer is a hungry ballplayer.' I don't want any hungry athletes around me. The way to win games and titles is with 40 players who are free to give their undivided attention to football because they don't have a worry in the world."

"He created the winning atmosphere in Baltimore," said Harry Hulmes, a former Colt general manager who now is an executive with the New Orleans Saints. "When I left him, Carroll asked me if I'd got rid of my Baltimore house yet. I told him no. He said: 'If nobody meets your offer, let me know, I'll buy it.' I thought that was generous, but I never intended to call on him until he telephoned me six or eight weeks later in New Orleans. He wanted to know if I was setteled and I told him we had a house we couldn't put a deposit on because we hadn't sold in Baltimore yet. 'How much is the deposit?' he asked. I told him $10,000. 'I'll have the check there in the morning,' he said. No strings, no interest, no note—and I'm not even working for him anymore. That's Carroll."

Ram players must have been happy to learn of the team's sale. Those in the front office had a somewhat different reaction. They didn't know what to think. The reorganization of executives included, besides Rosenbloom, Don Klosterman, who operated as general manager in Baltimore. In Los Angeles, Klosterman's title was "assistant to the owner." Suddenly, the Rams had more high-priced help than any team in football. Bill Barnes, Jack Teele and Johnny Sanders were all still around, as were the club's two public relations directors, Jerry Wilcox and Jack Geyer.

There was also the possibility that Rosenbloom's son, Steve, president of the Colts in 1970-71, would move to Los Angeles soon to join the Rams in some high-ranking capacity.

Thus, in the Rams' second year under Prothro, there was once again a question concerning balance of power. Klosterman, a man of charming persuasion, was the strong, new influence. His reputation was that of one of the most knowledgeable men in the league when it came to personnel.

The 1972 Ram season began, characteristically, when, early in the summer, Roman Gabriel went out with a collapsed lung. He made a re-

As the 1973 season approached, the Rams were led by a new regime: Carroll Rosenbloom (far left), who acquired ownership of the team in a unique swap during 1972 in which he gave up control of the Baltimore Colts; Don Klosterman, Rosenbloom's aide first in Baltimore and now in Los Angeles; and Chuck Knox, named head coach for '73.

markable recovery, but soon was flattened again by a strange arm ailment.

It was that kind of up and down year for the Rams, who, somehow, still managed to remain in contention in a National Football Conference Western Division race nobody wanted to win.

It did seem typical of this team, though, for people in Los Angeles to pick up a newspaper on a December morning and read: "Prothro's Job May Be At Stake Tonight." The Rams had appeared as if they weren't motivated through much of the season, and, naturally, the blame was being placed on Prothro. That is how quickly life can change for a head coach in Los Angeles.

Another headline, just a few days later, may have said it even better. "Rams Evade Man With Net," it read. It seemed as if that had been the case for years. Carroll Rosenbloom had said when he bought the team he wanted, among other things, sunshine and relaxation.

"It has been a harrowing first year for Rosenbloom in Los Angeles," wrote Melvin Durslag in the *Herald-Examiner,* "and the next time he is looking for sunshine and relaxation, he will trade for a franchise in Philadelphia."

Rosenbloom was in Los Angeles now, though. For better or worse. And when the Rams closed out with a 6-7-1 record, he carefully surveyed the situation and then fired Prothro.

The move was not universally applauded. Prothro remains a coach who is widely respected by a large segment of the football community. He was not dispatched for lack of intelligence. If anything, perhaps Tommy was too smart. He expected his players to be mature enough to rouse themselves once a week. He felt professionals didn't need collegiate prep talks. He thought money and pride would be enough.

Chuck Knox was named coach of the Rams in February 1973. Experienced, with solid cre-

dentials in Detroit and New York, he is, at 40, among the handsomest coaches in the NFL.

Knox inherited a controversy at quarterback. Roman Gabriel's arm problems convinced the Rams that more insurance was required at the position, so they traded a prime defensive lineman, Coy Bacon, and a young runner, Bob Thomas, to San Diego for John Hadl. Immediately, longtime Ram boosters flashed back to the days of Van Brocklin-Waterfield, Wade-Van Brocklin and Gabriel-Munson. Gabriel asked to be traded to Washington and his old coach George Allen, stating that he would never play for the L.A. organization again. Ah, the Rams. There is no one else like them.

Still, for all the problems, Rosenbloom is an owner in the style of his predecessor. Given a choice, in fact, it is a good bet that Dan Reeves would have chosen his old friend from Baltimore as his successor.

More than two years after his death, Reeves continues to have a large influence on this team and on the game of professional football. The people he trained can now be seen in prominent positions throughout the National Football League—men such as Pete Rozelle, Tex Schramm, Don Klosterman, Sid Gillman, Norm Van Brocklin, Fred Gehrke, Harland Svare and Bill Granholm.

To those who knew and loved Reeves, the unfortunate part of his final years was the fact that part of the public turned against him. Unaware of both sides of the problem, the man on the street in Los Angeles favored George Allen in his dispute with the Rams' owner. Dan's reputation as a hard, cold "firing owner" spread. Nothing could have been further from the truth.

Reeves cared deeply about his employees. He proved it continuously. Almost everyone ever employed by the Rams had a lifetime job with Dan if he so chose. Long after their coaching careers were over, Waterfield and Pool returned to join the Los Angeles scouting staff under Reeves.

"Dan Reeves was," says Pete Rozelle, "a man of great integrity who placed strong emphasis on loyalty. He, himself, generated great loyalty. I think his biggest impact was in making football a year-round operation. Scouting was the focal point, but it extended into other areas, too. He was convinced that to be a success, you had to work all year at it. Before the Rams, it was common to hire six-month assistant coaches. You don't see it now. Of course, he truly did open the West to major professional sports. All you have to do is add up the teams operating west of Missouri to realize that. And I'm talking about all sports, not just football. He was the first major league owner to gamble. All the rest came later. Around the National Football League, I think his greatest contribution of all was that he helped generate more of a commitment to excellence on everyone's part. He was, needless to say, quite a man."

In 1967, Reeves was inducted into the Professional Football Hall of Fame in Canton, Ohio. "It's a great honor," he said, "but I wish they'd held it off for 20 years. It makes me feel a little bit Forest Lawnish." The sense of humor was always there. Once, while giving a writer a tour of the team's new office facilities in West Los Angeles, Dan smiled and said, "Don't make it sound too lavish. My stockholders haven't seen it yet." While trying to talk Vince Lombardi into coaching his football team one afternoon, he offered a 10-year contract for $100,000 annually. "But what I'm looking for," protested Lombardi, "is security." Dan looked up and smiled. "Wonderful. In that case, make it $10,000 for a hundred years."

"More often than not," said Lamar Hunt, president of the Kansas City Chiefs, "Dan would be the butt of his own jokes. One I remember in particular was in the fall of 1966. He asked me how Mike Garrett was doing. Mike was having

a fine rookie year with the Chiefs, which I told Dan with some pride. After all, we had signed him in competition with the Rams. Dan's reply, with a twinkle in his eye, was, 'Oh, well! He was too small to play for the Rams anyway!'"

To understand the full impact of Dan Reeves, one need only listen to other prominent football people talk about him.

Bob Waterfield: "I'll tell you what kind of a guy Dan was. If you were in trouble, you didn't need to go looking for him to help. He found you first. He's the best friend I ever had. The best friend anybody ever had."

Sid Gillman: "He's the greatest man I've ever known in football.

George Halas: "Dan was every bit the pioneer, in the sense of staking out new territory for the NFL, as those who were in it at the beginning. His move to Los Angeles was a giant step forward. As time went on and our game broadened into a national attraction through television, Dan's imaginative zeal was more than justified. I believe what I admired most about him were two distinctive personal traits. He was loyal to everyone in his organization, but he demanded loyalty in return. He had the old fashioned competitive drive that all the early owners had as part of their makeup. He loved to win and he suffered deep anguish when he lost, but he did his best to hide his feelings."

Art Rooney: "In the '30s much of the publicity was centered around George Halas, George Preston Marshall, Curly Lambeau and Tim Mara. But later, inside the meetings there were other voices who were more reserved, but who still had a great impact on the growth of the game. Take Dan Reeves. He was a reserved man, a man who never sought the headlines, but behind the closed doors of the annual meetings his voice, his ideas, were listened to and acted upon by his fellow owners."

Don Klosterman: "Dan's ability to organize

Dan Reeves

and delegate authority left an indelible impression upon me. He was a man of tremendous foresight. He and Carroll Rosenbloom were the two major architects in the merger between the American and National Football Leagues, but I can never recall these two men being given the credit that is unquestionably due them."

Carroll Rosenbloom: "Always I will remember Dan as a tough competitor, a wise and fair adminstrator and a completely unselfish person. When my son Steve took over the presidency of the Colts, I told him if I could give him a man to emulate and a man who wanted to be helpful to our great sport, Dan Reeves is the man I would point to."

In the new era of Carroll Rosenbloom, the memories linger on. But as the 1970s churn to midpoint, there are fresh faces and new names.

From the beginning, the Rams have been a team of color, a team that won some and lost some, a team that has had more than its share of headlines.

If the Rams' past is a reflection of the Rams' future, the story has only begun.

The Names
and Numbers

YEAR-BY-YEAR RAMS' SCORES

Cleveland Rams, 1937–42, 1944–45
Los Angeles Rams, 1946–72

1937

(1–10–0, fifth place)
Coach: Hugo Bezdek

	Rams	Opp.
Detroit ....(H)	0	28
Philadelphia ....(A)	21	3
Brooklyn ....(A)	7	9
Chicago Cards ....(H)	0	6
Chicago Bears ....(H)	2	20
Green Bay ....(H)	10	35
Green Bay ....(A)	7	35
Chicago Cards ....(A)	7	13
Detroit ....(A)	7	27
Washington ....(H)	7	16
Chicago Bears ....(A)	7	15
	75	207

1938

(4–7–0, fourth place)
Coach: Hugo Bezdek (3 games)
Coach: Art Lewis (8 games)

	Rams	Opp.
Green Bay ....(A)	17	26
Chicago Cards ....(H)	6	7
Washington ....(A)	13	37
Detroit ....(H)	21	17
Chicago Bears ....(H)	14	7
Chicago Bears ....(A)	23	21
Green Bay ....(H)	7	28
Detroit ....(A)	0	6
New York ....(A)	0	28
Chicago Cards ....(A)	17	31
Pittsburgh ....(*)	13	7
	131	215

*Played in New Orleans

1939

(5–5–1, fourth place)
Coach: Earl "Dutch" Clark

	Rams	Opp.
Chicago Bears ....(A)	21	30
Brooklyn ....(A)	12	23
Green Bay ....(A)	27	24
Chicago Bears ....(H)	21	35
Detroit ....(A)	7	15
Chicago Cards ....(A)	24	0
Pittsburgh ....(H)	14	14
Chicago Cards ....(H)	14	0
Detroit ....(H)	14	3
Green Bay ....(H)	6	7
Philadelphia ....(*)	35	13
	195	164

*Played in Colorado Springs

1940

(4–6–1, fourth place)
Coach: Earl "Dutch" Clark

	Rams	Opp.
Philadelphia ....(H)	21	13
Detroit ....(A)	0	6
Chicago Bears ....(H)	14	21
Green Bay ....(A)	14	31
Chicago Cards ....(H)	26	14
Chicago Cards ....(A)	7	17
Detroit ....(H)	14	0
New York ....(A)	13	0
Brooklyn ....(A)	14	29
Chicago Bears ....(A)	25	47
Green Bay ....(H)	13	13
	171	191

1941

(2–9–0, fifth place)
Coach: Earl "Dutch" Clark

	Rams	Opp.
Pittsburgh ....(*)	17	14
Chicago Cards ....(A)	10	6
Green Bay ....(A)	7	24
Chicago Bears ....(H)	21	48
Detroit ....(A)	7	17
Green Bay ....(H)	14	17
Washington ....(A)	13	17
Detroit ....(H)	0	14
Chicago Bears ....(A)	13	31
New York ....(A)	14	49
Chicago Cards ....(H)	0	7
	116	244

*Played in Akron

1942

(5–6–0, third place)
Coach: Earl "Dutch" Clark

	Rams	Opp.
Chicago Cards ....(*)	0	7
Philadelphia ....(H)	24	14
Detroit ....(A)	14	0
Chicago Bears ....(H)	7	21
Chicago Cards ....(H)	7	3
Brooklyn ....(A)	17	0
Green Bay ....(H)	12	30
Washington ....(A)	14	33
Green Bay ....(A)	28	45
Detroit ....(H)	27	7
Chicago Bears ....(A)	0	47
	150	207

*Played in Buffalo

Rams Suspended Operations in 1943.

1944

(4–6–0, fourth place)
Coach: Aldo "Buff" Donelli

	Rams	Opp.
Card-Pitt ....(*)	30	28
Chicago Bears ....(H)	19	7
Detroit ....(A)	20	17
Green Bay ....(A)	21	30
Chicago Bears ....(A)	21	28
Washington ....(A)	10	14
Green Bay ....(H)	7	42
Card-Pitt ....(+)	33	6
Detroit ....(H)	14	26
Philadelphia ....(A)	13	26
	188	224

*Played in Pittsburgh
+Played in Chicago

1945

(9–1–0, first place)
Coach: Adam walsh

	Rams	Opp.
Chicago Cards ....(H)	21	0
Chicago Bears ....(H)	17	0
Green Bay ....(A)	27	14
Chicago Bears ....(A)	41	21
Philadelphia ....(A)	14	28
New York ....(A)	21	17
Green Bay ....(H)	20	7
Chicago Cards ....(A)	35	21
Detroit ....(A)	28	21
Boston ....(H)	20	7
	244	136

NFL Championship

Washington ....(H)	15	14

1946

(6–4–1, second place)
Coach: Adam Walsh

	Rams	Opp.
Philadelphia ....(H)	14	25
Green Bay ....(A)	21	17
Chicago Bears ....(A)	28	28
Detroit ....(H)	35	14
Chicago Cards ....(A)	10	34
Detroit ....(A)	41	20
Chicago Bears ....(H)	21	27
Chicago Cards ....(H)	17	14
Boston.......................(A)	21	40
New York ....(A)	31	21
Green Bay ....(H)	38	17
	277	257

1947

(6–6–0, fourth place)
Coach: Bob Snyder

	Rams	Opp.
Pittsburgh ....(A)	48	7
Green Bay ....(A)	14	17
Detroit ....(A)	27	13
Chicago Cards ....(H)	27	7
Philadelphia ....(A)	7	14
Chicago Cards ....(A)	10	17
Boston ....(H)	16	27
Chicago Bears ....(H)	21	41
Detroit ....(H)	28	17
Green Bay ....(H)	10	30
Chicago Bears ....(A)	17	14
New York ....(H)	34	10
	259	214

1948

(6−5−1, third place)
Coach: Bob Snyder (Preseason only)

Coach: Clark Shaughnessy	Rams	Opp.
Detroit ....(H)	44	7
Philadelphia ....(H)	28	28
Chicago Bears ....(A)	21	42
Green Bay ....(A)	0	16
Detroit ....(A)	34	27
Chicago Cards......................(H)	22	27
Chicago Bears ....(H)	6	21
New York ....(A)	52	37
Chicago Cards ....(A)	24	27
Green Bay ....(H)	24	10
Washington ....(A)	41	13
Pittsburgh ....(H)	31	14
	327	269

1949

(8−2−2, first place)

Coach: Clark Shaughnessy	Rams	Opp.
Detroit ....(H)	27	24
Green Bay ....(A)	48	7
Chicago Bears ....(A)	31	16
Detroit ....(A)	21	10
Green Bay ....(H)	35	7
Chicago Bears ....(H)	27	24
Philadelphia ....(A)	14	38
Pittsburgh ....(A)	7	7
Chicago Cards ....(A)	28	28
New York Bulldogs................(H)	42	20
Chicago Cards ....(H)	27	31
Washington ....(H)	53	27
	360	239

NFL Championship
| Philadelphia ....(H) | 0 | 14 |

1950

(9−3−0, first place)

Coach: Joe Stydahar	Rams	Opp.
Chicago Bears ....(H)	20	24
New York Yanks ....(H)	45	28
San Francisco ....(A)	35	14
Philadelphia ....(A)	20	56
Detroit ....(A)	30	28
Baltimore ....(H)	70	27
Detroit ....(H)	65	24
San Francisco ....(H)	28	21
Green Bay ....(A)	45	14
New York Yanks....................(A)	43	35
Chicago Bears ....(A)	14	24
Green Bay ....(H)	51	14
	466	309

Play-off
| Chicago Bears ....(H) | 24 | 14 |

NFL Championship
| Cleveland ....(A) | 28 | 30 |

1951

(8−4−0, first place)

Coach: Joe Stydahar	Rams	Opp.
New York Yanks ....(H)	54	14
Cleveland ....(H)	23	38
Detroit ....(A)	27	21
Green Bay ....(A)	28	0
San Francisco ....(A)	17	44
San Francisco ....(H)	23	16
Chicago Cards.......................(H)	45	21
New York Yanks ....(H)	48	21
Washington ....(A)	21	31
Chicago Bears ....(A)	42	17
Detroit ....(H)	22	24
Green Bay ....(H)	42	14
	392	261

NFL Championship
| Cleveland ....(H) | 24 | 17 |

1952

(9−3−0, second place)
Coach: Joe Stydahar (one game)

Coach: Hamp Pool	Rams	Opp.
Cleveland ....(A)	7	37
Detroit ....(H)	14	17
Green Bay ....(A)	30	28
Detroit ....(A)	16	24
Chicago Bears ....(H)	31	7
Dallas ....(H)	42	20
Dallas ....(A)	27	6
Chicago Bears ....(A)	40	24

1952 (con't)

	Rams	Opp.
San Francisco.......................(H)	35	9
San Francisco.......................(A)	34	21
Green Bay ....(H)	45	27
Pittsburgh ....(H)	28	14
	349	234

Play-off
| Detroit ....(A) | 21 | 31 |

1953

(8−3−1, third place)

Coach: Hamp Pool	Rams	Opp.
New York ....(H)	21	7
San Francisco ....(A)	30	31
Green Bay ....(A)	38	20
Detroit ....(A)	31	19
Chicago Bears ....(H)	38	24
Detroit ....(H)	37	24
San Francisco ....(H)	27	31
Chicago Cards ....(A)	24	24
Baltimore ....(A)	21	13
Chicago Bears ....(A)	21	24
Baltimore ....(H)	45	2
Green Bay ....(H)	33	17
	366	236

1954

(6−5−1, fourth place)

Coach: Hamp Pool	Rams	Opp.
Baltimore ....(A)	48	0
San Francisco ....(H)	24	24
Detroit ....(A)	3	21
Green Bay ....(A)	17	35
Chicago Bears ....(H)	42	38
Detroit ....(H)	24	27
San Francisco ....(A)	42	34
Chicago Cards ....(H)	28	17
New York ....(A)	17	16
Chicago Bears ....(A)	13	24
Baltimore ....(H)	21	22
Green Bay ....(H)	35	27
	314	285

1955

(8−3−1, first place)

Coach: Sid Gillman	Rams	Opp.
San Francisco ....(A)	23	14
Pittsburgh ....(H)	27	26
Detroit ....(A)	17	10
Green Bay ....(A)	28	30
Detroit ....(H)	24	13
Chicago Bears ....(H)	20	31
San Francisco ....(H)	27	14
Chicago Bears ....(A)	3	24
Baltimore ....(A)	17	17
Philadelphia ....(A)	23	21
Baltimore ....(H)	20	14
Green Bay ....(H)	31	17
	260	231

NFL Championship
| Cleveland ....(H) | 14 | 38 |

1956

(4−8−0, fifth place)

Coach: Sid Gillman	Rams	Opp.
Philadelphia ....(H)	27	7
San Francisco ....(A)	30	33
Detroit ....(A)	21	24
Green Bay ....(A)	17	42
Detroit ....(H)	7	16
Chicago Bears ....(H)	24	35
San Francisco ....(H)	30	6
Chicago Bears ....(A)	21	30
Baltimore ....(A)	21	56
Pittsburgh ....(A)	13	30
Baltimore ....(H)	31	7
Green Bay ....(H)	49	21
	291	307

1957

(6−6−0, fourth place)

Coach: Sid Gillman	Rams	Opp.
Philadelphia ....(H)	17	13
San Francisco ....(A)	20	23
Detroit ....(A)	7	10
Chicago Bears ....(A)	26	34
Detroit ....(H)	35	17
Chicago Bears ....(H)	10	16

	Rams	Opp.
San Francisco..........................(H)	37	24
Green Bay ....(A)	31	27
Cleveland ....(A)	31	45
Baltimore ....(A)	14	31
Green Bay ....(H)	42	17
Baltimore ....(H)	37	21
	307	278

1958

(8–4–0, second place)
Coach: Sid Gillman

	Rams	Opp.
Cleveland ....(H)	27	30
San Francisco..........................(A)	33	3
Detroit ....(A)	42	28
Chicago Bears ....(A)	10	31
Detroit ....(A)	24	41
Chicago Bears ....(H)	41	35
San Francisco..........................(H)	56	7
Green Bay ....(A)	20	7
Baltimore ....(A)	7	34
Chicago Cards..........................(A)	20	14
Baltimore ....(H)	30	28
Green Bay ....(H)	34	20
	344	278

1959

(2–10–0, sixth place)
Coach: Sid Gillman

	Rams	Opp.
New York ....(H)	21	23
San Francisco..........................(A)	0	34
Chicago Bears ....(A)	28	21
Green Bay ....(A)	45	6
Detroit ....(H)	7	17
Chicago Bears ....(H)	21	26
San Francisco..........................(H)	16	24
Detroit ....(A)	17	23
Philadelphia ....(A)	20	23
Baltimore ....(H)	21	35
Green Bay ....(H)	20	38
Baltimore ....(H)	26	45
	242	315

1960

(4–7–1, sixth place)
Coach: Bob Waterfield

	Rams	Opp.
St. Louis ....(H)	21	43
San Francisco..........................(A)	9	13
Chicago....................................(A)	27	34
Baltimore ....(A)	17	31
Chicago....................................(H)	24	24
Detroit ....(H)	48	35
Dallas......................................(A)	38	13
Detroit ....(A)	10	12
Green Bay ....(A)	33	31
San Francisco..........................(H)	7	23
Baltimore ....(H)	10	3
Green Bay ....(H)	21	35
	265	297

1961

(4–10–0, sixth place)
Coach: Bob Waterfield

	Rams	Opp.
Baltimore ....(A)	24	27
Chicago....................................(H)	17	21
Pittsburgh ....(H)	24	14
San Francisco..........................(A)	0	35
Detroit ....(A)	13	14
New York ....(A)	14	24
Detroit ....(H)	10	28
Minnesota................................(H)	31	17
San Francisco..........................(H)	17	7
Green Bay ....(A)	17	35
Chicago....................................(A)	24	28
Minnesota................................(A)	21	42
Baltimore ....(H)	34	17
Green Bay ....(H)	17	24
	263	333

1962

(1–12–1, seventh place)
Coach: Bob Waterfield (eight games)
Coach: Harland Svare (six games)

	Rams	Opp.
Baltimore ....(A)	27	30
Chicago....................................(A)	23	27
Dallas ....(H)	17	27
Washington ....(A)	14	20
Detroit ....(A)	10	13

	Rams	Opp.
Minnesota................................(H)	14	38
San Francisco..........................(A)	28	14
Detroit ....(H)	3	12
Baltimore ....(H)	2	14
San Francisco..........................(H)	17	24
Minnesota................................(A)	24	24
Green Bay ....(A)	10	41
Chicago....................................(A)	14	30
Green Bay ....(H)	17	20
	220	334

1963

(5–9–0, sixth place)
Coach: Harland Svare

	Rams	Opp.
Detroit ....(H)	2	23
Washington..............................(H)	14	37
Cleveland ....(A)	6	20
Green Bay ....(A)	10	42
Chicago....................................(H)	14	52
Minnesota................................(H)	27	24
San Francisco..........................(H)	28	21
Minnesota................................(A)	13	21
Chicago....................................(A)	0	6
Detroit ....(A)	28	21
Baltimore ....(H)	17	16
San Francisco..........................(A)	21	17
Green Bay ....(H)	14	31
Baltimore ....(A)	16	19
	210	350

1964

(5–7–2, fifth place)
Coach: Harland Svare

	Rams	Opp.
Pittsburgh ....(A)	26	14
Detroit ....(H)	17	17
Minnesota................................(H)	22	13
Baltimore ....(A)	20	35
Chicago....................................(A)	17	38
San Francisco..........................(H)	42	14
Green Bay ....(A)	27	17
Detroit ....(A)	17	37
Philadelphia ....(H)	20	10
Chicago....................................(H)	24	34
Baltimore ....(H)	7	24
Minnesota................................(A)	13	34
San Francisco..........................(A)	7	28
Green Bay ....(H)	24	24
	283	339

1965

(4–10–0, seventh place)
Coach: Harland Svare

	Rams	Opp.
Detroit ....(A)	0	20
Chicago....................................(H)	30	28
Minnesota................................(H)	35	38
Chicago....................................(A)	6	31
San Francisco..........................(H)	21	45
Baltimore ....(A)	20	35
Detroit ....(H)	7	31
Minnesota................................(A)	13	24
Green Bay ....(A)	3	6
San Francisco..........................(A)	27	30
Green Bay ....(H)	21	10
St. Louis ....(A)	27	3
Cleveland ....(H)	42	7
Baltimore ....(H)	17	20
	269	328

1966

(8–6–0, third place)
Coach: George Allen

	Rams	Opp.
Atlanta....................................(A)	19	14
Chicago....................................(H)	31	17
Green Bay ....(A)	13	24
San Francisco..........................(H)	34	3
Detroit ....(A)	14	7
Minnesota................................(A)	7	35
Chicago....................................(A)	10	17
Baltimore ....(H)	3	17
San Francisco..........................(A)	13	21
New York ....(H)	55	14
Minnesota................................(H)	21	6
Baltimore ....(A)	23	7
Detroit ....(H)	23	3
Green Bay ....(H)	23	27
	289	212

1967

(11−1−2, first place)
Coach: George Allen

	Rams	Opp.
New Orleans.....................(A)	27	13
Minnesota..........................(H)	39	3
Dallas................................(A)	35	13
San Francisco...................(H)	24	27
Baltimore..........................(A)	24	24
Washington.......................(H)	28	28
Chicago.............................(A)	28	17
San Francisco...................(A)	17	7
Philadelphia.....................(H)	33	17
Atlanta..............................(A)	31	3
Detroit..............................(A)	31	7
Atlanta..............................(H)	20	3
Green Bay.........................(H)	27	24
Baltimore..........................(H)	34	10
	398	196

Play-off

Green Bay.........................(A)	7	28

1968

(10−3−1, second place)
Coach: George Allen

	Rams	Opp.
St. Louis...........................(A)	24	13
Pittsburgh.........................(H)	45	10
Cleveland..........................(A)	24	6
San Francisco...................(H)	24	10
Green Bay.........................(A)	16	14
Atlanta..............................(H)	27	14
Baltimore..........................(A)	10	27
Detroit..............................(H)	10	7
Atlanta..............................(A)	17	10
San Francisco...................(A)	20	20
New York..........................(H)	24	21
Minnesota..........................(A)	31	3
Chicago.............................(H)	16	17
Baltimore..........................(H)	24	28
	312	200

1969

(11−3−0, first place)
Coach: George Allen

	Rams	Opp.
Baltimore..........................(A)	27	20
Atlanta..............................(H)	17	7
New Orleans......................(H)	36	17
San Francisco...................(A)	27	21
Green Bay.........................(H)	34	21
Chicago.............................(A)	9	7
Atlanta..............................(A)	38	6
San Francisco...................(H)	41	30
Philadelphia.....................(A)	23	17
Dallas................................(H)	24	23
Washington.......................(A)	24	13
Minnesota..........................(H)	13	20
Detroit..............................(A)	0	28
Baltimore..........................(H)	7	13
	320	243

Play-off

Minnesota..........................(A)	20	23

1970

(9−4−1, second place)
Coach: George Allen

	Rams	Opp.
St. Louis...........................(H)	34	13
Buffalo..............................(A)	19	0
San Diego.........................(H)	37	10
San Francisco...................(H)	6	20
Green Bay.........................(A)	31	21
Minnesota..........................(A)	3	13
New Orleans......................(A)	30	17
Atlanta..............................(H)	10	10
New York Jets...................(H)	20	31
Atlanta..............................(A)	17	7
San Francisco...................(A)	30	13
New Orleans......................(H)	34	16
Detroit..............................(A)	23	28
New York Giants...............(A)	31	3
	325	202

1971

(8−5−1, second place)
Coach: Tommy Prothro

	Rams	Opp.
New Orleans......................(A)	20	24
Atlanta..............................(H)	20	20
Chicago.............................(H)	17	3
San Francisco...................(A)	20	13
Atlanta..............................(A)	24	16
Green Bay.........................(H)	30	13

1971 (con't)

	Rams	Opp
Miami................................(H)	14	20
Baltimore..........................(A)	17	24
Detroit..............................(A)	21	13
San Francisco...................(H)	17	6
Dallas................................(A)	21	28
New Orleans......................(H)	45	28
Washington.......................(H)	24	38
Pittsburgh.........................(A)	23	14
	313	260

1972

(6−7−1, third place)
Coach: Tommy Prothro

	Rams	Opp.
New Orleans......................(H)	34	14
Chicago.............................(A)	13	13
Atlanta..............................(A)	3	31
San Francisco...................(H)	31	7
Philadelphia.....................(A)	34	3
Cincinnati.........................(H)	15	12
Oakland............................(A)	17	45
Atlanta..............................(H)	20	7
Denver..............................(H)	10	16
Minnesota..........................(H)	41	45
New Orleans......................(A)	16	19
San Francisco...................(A)	26	16
St. Louis...........................(A)	14	24
Detroit..............................(H)	17	34
	291	286

LOS ANGELES RAMS, 1937—72

Adams, Chester, T, Ohio ....1939 – 42
Adams, John, TE, CAl State-L.A. 1963
Agajanian, Ben, PK, New Mexico 1953
Agler, Bob, RB, Otterbein ....1948 – 49
Alexander, Kermit, DB, UCLA ....1970 – 71
Alfonse, Jules, B, Minnesota................1937 – 38
Allen, Duane, E, Santa Ana J.C. ....1961 – 64
Anderson, Bruce, DE, Willamette 1966
Anderson, Stanley, E, Stanford ....1941 – 42
Andrako, Stephen, C, Ohio State 1941
Armstrong, Graham, T, John Carroll.....1941, 1945
Arnett, Jon, RB, So. California ....1957 – 63
Atkins, Pervis, RB, New Mexico State.....1961 – 63
Atty, Alexander, G, West Virginia.................1939

B

Bacon, Coy, DT, Jackson State..............1968 – 72
Bagarus, Steve, RB, Notre Dame.................1947
Baker, John, DT, No. Carolina Coll. ....1958 – 61
Baker, Terry, QB-RB, Oregon State........1963 – 65
Banta, Jack, RB, So. California ....1946 – 48
Barber, Mark, B, So. Dakota State.............1937
Barle, Louis, T,.......................................1939
Barry, Paul, RB, Tulsa ....1950 – 52
Bass, Dick, RB, Pacific ....1960 – 69
Baughan, Maxie, LB, Georgia Tech ....1966 – 70
Beathard, Pete, QB, So. California 1972
Benton, Jim, E, Arkansas.......1938 – 42, 1944 – 47
Bernard, David, B, Mississippi ....1944 – 45
Berry, Cornelius, E, No. Carolina State.........1940
Bertelsen, Jim, RB, Texas 1972
Bettridge, John, B, Ohio State 1937
Bighead, Jack, E, Pepperdine 1955
Bleeker, Mel, RB, So. California 1947
Boone, Robert, B, Elon 1942
Bostick, Lewis, G, Alabama ....1939 – 42
Bouley, Gil, T, Boston College...............1945 – 50
Bowers, Bill, DB, So. California 1954
Boyd, Bob, E, Loyola-L.A..........................1950 – 57
Boeke, Jim, T, Heidelberg ....1960 – 63
Braatz, Tom, E, Marquette 1958
Bradshaw, Charles, T, Baylor ....1958 – 60
Brahm, Lawrence, G, Temple 1942
bratkowski, Zeke, QB, Georgia.............1961 – 63
Bravo, Alex, DB, Cal Poly-Obispo ....1957 – 58
Brazell, Carl, B, Baylor 1938
Breen, Gene, LB, Virginia Tech ....1967 – 68
Brink, Larry, DE, No. Illinois ....1948 – 53
Brito, Gene, DE, Loyola-L.A..................1959 – 60
Britt, Charley, DB, Georgia ....1960 – 63

Brooks, Larry, DT, Virginia State 1972
Brown, Bob, T, Nebraska1969 – 70.....................
Brown, Fred, LB, Miami 1965
Brown, Willie, E-RB, So. California ....1964 – 65
Brumbaugh, Carl, B, Florida.........................1937
Bruney, Fred, DB, Ohio State 1948
Buckley, Philip, E, Xavier 1937
Budka, Frank, DB, Notre Dame...................1964
Bukich, Rudy, QB, So. California ....1953 – 56
Burman, George, C-G, Northwestern......1967 – 70
Burmeister, Forrest, B, Purdue......................1937
Burroughs, Don, DB, Colorado A&M.......1955 – 59
Busich, Samuel, E, Ohio State 1937
Buzin, Rich, T, Penn State.........................1971
Byrd, Mac, LB, So. California 1965

C

Cahill, Dave, DT, No. Arizona 1967
Carey, Bob, E, Michigan State 1952, 1954, 1956
Carollo, Joe, T, Notre Dame ....1962 – 68, 1971
Casey, Bernie, FL, Bowling Green..........1967 – 68
Cash, Rick, DE, N.E. Missouri...............1969 – 70
Casner, Ken, T, Baylor 1952
Cason, Jim, DB, LSU ....1955 – 56
Castete, Jesse, DB, McNeese State ....1956 – 57
Champagne, Ed, T, LSU ....1947 – 50
Chapple, Dave, P, Cal State-Santa Barbara ...1972
Cherundolo, Charles, C, Penn State......1937 – 39
Chesbro, Marcel, G, Colgate 1938
Chuy, Don, G, Clemson ....1963 – 68
Clark, Al, CB-S, E. Michigan.......................1972
Clarke, Leon, E, So. California ....1956 – 59
Clay, Boyd, T, Tennessee ....1940 – 42, 1944
Colella, Thomas, B, Canisius ....1944 – 45
Collier, Bob, T, SMU 1951
Conkright, William, C, Oklahoma ....1939 – 45
Conlee, Gerald, C, St. Mary's 1938
Cooper, William, T, Oberlin 1937
Corbo, Thomas, G, Duquesne 1944
Cordileone, Lou, LB, Clemson 1962
Cordill, Oliver, B, Rice 1940
Corn, Joe, RB, No college 1948
Cothren, Paige, PK, Mississippi..............1957 – 58
Cowan, Charlie, T, New Mex. Highlands .1961 – 72
Cowhig, Jerry, RB, Notre Dame...........1947 – 49
Coyle, Ross, DB, Oklahoma 1961
Crabb, Claude, DB, Colorado ....1966 – 68
Cross, Bobby, T, Kilgore J.C. ....1954 – 55
Cross, Irv, DB, Northwestern.................1966 – 68
Crow, Lindon, DB, So. California ....1961 – 64
Crowder, Earl, B, Oklahoma.......................1940
Curran, Pat, TE-RB, Lakeland ....1969 – 72
Currie, Dan, LB, Michigan State............1965 – 66
Currivan, Don, DE, Boston College........1948 – 49

D

Dahms, Tom, T, San Diego State...........1951 – 54
Dale, Carroll, E, VPI...............................1960 – 64
Dalsasso, Christopher, T, Indiana.................1937
Daniel, Willie, DB, Mississippi State ....1967 – 69
Daugherty, Dick, LB, Oregon ....1951 – 58
David, Bob, G, Villanova.........................1947 – 48
Davis, Corbett, QB, Indiana ....1938 – 42
Davis, Glenn, RB, Army.........................1950 – 51
Davis, Roger, G, Syracuse 1964
Dean, Hal, G, Ohio State ....1947 – 49
DeFruiter, Bob, DB, Nebraska.......................1948
DeLauer, Robert, C, So. California ....1945 – 46
Dennis, Mike, RB, Mississippi ....1968 – 69
Dickson, Paul, T, Baylor............................1959
Doll, Don, DB, So. California 1954
Dougherty, Bob, LB, Kentucky 1947
Dowd, Gerald, C, St. Mary's 1939
Drake, John, B, Purdue........................1937 – 41
Dryer, Fred, DE, San Diego State 1972
Dunstan, Elwyn, T, Portland..................1939 – 41
Dwyer, Jack, DB, Loyola-L.A.................1952 – 54
Dyer, Henry, RB, Grambling ....1966 – 68

E

Eason, Roger, G, Oklahoma ....1945 – 48
Ellena, Jack, MG, UCLA.......................1955 – 56
Ellersick, Don, DB, Washington State 1960
Ellison, Willie, RB, Texas Southern ....1967 – 72
Elmendorf, Dave, S, Texas A&M ....1971 – 72
Elston, Arthur, C, So. California 1942

Emerick, Robert, T, Miami, Ohio...................1937
Evey, Dick, DT, Tennessee 1970
Ezerins, Vilnis, RB, Whitewater State...........1968

F

Fanning, Stan, DE, Idaho............................1963
Farmer, Tom, RB, Iowa 1946
Fawcett, Jake, T, SMU 1942, 1944, 1946
Fears, Tom, E, UCLA ....1948 – 54
Ferris, Neil, DB, Loyola-L.A. 1953
Finch, Karl, E, Cal Poly-Pomona 1962
Finlay, Jack, G, UCLA ....1947 – 51
Fournet, Sid, DT, LSU ....1955 – 56
Franckhauser, Tom, DB, Purdue 1959
Friend, Benjamin, T, LSU 1939
Fry, Bob, T, Kentucky ....1953 – 59
Fuller, Frank, DT, Kentucky.....................1953 – 58

G

Gabriel, Roman, QB, No. Carolina State .1962 – 72
Gallovich, Anthony, B, Wake Forest.............1941
Geddes, Ken, LB, Nebraska ....1971 – 72
Gehrke, Fred, B, Utah.................1940, 1945 – 49
George, Bill, LB, Wake Forest 1966
Giannoni, John, E, St. Mary's.......................1938
Gibson, Billy Joe, C, Tulsa...................1942, 1944
Gift, Wayne, B, Purdue............................1937
Goddard, Ed, B, Washington State ....1937 – 38
Godfrey, Herb, E, Washington State.............1942
Goodnight, Owen, B, Hardin-Simmons.........1941
Goolsby, James, C, Mississippi State 1940
Gordon, Dick, WR, Michigan State...............1972
Gossett, Bruce, PK, Richmond...............1964 – 68
Greenwood, Don, B, Missouri.......................1945
Gregory, John, G, Chattanooga ....1941 – 42
Gremminger, Hank, DB, Baylor 1966
Grier, Roosevelt, DT, Penn State............1963 – 66
Griffin, Bob, C, Arkansas ....1953 – 57
Griffin, John, DB, Memphis State 1963
Gudauskas, Peter, G, Murray State.............1940
Guillory, Tony, LB, Lamar Tech ...1965, 1967 – 68
Guzik, John, LB, Pittsburgh ....1959 – 60

H

Hall, Alvin, DB, No college ....1961 – 63
Hall, Parker, QB, Mississippi ....1939 – 42
Halleck, Paul, B, Ohio................................1937
Halliday, Jack, DT, SMU 1951
Halverson, Dean, LBO, Washington
....1968, 1971 – 72
Haman, John, C, Northwestern..............1940 – 41
Hamilton, Ray, E, Arkansas ....1938, 1944 – 47
Harding, Roger, C, California........................1946
Hardy, Jim, QB, So. California ....1946 – 48
Harmon, Tom, RB, Michigan..................1946 – 47
Harris, Jim, DB, Oklahoma 1958
Harris, Marv, LB, Stanford 1964
Hauser, Art, DT, Xavier ....1954 – 57
Hayes, Larry, C, Vanderbilt...................1962 – 63
Haymond, Alvin, DB, Southern U. ....1969 – 71
Haynes, Hall, DB, Santa Clara ....1954 – 55
Heckard, Steve, E, Davidson ....1965 – 66
Hecker, Bob, DB, Baldwin-Wallace 1952
Hecker, Norb, DB, Baldwin-Wallace ......1951 – 53
Hector, Willie, T, Pacific 1961
Heineman, Ken, B, Texas Mines ....1940 – 41
Henry, Mike, LB, So. California ....1962 – 64
Henry, Urban, DT, Georgia Tech.................1961
Hershey, Kirk, E, Cornell..........................1941
Hickey, Howard, E, Arkansas ....1941, 1945 – 48
Hightower, John, E, Sam Houston...............1942
Hirsch, Eroly, E-RB, Wisconsin ....1949 – 57
Hock, John, G, Santa Clara ....1953 – 57
Hoerner, Dick, RB, Iowa ....1947 – 51
Hoffman, Bob, RB, So. California ....1946 – 48
Holladay, Bob, RB, Tulsa 1956
Holovak, Mike, RB, Boston College............1946
Holtzman, Glen, T, No. Texas State ....1955 – 58
Hord, Roy, G, Duke..............................1960 – 62
Horvath, Les, RB, Ohio State ....1947 – 48
Houser, John, C-G, Redlands................1957 – 59
Howard, Gene, DB, Langston ....1971 – 72
Hubbell, Frank, DE-TE, Tennessee.........1947 – 49
Huffman, Dick, T, Tennessee.................1947 – 50
Huggins, Roy, B, Vanderbilt 1944
Hughes, Ed, DB, Tulsa ....1954 – 55

Humphrey, Buddy, QB, Baylor ....1959 – 60
Hunter, Art, C, Notre Dame ....1960 – 64
Hupke, Thomas, G, Alabama ....1938 – 39

I

Iglehart, Floyd, DB, Wiley 1958
Iman, Ken, C, S. E. Missouri State...........1965 – 72
Isselhardt, Ralph, G, Franklin......................1937

J

Jackson, Harold, FL, Jackson State.............1968
Jacobs, Jack, QB, Oklahoma 1942, 1945
Janerette, Charlie, G, Penn State.................1960
Janiak, Leonard, B, Ohio ....1940 – 42
Jobko, Bill, LB, Ohio State ....1958 – 62
Johnson, Clyde, T, Kentucky...................1946 – 47
Johnson, Donals, C, Northwestern...............1942
Johnson, Marvin, DB, San Jose State .....1951 – 52
Johnson, Mitch, T, UCLA ....1969 – 70
Jones, David, DE, So. Carolina State ....1961 – 71
Jones, Harvey, B, Baylor ....1944 – 45
Jones, Jimmy, RB, Washington 1958
Jordan, Jeff, RB, Washington 1970
Josephson, Les, RB, Augustana
....1964 – 67, 1969 – 72

K

Kablealo, Michael, B, Ohio State 1944
Kalmanir, Tom, RB, Nevada ....1949 – 51
Karilivacz, Carl, DB, Syracuse ....1959 – 60
Karras, Ted, G, Indiana...............................1966
Karrs, John, B, Duquesne 1944
Keane, Tom, DB, West Virginia...............1948 – 51
Keeble, Joe, B, UCLA 1937
Kenerson, John, T, Kentucky State 1960
Kilgore, Jon, P, Auburn ....1965 – 67
Kimbrough, Elbert, DB, Northwestern 1961
Kinek, Michael, E, Michigan State 1940
Kirk, Ken, C, Mississippi 1963
Klein, Bob, TE, So. California ....1969 – 72
Klosterman, Don, QB, Loyola-L.A.................1952
Koch, George, B, Baylor 1945
Konetsky, Floyd, E, Florida....................1944 – 45
Kovatch, John, E, Northwestern 1938
Krause, Paul, G, DePaul 1938
Ksionyak, John, QB, St. Bonaventure...........1947

L

LaHood, Mike, G, Wyoming..........1969, 1971 – 72
Lamson, Chuck, DB, Wyoming ....1965 – 67
Lane, Dick, DB, Scottsbluff J.C.............1952 – 53
Lang, Israel, RB, Tennessee State 1969
Lange, Bill, G, Dayton ....1951 – 52
Lansford, Buck, G, Texas ....1958 – 60
Larsen, Gary, DT, Concordia 1964
Lazetich, Milan, G, Michigan ....1945 – 50
Lazetich, William, B, Montana ....1939, 1941 – 42
Lear, Les, G, Manitoba, Canada.............1944 – 46
Leggett, Earl, DT, LSU 1966
Levy, Len, G, Minnesota ....1945 – 46
Lewis, Arthur, T, Ohio ....1938 – 39
Lewis, Woodley, DB-E, Oregon ....1950 – 55
Liles, Elvin, G, Oklahoma A&M....................1945
Lipscomb, Gene, DT, No college ....1953 – 55
Littlefield, Carl, B, Washington State 1938
Livingston, Cliff, LB, UCLA ....1963 – 65
Livingston, Ted, T, Indiana....................1937 – 40
Long, Bob, LB, UCLA ....1960 – 61
Long, Bob, WR, Wichita State 1970
Lothridge, Billy, P, Georgia Tech..................1965
LoVetere, John, DT, Compton J.C. ....1959 – 62
Lundy, Lamar, DE-TE, Purdue...............1957 – 69

M

Mack, Tom, G, Michigan ....1966 – 72
Magnani, Dante, B, St. Mary's 1940 – 42, 1947 – 48
Maher, Francis, B, Toledo............................1941
Marchlewski, Frank, C, Minnesota ....1965 – 69
Marconi, Joe, RB, West Virginia ....1959 – 61
Markov, Victor, T, Washington 1938
Martin, Aaron, DB, No. Carolina Coll. .....1964 – 65
Martin, John, C, Navy............................1947 – 49
Maslowski, Matt, WR, San Diego 1971
Mason, Tommy, RB, Tulane...................1967 – 70

Matheson, Riley, G, Texas Mines
..............................1939 – 42, 1944 – 47
Matson, Oillie, RB-E, San Francisco.......1959 – 62
Mattos, Harry, B, St. Mary's 1937
Mayes, Carl, RB, Texas...............................1952
McCormick, Tom, RB, Pacific ....1953 – 55
McDonald, Tommy, FL, Oklahoma ....1965 – 66
McDonough, Paul, E, Utah 1938
McFadin, Bud, DT-T, Texas ....1952 – 56
McGarry, Bernard, G, Utah....................1939 – 42
McIlhany, Dan, DB, Texas A&M 1965
McKeever, Marlin, LB-TE, So. California
..............................1961 – 66, 1971 – 72
McLaughlin, Leon, C, UCLA....................1951 – 55
Meador, Ed, DB, Arkansas Tech ....1959 – 70
Mello, Jim, RB, Notre Dame.........................1948
Mergenthal, Art, G, Notre Dame ....1945 – 46
Michaels, Lou, DE, Kentucky..................1958 – 60
Miller, Charles, C, Purdue 1937
Miller, Clark, DE, Utah State 1970
Miller, Paul, DE, LSU ....1954 – 57
Miller, Ralph, T, Rice.............................1937 – 38
Miller, Ron, E, So. California.........................1956
Miller, Ron, QB, Wisconsin..........................1962
Moan, Emmett, B, West Virginia 1937
Molden, Frank, DT, Jackson State 1965
Monaco, Raymond, G, Holy Cross 1945
Moore, Tom, RB, Vanderbilt.........................1966
Morris, George, B, Baldwin-Wallace.......1941 – 42
Morris, Jack, DB, Oregon.......................1958 – 60
Morris, Larry, LB, Georgia Tech ....1955 – 57
Morrow, John, C, Michigan ....1956 – 59
Mucha, Rudolph, QB, Washington 1941, 1945
Munson, Bill, QB, Utah State ....1964 – 67
Myers, Brad, RB, Bucknell ....1953 – 56
Myers, Jack, RB-DB, UCLA 1952

N

Naumetz, Fred, LB-C, Boston College ....1946 – 50
Neihaus, Ralph, T, Cincinnati 1939
Nelson, Bill, DT, Oregon State ....1971 – 72
Nemeth, Steve, B, Notre Dame 1945
Nettles, Jim, DB, Wisconsin ....1969 – 72
Nichols, Bob, T, Stanford.......................1966 – 67

O

Olsen, T, ...1944
Olsen, Merlin, DT, Utah State ....1962 – 72
Olsen, Phil, DT, Utah State ....1971 – 72
O'Neill, William, B, George Washington.........1937

P

Pardee, Jack, LB, Texas A&M 1957 – 64, 1966 – 70
Parish, Don, LB, Stanford............................1971
pasque, Joe, T, SMU 1942, 1946
Pasquariello, Ralph, RB, Villanova 1950
Patt, Maurice, E, Carnegie Tech.............1939 – 42
Paul, Don, LB, UCLA.............................1948 – 55
Pergine, John, LB, Notre Dame ....1969 – 72
Perkins, Art, RB, No. Texas State..........1962 – 63
Petchell, John, B, Duquesne 1942, 1944
Peterson, Nelson, B, West Virginia Wesleyan 1938
Petitbon, Richie, DB, Tulane...................1969 – 70
Phillips, George, B, UCLA 1945
Phillips, Jim, E, Auburn ....1958 – 64
Pillath, Roger, T, Wisconsin.........................1965
Pincura, Stanley, B, Ohio State ....1937 – 38
Pitts, Elijah, RB, Philander Smith 1970
Pitts, Hugh, LB, TCU...................................1956
Pivec, Dave, TE, Notre Dame ....1966 – 68
Platukas, George, E, Duquesne ....1941 – 42
Plum, Milt, QB, Penn State 1968
Plunkett, Warren, B, Minnesota 1942
Pope, Bucky, FL, Catawba ....1964, 1966 – 67
Pottios, Myron, LB, Notre Dame ....1966 – 70
Powell, Tim, DE, Northwestern 1965
Prather, Dale, E, George Washington .....1938 – 39
Pritchard, Abisha, B, VMI 1942
Pritko, Steve, DE, Villanova ....1946 – 47
Prochaska, Ray, E, Nebraska.......................1941
Pudloski, Chester, T, Villanova 1944
Purnell, Jim, LB, Wisconsin ....1969 – 72
Putnam, Duane, G, Pacific ....1952 – 59, 1962

Q

Quinlan, Skeet, RB, San Diego State ......1952 – 56

R

Ragazzo, Philip, T, Western Reserve ......1938 – 39
Rapp, Manuel, B, St. Louis ....1941 – 42
Ray, David, PK-WR, Alabama ....1969 – 72
Ream, Charles, T, Ohio State 1938
Reisz, Albert, B, S. E. Louisiana ....1944 – 46
Reinhard, Bob, T-DT, California 1950
Reid, Joe, LB, LSU 1941
Rentzel, Lance, WR, Oklahoma ....1971 – 72
Repko, Joe, DT, Boston College.............1948 – 49
Reynolds, Jack, LB, Tennessee ....1970 – 72
Rhome, Jerry, QB, Tulsa 1971
Rich, Herb, DB, Vanderbilt ....1951 – 53
Richardson, Jerry, DB, W. Texas State ...1964 – 65
Richter, Les, LB, California ....1954 – 62
Rickards, Paul, QB, Pittsburgh 1948
Rieth, William, G, Carnegie Tech
....1941 – 42, 1944 – 45
Riffle, Charles, G, Notre Dame 1944
Robertson, Isiah, LB, Southern U. ....1971 – 72
Robinson, John, T, N. E. Missouri 1938
Robustelli, Andy, DE, Arnold ....1951 – 55
Rockwell, Henry, C, Arizona State..........1940 – 42
Rodak, Michael, G, Western Reserve ......1939 – 40
Rosequist, Ted, T, Ohio State 1937
Russell, Douglas, B, Kansas 1939
Russsll, Lloys, B, Baylor 1939
Ruthstrom, Ralph, RB, SMU ....1945 – 46
Ryan, Frank, QB, Rice ....1958 – 61

S

Saul, Rich, C-G, Michigan State ....1971 – 72
Savatsky, Oliver, E, Miami, Ohio 1937
Scarry, Michael, C, Waynesburg ....1944 – 45
Schenken, Nathan, T, Howard 1939
Schuh, Harry, T, Memphis State ....1971 – 72
Schultz, Eberle, T, Oregon State ....1946 – 47
Schumacher, Gregg, DE, Illinois ....1967 – 68
Schupbach, O. T., T, West Texas State ...1941 – 42
Scibelli, Joe, G, Notre Dame ....1961 – 72
Seabright, Charles, QB, West Virginia 1941
Sebastian, Michael, B, Pittsburgh 1937
Selawski, Gene, T, Purdue 1959
Sewell, Harley, G, Texas 1963
Shannon, Carver, DB-RB, So. Illinois...1962 – 64
Shaw, Bob, E, Ohio State.......................1945 – 49
Shaw, Glenn, RB, Kentucky 1962
Shaw, Nate, DB, So. California ....1969 – 70
Sherman, Will, DB, St. Mary's ....1954 – 60
Shirey, Fred, T, Nebraska.......................1940 – 41
Shiver, Ray, DB, Miami.................................1956
Shofner, Del, E, Baylor ....1957 – 60
Sikich, Rudy, T, Minnesota 1945
Simensen, Don, T, St. Thomas ....1951 – 52
Simington, Milton, G, Arkansas 1941
Sims, George, DB, Baylor ....1949 – 50
Skooczen, Stanley, B, Western Reserve........1944
Skoronski, Ed, C, Purdue 1937
Slovak, Martin, B, Toledo ....1939 – 41
Smith, Billy Ray, DE, Arkansas 1957
Smith, Bobby, DB, UCLA ....1962 – 65
Smith, Bruce, RB, Minnesota 1948
Smith, Gaylon, B, Southwestern.............1939 – 42
Smith, Larry, RB, Florida ....1969 – 72
Smith, Ron, QB, Richmond 1965
Smith, Ron, DB, Wisconsin 1969
Smith, V. T., RB, Abilene Christian ....1949 – 53
Smyth, Bill, T-TE, Cincinnati ....1947 – 50
Snow, Jack, WR, Notre Dame.................1965 – 72
Snyder, Robert, B, Ohio ....1937 – 38
Spadaccini, Vic, B, Minnesota ....1938 – 40
Sparkman, Alan, DT, Texas A&M ....1948 – 49
Stalcup, Jerry, LB, Wisconsin 1960
Statuto, Art, C, Notre Dame 1950
Stephens, John, E, Marshall 1938
Stephens, Larry, DT, Texas 1962
Stephenson, Dave, G, West Virginia..............1950
Stevenson, Ralph, B, Oklahoma 1940
Stiger, Jim, RB, Washington ....1965 – 67
Strode, Woody, E, UCLA 1946
Strofolino, Mike, LB, Villanova......................1965
Strugar, George, DT, Washington...........1957 – 61
Studstill, Pat, WR-P, Houston.................1968 – 71
Stuart, Roy, B, Tulsa 1942
Sucic, Steve, RB, Illinois 1946
Svare, Harland, LB, Washington State ....1953 – 54
Swain, Bill, LB, Oregon 1963

Sweet, Joe, WR, Tennessee State.................1972
Sweetan, Karl, QB, Wake Forest............1969 – 70

T

Talbert, Diron, DT, Texas.......................1967 – 70
Tarbox, Bruce, G, Syracuse 1961
Taylor, Corky, RB, Kansas State ....1955 – 57
Teeuws, Len, T, Tulane ....1952 – 53
Thomas, Bob, RB, Arizona State ....1971 – 72
Thomason, Bob, QB, VMI 1949
Thompson, Harry, G, UCLA ....1950 – 54
Toogood, Charley, DT-T, Nebraska.........1951 – 56
Towler, Dan, RB, Washington & Jefferson
....1950 – 55
Truax, Billy, TE, LSU ....1964 – 70
Tucker, Wendell, FL, So. Carolina State..1967 – 70
Tuckey, Richard, B, Manhattan 1938
Turner, James, B, Oklahoma A&M................1937

U

Underwood, Forrest, T, Davis-Elkins.............1937
Uzdavinis, Walter, E, Fordham 1937

V

Valdez, Bernon, DB, San Diego 1960
Van Brocklin, Norm, QB, Oregon ....1949 – 57
Varrichione, Frank, T, Notre Dame ....1961 – 65
Vasicek, Vic, LB, Texas 1950
Villanueva, Danny, K, New Mexico State 1960 – 64
Von Sonn, Andy, LB, UCLA 1964

W

Wade, Bill, QB, Vanderbilt ....1954 – 60
Waller, Ron, RB, Maryland ....1955 – 58
Wardlow, Duane, DE, Washington..........1954 – 56
Washington, Ken, RB-DB, UCLA ....1946 – 48
Waterfield, Bob, QB-DB-K, UCLA ....1945 – 52
Weisgerber, Richard, B, Willamette 1938
Wendryhoski, Joe, C, Illinois..................1964 – 66
West, Pat, RB, So. California ....1944 – 48
West, Stan, MG, Oklahoma ....1950 – 54
White, Lee, RB, Weber State 1971
Whitmyer, Nat, DB, Washington 1963
Whittenton, Jesse, DB, Texas Western ...1956 – 57
Whittingham, Fred, LB, Cal Poly-Obispo......1964
Wilbur, John, G, Stanford 1970
Wilkins, Roy, LB, Georgie ....1958 – 59
Williams, Charlie, WR, Prairie View..............1970
Williams, Clarence, DB, Washington State
....1965 – 72
Williams, Frank, RB, Pepperdine............1961 – 64
Williams, Jerry, DB, Washington State....1949 – 52
Williams, Roger, DB, Grambling ....1971 – 72
Williams, Sam, DE, Michigan State 1959
Williams, Travis, RB, Arizona State 1971
Wilson, Ben, RB, So. California ....1963 – 65
Wilson, Jack, RB, Baylor ....1946 – 47
Wilson, Jim, T, Georgia 1968
Wilson, John, E, Western Reserve ....1939 – 42
Wilson, Tom, RB, No college ....1956 – 61
Winkler, Jim, DB, Texas A&M ....1951 – 52
Winkler, Joe, C, Purdue 1945
Winston, Kelton, DB, Wiley ....1967 – 68
Wojcik, Greg, DT, So. California 1971
Woodlief, Doug, LB, Memphis State ....1965 – 69
Worden, James, B, Waynesburg...................1945

Y

Yagiello, Ray, G, Catawba ....1948 – 49
Youngblood, Jack, DE, Florida................1971 – 72
Younger, Paul, RB-LB, Grambling ....1949 – 57

Z

Zilly, Jack, TE-DT, Notre Dame...............1947 – 51
Zirinsky, Walt, B, Lafayette 1945
Zoll, Richard, G, Indiana ....1937 – 38

RAMS' INDIVIDUAL RECORDS

SERVICE

Most Seasons—13, Lamar Lundy, 1957 – 69; Jack Pardee, 1957 – 64, 1966 – 70
Most Games—169, Jack Pardee, 1957 – 64, 1966 – 70
Most Consecutive Games—159, Ed Meador, 1959 – 70

SCORING

Most Points
  Lifetime—573, Bob Waterfield, 1945 – 52
  Season—121, David Ray, 1970 (34 PATs, 29 FGs)
  Game—24, Elroy Hirsch, 1951 v. New York Yanks
  24, Bob Shaw, 1949 v. Washington
Most Touchdowns
  Lifetime—55, Elroy Hirsch, 1949 – 57
  Season—17, Elroy Hirsch, 1951
  Game—4, Elroy Hirsch, 1941 v. New York Yanks
  4, Bob Shaw, 1949 v. Washington
Most Points After Touchdown
  Lifetime—315, Bob Waterfield, 1945 – 52
  Season—54, Bob Waterfield, 1950
  Game—9, Bob Waterfield, 1950 v. Baltimore
Most Field Goals Made
  Lifetime—120, Bruce Gossett, 1964 – 69
  Season—29, David Ray, 1970
  Game—5, Bob Waterfield, 1951 v. Detroit
Longest Field Goal—51, Danny Villanueva, 1962 v. Dallas
  51, Lou Michaels, 1960 v. Baltimore

RUSHING

Most Attempts
  Lifetime—1,218, Dick Bass, 1960 – 69
  Season—248, Dick Bass, 1966
  Game—31, Ollie Matson, 1959 v. Chicago Bears (gained 199 yards)
Most Yards Gained
  Lifetime—5,417, Dick Bass, 1960 – 69 (1,218 atts., 4.5 avg.)
  Season—1,090, Dick Bass, 1966 (248 atts., 4.4 avg.)
  Game—247,* Willie Ellison, 1971 v. New Orleans (26 atts., 9.5 avg.)
Longest Run from Scrimmage—92, Kenny Washington, 1947 v. Chicago Cardinals

PASSING

Most Attempts
  Lifetime—3,313, Roman Gabriel, 1962 – 72
  Season—407, Roman Gabriel, 1970
  Game—53, Jim Hardy, 1948 v. Chicago Cardinals
Most Completions
  Lifetime—1,705, Roman Gabriel, 1962 – 72
  Season—217, Roman Gabriel, 1966 (397 atts., 54.7%)
  217, Roman Gabriel, 1969 (399 atts., 54.4%)
  Game—28, Jim Hardy, 1948 v. Chicago Cardinals (53 atts.)
Best Passing Efficiency
  Lifetime—54.0%, Bill Wade, 1954 – 60 (1,116 atts., 603 comp.)
  (500 or more)
  Season—58.6%, Bill Wade, 1959 (261 atts., 153 comp.)
  (100 or more)
  Game—81.8%, Roman Gabriel, 1967 v. Baltimore (22 atts., 18 comp.)
  (20 or more)
Longest Passing Gain—96, Frank Ryan to Ollie Matson, 1961 v. Pittsburgh
Most Yards Gained
  Lifetime—22,223, Roman Gabriel, 1962 – 72
  Season—2,875, Bill Wade, 1958 (341 atts., 181 comp.)
  Game—554,* Norm Van Brocklin, 1951 v. N.Y. Yanks (41 atts., 27 comp.)
Most Touchdown Passes
  Lifetime—154, Roman Gabriel, 1962 – 72
  Season—25, Roman Gabriel, 1967
  Game—5, Bob Waterfield, 1949 v. New York Bulldogs
  5, Norm Van Brocklin, 1950 v. Detroit
  5, Norm Van Brocklin, 1951 v. New York Yanks
  5, Roman Gabriel, 1965 v. Cleveland
Most Passes Had Intercepted
  Lifetime—128, Bob Waterfield, 1945 – 52
  Season—24, Bob Waterfield, 1949
  Game—7, Bob Waterfield, 1948 v. Green Bay
Fewest Passes Had Intercepted
  Season—2, Roman Gabriel, 1962 (101 atts.)
  (100 atts.)
Most Consecutive Passes Attempted, None Intercepted—206, Roman Gabriel, 1968 – 70
Lowest Percentage, Passes Had Intercepted
  Lifetime—3.4,* Roman Gabriel, 1962 – 72
  Season—1.8, Roman Gabriel, 1969 (7/399)
  (100 atts.)

PASS RECEIVING

Most Receptions
  Lifetime—400, Tom Fears, 1948 – 56
  Season—84, Tom Fears, 1950
  Game—18,* Tom Fears, 1950 v. Green Bay
Most Yards Gained Receiving
  Lifetime—6,289, Elroy Hirsch, 1949 – 57
  Season—1,495, Elroy Hirsch, 1951
  Game—303,* Jim Benton, 1945 v. Detroit
Most Consecutive Games, Pass Receiving—68, Jim Phillips, 1958 – 63
Most Touchdowns Receiving
  Lifetime—53, Elroy Hirsch, 1949 – 57
  Season—17,# Elroy Hirsch, 1951
  Game—4, Bob Shaw, 1949 v. Washington
  4, Elroy Hirsch, 1951 v. New York Yanks
Most Consecutive Games Touchdown Passes Received—11,# Elroy Hirsch, 1950 – 51

INTERCEPTIONS

Most Interceptions
  Lifetime—46, Ed Meador, 1959 – 70
  Season—14,* Night Train Lane, 1952
  Game—3, by 12 players (most recent, Gene Howard v. San Francisco, 1971)
Most Consecutive Games, Passes Intercepted By—6, Will Sherman, 1954 – 55
Longest Intercepted Pass Return—97, Herb Rich, 1952 v. Dallas Texans
  97, Bobby Smith, 1964 v. San Francisco

PUNTING

Most Punts
  Lifetime—356, Norm Van Brocklin, 1949 – 57
  Season—87, Danny Villanueva, 1962 (45.5 avg.)
  Game—12, Parker Hall, 1939 v. Green Bay (39.3 avg.)
Best Punting Average
  Season—45.5, Danny Villanueva, 1962 (87 punts)
  Game—52.5, Danny Villanueva, 1962 v. San Francisco (6,315 yds.)
  (4 or more)
Longest Punt—88, Bob Waterfield, 1948 v. Green Bay

PUNT RETURNS

Most Punt Returns
  Lifetime—110, Alvin Haymond, 1969 – 71
  Season—53, Alvin Haymond, 1970
  Game—7, Alvin Haymond, 1970 v. Atlanta
Highest Average Punt Return
  Lifetime—10.9, V. T. Smith (75), 1949 – 53
  Season—18.5, Woodley Lewis, 1952
Longest Punt Return—90, Dick Bass, 1961 v. Green Bay

KICKOFF RETURNS

Most Kickoff Returns
  Lifetime—109, Woodley Lewis, 1950 – 55
  Season—35, Alvin Haymond, 1970
  Game—6, Carver Shannon, 1963 v. Chicago; 1964 v. Detroit
  6, Woodley Lewis, 1953 v. Green Bay
Most Yards Kickoff Returns
  Lifetime—2603, Woodley Lewis, 1950 – 55
  Season—836, Woodley Lewis, 1954
  Game—202, Carver Shannon, 1963 v. Chicago
Most Kickoff Returns for Touchdowns
  Lifetime—3, V. T. Smith, 1949 – 53
  Season—3, V. T. Smith, 1950
Highest Average Kickoff Return
  Season—33.7, V. T. Smith, 1950
Longest Kickoff Return—105, Jon Arnett, 1961 v. Detroit
  105, Travis Williams, 1971 v. New Orleans

FIELD GOAL RETURNS

Longest Field Goal Return—99, Jerry Williams, 1951 v. Green Bay

COMBINED YARDAGE

(Includes rushes, pass receptions, returns of interceptions, punts, kickoffs and fumbles)
Most Combined Yards
  Lifetime—9,213, Dick Bass, 1960 – 69

*NFL record
#Ties NFL record

RAMS' TEAM RECORDS

SCORING

Most Points
  Season—466, 1950
  Game—70, 1950 (Rams 70 – Baltimore 27)
  Quarter—41, 1950 v. Detroit (3rd quarter)
Fewest Points
  Season—75, 1937
  Game—0 (14 games)
Fewest Points Allowed
  Season—136, 1945

Most Touchdowns
Season—64, 1950
Game—10,# 1950 v. Baltimore
Fewest Touchdowns
Season—10, 1937
Most Touchdowns Rushing
Season—33, 1950
Game—6, 1949 v. Green Bay; 1951 v. New York Yanks
Most Touchdowns Passing
Season—31, 1950
Game—6, 1959 v. New York Bulldogs; 1949 v. Washington; 1950 v. Detroit
Most Points After Touchdowns
Season—59, 1950
Game—10, 1950 v. Baltimore
Most Field Goals
Season—29, 1970
Game—5, 1951 v. Detroit
Most Field Goals Attempted
Season—49,# 1966

FIRST DOWNS

Most First Downs
Season—278, 1950
Game—38,* 1966 v. New York Giants
Fewest First Downs
Season—88, 1937
Game—2, 1937 v. Washington
Most First Downs Rushing
Season—118, 1955
Most First Downs Passing
Season—153, 1965
Most First Downs Penalties
Season—28, 1951
Fewest First Downs Allowed
Game—6, 1968 v. Cleveland Browns; 1965 v. Cleveland Browns

RUSHING

Most Yards Gained Rushing
Season—2,210, 1951
Game—371, 1951 v. New York Yanks
Fewest Yards Gained Rushing
Season—798, 1938
Fewest Yards Allowed Rushing
Season—1,119, 1967
Game—19, 1954 v. Baltimore

PASSING

Moet Yards Gained Passing
Season—3,709, 1950
Game—554,* 1951 v. New York Yanks
Fewest Yards Gained Passing
Season—839, 1937
Game—0, 1949 v. Pittsburgh
Fewest Yards Allowed Passing
Season—1,813, 1968
Most Passes Attempted
Season—453, 1950
Game—55, 1950 v. Philadelphia
Most Passes Completed
Season—253, 1950
Game—32, 1950 v. Green Bay
Fewest Passes Attempted
Season—168, 1937
Game—4, 1937
Most Passes Had Intercepted
Season—35, 1941
Game—7, Many times
Fewest Passes Had Intercepted
Season—7, 1969
Most Times Opponent Passer Tackled
Season—53, 1970
Fewest Times Passer Tackled
Season—16, 1972
Best Passing Percentage
Season—55.8, 1950

TOTAL YARDS

Most Yards Gained
Season—5,506, 1951
Game—735,* 1951 v. New York Yanks
Fewest Yards Gained
Season—1,794, 1937
Game—58, 1942 v. Chicago Bears
Fewest Yards Allowed
Season—3,118, 1968
Game—70, 1953 v. Baltimore

INTERCEPTIONS

Most Interceptions
Season—38, 1952
Game—7, 1964 v. San Francisco
Most YardsReturning Interceptions
Season—712, 1952
Game—314,* 1964 v. San Francisco

PUNTING

Most Punts
Season—87, 1962
Game—12, 1938 v. Chicago Bears; 1939 v. Green Bay; 1940 v. New York Giants
Best Punting Average
Season—45.5, 1962
Game—52.5, 1939 v. Green Bay; 1962 v. San Francisco
(4 or more)

PENALTIES

Most Penalties
Season—110, 1950
Fewest Penalties
Season—29, 1941
Most Yards Penalized
Season—1,038, 1950
Fewest Yards Penalized
Season—195, 1938

FUMBLES

Most Fumbles
Season—40, 1964, 1965
Game—8, 1964 v. Detroit
Fewest Fumbles
Season—17, 1960
Game—0, Many games
Most Opponents Fumbles Recovered
Season—24, 1947, 1948
Game—5, 1938 v. Chicago Cardinals; 1954 v. Detroit; 1966 v. Green Bay

*NFL record
#Ties NFL record

Photography Credits
George Bartell 51
Phil Bath 178
David Boss 9, 55B, 96, 97AB, 99, 109, 139, 140, 141B, 162B, 164, 167, 179
Merv Corning Dust Jacket, 49B
Chance Brockway 94A
Chicago Daily News 165
Malcolm Emmons 174, 178
Nate Fine 168
James F. Flores 54, 56
Bart Forbes 55A
George Gellatly 125, 142
Grambling College 144
Green Bay Packers 108
Hall of Fame 49A, 50A, B, D, E; 65, 66, 67, 78, 120, 134, 138, 144, 152B
Los Angeles Rams 15, 19, 20, 28AB, 33, 36A, 40AB, 43, 44AB, 49C, 50C, 62, 74, 80-81, 94B, 98A, 104, 106AB, 110, 118, 126, 128, 141A, 145BC, 146, 152A, 155, 156, 157, 158, 159B, 160, 161, 170, 171, 180AB, 181
Darryl Norenberg 52-53, 91, 176
Frank Rippon 25, 34B, 121, 137, 154B
Russ Russell 163
Shankle Photographers 152B
Vic Stein 6, 13, 15, 16, 21, 22-23, 24, 26, 27, 30-31, 32, 35, 36B, 37, 38-39, 41, 42AB, 45, 70-71, 72, 73, 83B, 86, 89, 95, 102, 105, 112, 114, 122, 130, 131, 136, 141, 146, 148, 153, 154, 162A, 166, 169, 173, 177
Herb Weitman 87
University of Wisconsin 116
Wide World Photos 63
UPI 98B